I0827800

A FIGHT FOR
VISIBILITY

MAKING THE MODERN SOUTH

David Goldfield, Series Editor

BLACK MEMPHIS CONFRONTS THE LOST CAUSE

★★★

DONNA E. REEVES

LOUISIANA STATE UNIVERSITY PRESS  BATON ROUGE

Published by Louisiana State University Press
lsupress.org

DESIGNER: Emily A. Olson
TYPEFACES: Chaparral Pro, text; LTC Flash, Akzidenz-Grotesk Next, display

The manufacturer's authorized representative in the EU for product safety is Mare Nostrum Group B.V., Doelen 72, 4831 GR Breda, The Netherlands. Email: gpsr@mare-nostrum.co.uk.

Cover illustration adapted from rawpixel and Adobe Stock

LIBRARY OF CONGRESS CATALOGING-IN-PUBLICATION DATA

Names: Reeves, Donna E., author.
Title: A fight for visibility : Black Memphis confronts the Lost Cause / Donna E. Reeves.
Other titles: Making the modern South
Description: Baton Rouge : Louisiana State University Press, [2026] | Series: Making the modern South | Includes bibliographical references and index.
Identifiers: LCCN 2026020967 (print) | LCCN 2026020968 (ebook) | ISBN 978-0-8071-8656-5 (cloth) | ISBN 978-0-8071-8767-8 (epub) | ISBN 978-0-8071-8768-5 (pdf)
Subjects: LCSH: African Americans—Tennessee—Memphis—History | African Americans—Tennessee—Memphis—Social conditions | Lost Cause mythology | Memphis (Tenn.)—Race relations | Memphis (Tenn.)—History
Classification: LCC F444.M59 B53 2026 (print) | LCC F444.M59 (ebook)
LC record available at https://lccn.loc.gov/2026020967
LC ebook record available at https://lccn.loc.gov/2026020968

CONTENTS

ACKNOWLEDGMENTS

As I complete work on this book, my heart is full of gratitude. From Drs. Wanda Hendricks and Cynthia Kierner, who set me off on the voyage of historical scholarship, to Drs. Kenneth Goings, Beverly Bond, and Janann Sherman, who cultivated the seeds that my professors at UNCC planted, I am thankful for all the help along the way. My advisors believed in me, and at the time I do not think I appreciated all the effort that went into their mentoring, but now I see clearly that what seemed tough at the time was just their making sure that I was ready for the rigorous journey ahead. I cannot thank them enough.

I would also like to dedicate this book to my parents. My mom worked as a barber her entire life, and my father worked as a general laborer. Though they did not always understand what I was doing in graduate school, they were right there cheering me on. They propelled me to go faster and further than they did in school. They saw many of their dreams realized through me.

A FIGHT FOR VISIBILITY

INTRODUCTION

The Struggle over the Meaning of the Lost Cause

On May 16, 1905, more than thirty thousand people gathered in Memphis, Tennessee, to pay homage to a man they understood to be a hero—a man they believed personified everything that was good about the Old South.[1] Excitement and anticipation mounted as Kathleen Bradley, the eight-year-old great-granddaughter of the honoree, came to the stage. Pulling a cord, the young girl stepped back as a red-and-white drop cloth fell to the ground, revealing a massive bronze statue standing over twenty-one feet tall. The crowd erupted with cheers and applause, as their eyes gazed upon the figure of Confederate General Nathan Bedford Forrest mounted on horseback.[2] One by one, both Union and Confederate veterans came forward and spoke eloquently about General Forrest's achievements on and off the battlefield. He was the "Wizard of the Saddle," he always strived to be the "first with the most men," and he "fought like a Titan and struck like a god, and his dust is our ashes of glory."[3] Former Union Colonel C. A. Stanton spoke to what Forrest's presence in bronze meant for the city of Memphis. He exhorted spectators: "Look with pride upon this monument [because] . . . this monument is history in bronze; it illustrates an eventful era in our national history; it commemorates General Forrest's fame and it represents all the gallant soldiers of his command . . . it stands for heroic deeds which are now the proud heritage of all American citizens."[4] There was an added air of reverence surrounding the statue as it also served as the final resting place for Forrest and his wife, Mary. The Forrest Foundation had the couple reinterred from the Forrest family plot in Elmwood Cemetery to beneath the foundation of the statue.[5]

Seventy years later, Al Lewis, an African American student at Shelby State Community College, could not look upon the Forrest statue with pride. From Shelby State's campus (across the street from Forrest Park), the mostly African American student population viewed the statue with contempt. The statue paid homage to a brute—to the person responsible for the massacre of African American soldiers at Fort Pillow in 1864 and the first imperial wizard of the Ku Klux Klan. Instead of taking any violent action against the statue, Lewis and other protesters stayed in line with the spirit of the civil rights movement and spent the next twenty-plus years seeking a peaceful way to rid the Memphis community of what they believed to be a horrid blight.[6]

Nathan Bedford Forrest's statue provides a compelling example of how public monuments evoke different meanings for different audiences. When city officials erected the statue in 1905, observers commented that it served as a good focal point to remember the South's past when the people would honor rebel soldiers and their commitment to liberty. Southern audiences often completed this ritual of commemoration without the slightest sense of irony. George Gordon, historian for the event, stated: "We are . . . here to attest in verbal, visible and permanent form the eminent esteem and increasing appreciation in which the noble and heroic services of this anomalous man are held by his countrymen. . . . We now declare this durable testimonial, so imposing, so impressive and so expressive of the character and career of the man, to be the permanent proclamation of our veneration for his memory, our gratitude for his services and sacrifices, and our admiration for his valor and genius."[7]

The Forrest statue is a powerful symbol in that it is the manifestation of a people and their values. Johan Fornäs, in his book *Signifying Europe,* explains that groups will use a person or an object to link the group's collective consciousness. An important aspect of a community's ability to make these connections to one another is not just the presence of the person or the object, but the interaction that occurs when the members of the group view the symbol.[8] The Forrest statue represents a time gone by, a time when white men were at the top of the social, political, and economic hierarchy. John Winberry states that the monuments had multiple, complex, and sometimes contradictory meanings. While the monuments represented the "loss of manhood" due to injuries and death in the war, they also represented the strength of the South to overcome the loss of blood and treasure. Further, the monuments resisted the notion of a New South that came from industrialists who looked to the region to develop its natural resources and wanted to focus on building the region without the racial baggage of the past. The statues served as a symbol of a previous point in history and gave their viewers something to fight for in the current tumultuous times. In some ways, the symbol becomes a mascot, and it represents the power of self-interpretation/representation.[9]

By erecting the Forrest statue, white southerners of Memphis seized the opportunity to define the public's memory of southern rebellion.[10] The memorialization of Forrest at the turn of the twentieth century represented just one success out of many for organizations like the United Daughters of the Confederacy (UDC). For more than a century this group was instrumental in enabling the white South to claim public space as white space. These women, often alongside other southern heritage groups, developed and possessed the official popular narrative for the causes of the Civil War and what transpired in its aftermath. What these groups created was a storybook version of southern history that reduced African Americans to little more than static afterthoughts in the world of the white planter.[11]

Initially the Ladies Memorial Association and UDC chapters across the South focused on assisting veterans who had been injured in the war, on widows left alone to care for their families because of the war, and on memorializing the soldiers who died fighting for the Confederacy, but there was a change. Over the years, these organizations were less about memorializing the soldiers or assisting the fatherless families. The UDC dedicated its existence to the justification of the southern cause and those souls who fought to protect it.[12] Members of the UDC approached their mission armed with sentimentality for the Old South and a determination to disseminate its values to future generations. These women, along with their social club counterparts, developed what they believed to be the true history of the Civil War and Reconstruction, one in which they shared an identity that was uniquely southern and definitely white.[13] UDC members infused these statues with meaning—a meaning that excluded the participation and experiences of Black people. Since Confederate sympathizers blocked the participation of Black people, southern history became white history. The dominant narrative was one in which Black people performed best when their masters guided them with a steady and disciplined hand.[14]

By honoring a man such as Nathan Bedford Forrest and by excluding the voices of the descendants of the freed people, the white Memphis community leaders denied them status as equal participants in southern history, and the ramifications of that marginalization are apparent today.[15] Southern African Americans were loathe to participate in the UDC's memory-making activities even if the white women bothered to ask. Black people focused on the future at the end of the nineteenth century, because to look at the past just reminded them of the pain and humiliation their family members had suffered. Regrettably, Black people did not heed the call of men like Frederick Douglass to actively participate in the creation of the narrative of southern history. The absence of Black southern voices is why white women's voices, which painted a decidedly supportive view of the Confederate cause, became the only voices that mattered in the development of southern history.[16]

African Americans in Memphis expressed quite a different opinion regarding the Forrest statue during the last half of the twentieth century. For this community, the statue served as an offensive symbol of the South's past, representing racism and segregation.[17] The transformation of the dominant meanings of the statue is not surprising as more people with various backgrounds came to have a political voice (and choice) about the types of monuments that reflect the collective history of the city.[18] Memphis is the site of Dr. Martin Luther King Jr.'s last march and his assassination. This burden has weighed heavily on its African American residents. When this shift in the focus of public history (and public space) moved away from the glories of the Confederacy and leaned more toward the meanings of the civil rights movement in the lives of Memphians, clashes over what group gets to tell whose history were bound to occur.

Throughout the nineteenth and twentieth centuries, African Americans sought to create an inclusive history. After the end of the Civil War, African Americans centered much of their public celebrations on how the conflict led to one America. As the Fourth of July lost luster among white southerners during and immediately after the war, Black southerners embraced the holiday wholeheartedly in order to claim their ownership of the promises of the Constitution.[19]

The Forrest statue was not the only site of contest over differing conceptions of southern and American history and over who held the power to define historical memory. The Cotton Carnival was also a public event in which white Memphians used the streets of the city to reinforce their white-supremacist version of southern history. Economic need converged with nostalgia to advertise the carnival. White business leaders designed the carnival in an effort to restore life to the depressed cotton market of the early 1930s. The theme of the first carnival was "The Old South." Of course, this was a reenactment of a mythical past. White men (dressed in tuxedoes) presented themselves as the captains of the cotton industry. One lucky man wore the crown of a king and greeted the city from atop a float, while standing next to him was his queen, who was a young lady from the Memphis social registry. She was dressed in a ballgown, with gloves up to her elbows, and wore her own crown. Cotton was king, all the white women were young, and all the white men were gallant. Unlike the Forrest dedication, Black people played a role in these festivities. Black women, dressed as the mythological mammies of the plantation, greeted festival goers. Black men acted as workhorses and pulled the floats, and Black children ran around and jumped from cotton bale to cotton bale, laughing and playing. While white Memphians took the role of leaders as king and queen, organizers relegated Black people to the subordinate place that white Memphians believed God had destined for all Black people. This carnival, like the Forrest statue, served as yet another monument to white history and supremacy.[20]

African American activists founded the Cotton Makers Jubilee in 1935 in direct response to the images that white Memphians displayed in the Cotton Carnival. In the jubilee, Black Memphis challenged the dominant narrative that Black people were happy slaves, plump mammies, and carefree pickaninnies. They presented an image of Black southerners that pointed out the common history of the two races in the South. Through material representation, they established the record that while they may have been slaves, African Americans became so much more. They were doctors, lawyers, teachers, and most of all hardworking citizens with something to contribute to the communities in which they lived. Unfortunately, the jubilee was also a divisive event within the Black community as later chapters will demonstrate.[21]

David Blight argues that W. E. B. Du Bois "was the self-conscious creator of Black counter memory," and while he may have created the response to white-supremacist history, it still remains a fledgling endeavor more than a century later. Despite the efforts of southern heritage organizations, the Black man and woman were not invisible actors in history. Their story is retrievable within newspapers, letters, and institutional papers.[22] Another significant counternarrative, which is explored extensively in this book, is the political nature of memory when it comes to the Civil War and Reconstruction. The desire of southern heritage groups to either erase or marginalize the experience of African Americans matters when they battle over whether the Forrest statue should be removed. The statue served to remind white southerners of the power of their history. Each time neo-Confederates were able to beat back a challenge to have the statue removed, they became more emboldened in their interpretations of southern history.

White southerners developed their version of the South's history following the Civil War. Wanting to redeem themselves from the failures of southern rebellion, white southerners advanced a philosophy of racial mythology, imagined persecution, and absolution of blame for the war. The people who subscribed to these views portrayed Confederates as the heroes of Reconstruction, who rescued the region from the ruination of Black domination and federal rule.[23] This work seeks to challenge the white-supremacist version of the Old South by emphasizing the often suppressed, ignored, and forgotten voices of disenfranchised Black men and women. Southern history is not something that can be shared especially from the standpoint of white southerners loyal to the Confederate cause. Their narrative is particularly insular, as well as violently opposed to African Americans interjecting the experience of slavery or freed people. To recognize this group would sully the purity of the southern story of gentlemen and belles because they would have to recognize that the aforementioned groups could not have existed without the suffering of Black Americans.[24] By focusing on the protests against the Forrest statue and the implementation of the Cotton Makers Jubilee, this book examines how African Americans in Memphis perceived their public role and memorialization in the Old and New Souths. What becomes clear is that the more white southerners used public space to proclaim their superiority, the more African Americans used that same space to stake their claim to equal citizenship.

In his article "The Contested Image of Nathan Bedford Forrest," Court Carney also addresses the change in attitude about the Forrest statue among white southerners over the course of the twentieth century. He points out that the activism of the sixties influenced some of these shifts in attitude as the Black struggle for freedom caused many Confederate loyalists to harden their positions. Carney takes an interesting look at how men and women approached the Forrest monument. He discusses how men found Forrest a more intriguing figure and an example of the ideal southern man. He argues that southern women felt a closer bond to Robert E. Lee, as he was a more refined and polished leader. In southern heritage circles, people believed Forrest to be an "outlaw rebel" and "the most man." Carney suggests that Forrest was the man more southern men wanted to imitate.[25] Further, in his book *Reckoning with the Devil,* Carney explains that, in many ways, Forrest's image was like a tabula rasa, or blank slate. As his supporters wove together a mixture of truth, exaggeration, and outright falsehoods to create the image they wanted to see, Forrest became a kind of shorthand for the meaning of the war for the white residents (especially white men) of Memphis. He also stood for "contemporary struggles over power, representation, and implications of the past." This idea that Forrest became a blank slate also came in handy when Black Memphians began to define their ancestors' experiences in Memphis during the Civil War and Reconstruction. While white southerners focused on the "wizard of the saddle," Black Memphians focused on the butcher of Fort Pillow and his leadership of the Ku Klux Klan.[26]

Using the foundation of these authors and many others, this book continues the efforts of historians who explore the topic of southern memory. This book is a microstudy of how one aspect of southern memory played out in the city of Memphis, Tennessee. What readers will find in the following pages is another example of an inward-looking southern community, and how southern memory peddlers actively reject the experiences of nonwhite groups who frustrate their account of a benevolent South whose inhabitants lived harmoniously with each other. This book points to the active exclusion of—and even hostility toward—African Americans by Confederate flame keepers. At the same time, it highlights the tension that impacts the fight to take down these monuments to the white South and wrest control of southern history from the clutches of neo-Confederates and their allies.

These statues and these memories do not exist in a vacuum. John Winberry, in his article "Lest We Forget," concludes that the meaning of a monument is based on the perceptions of people who interact with the monument, not just the intent of those who erected the statue.[27] Spectators in 1905 had a different conversation than Memphians just over a half century later. Jody Stokes-Casey explains that in 1905 white Memphians wanted to remember their Confederate ancestors and honor those who survived the war. The Forrest statue reminded white men and women of the tragic loss of their money, their manhood, and their way of life. At the same time, the statue proved the ability of Confederate descendants to reclaim all those things that they believed were rightfully theirs. Statues like the Forrest monument had a restorative quality.[28] However, as the decades rolled on, the statue did not retain that same meaning. Men like Al Lewis, and other Black Memphians, began to state out loud what their opinions were about Forrest and the impact of his legacy on them and their ancestors. The transition of perceptions and the friction in this transition are at the root of this book, where readers will determine for themselves what lies at the center of what scholars call southern history, and whether there is room for all southerners to be included in this narrative about the South.

The first chapter begins by discussing the lives of African Americans in Memphis during the ante- and postbellum periods. Black people in west Tennessee and northern Mississippi worked their way to Memphis because of the freedom that city life offered. Before the war, they wanted freedom from their "masters," and they wanted the freedom to work and keep their earnings. Even though the enslaved believed Memphis represented more opportunity, city officials saw the presence of enslaved people and free Black persons as a nuisance or a danger. Civil authorities constantly questioned the presence of both groups in public spaces, where their sheer numbers made white Memphians uncomfortable.[29] Unfortunately, that meant that Black people in Memphis continued to experience discrimination from the state and local legislative bodies before and after the war. They also witnessed, and were the victims of, massive physical violence in 1866. Through rioting, white Memphians decided to use the public streets on which they felt threatened in order to cement their supposed superior position.[30]

Chapter 2 explores differing meanings of freedom among the classes of African Americans living in Memphis in a post-Reconstruction society. Leaders in the African American community tended to accept the negative stereotypes that southern loyalists presented about their race, especially as they applied to poorer Black people. Thus, the focus of the members of the talented tenth and accommodationist classes turned to uplift. In their minds, if they could lift up the race from poverty and degradation, then the entire race could move forward.[31] The chapter discusses attempts by Black women such as Ida B. Wells and Julia Hooks to uplift the "less fortunate" members of their race.

Chapter 3 describes the dedication ceremony for the Forrest statue. None of the stories told about Forrest at the dedication offered a complex view of the general or his work; speakers portrayed, rather, a savior of the South. As there were no African American participants, the ceremony drove home the point that the history being celebrated was white history. It is in this ceremony that one can see the intersection of white supremacy and memory in the mid-South. The remarks of city and business leaders highlight that they defined their history in terms of the nobility of all white men who fought in the war. The men linked themselves to the principles and values of their ancestors and promised to transmit this pride to their descendants. This transmission of pride provides the context for the modern era's upheavals surrounding Confederate memorabilia. It is the narrative that white southerners delivered at the Forrest monument dedication ceremony (and numerous other dedication ceremonies) that has allowed neo-Confederates to couch their arguments for keeping these relics in terms of liberty and independence without having to even recognize the peculiar institution.

Chapter 4 details the beginnings of the Cotton Carnival. The carnival began when local white business leaders decided to lift the spirits and economic well-being of Memphians during the early days of the Depression. They decided that they needed to remind the city and the region of what made west Tennessee great—not new industry or federal government relief, but the strength of agriculture. They believed the cotton crop was the key to pulling Memphis out of economic desperation. The organizers gave the first carnival a theme, "The Old South," so that every white person could celebrate the imagined good old days. The carnival came complete with Black men and women singing plantation hymns and Black men pulling floats of white women dressed as plantation mistresses. Every segment of the population participated. Organizers even paid Black children to jump on bales of cotton so that they could play the irrepressible pickaninnies of the nineteenth century.[32] While the organizers of the carnival focused on promoting economic prosperity for the region, they also provided the people with a demonstration of their preferred racial order.

The last chapters of this book explore how African Americans responded to white southerners' mythmaking efforts throughout the twentieth century. The meaning of the Forrest statue changed over time, and that moves us to Fornäs's conclusion that the meaning of a symbol is "context-dependent." When and how a community uses a symbol will determine how people interact with the symbol and how the people come to see what it means. Therefore, the symbol, according to Fornäs, is always "fluid and contextual, contested and contingent."[33] John Winberry posits that a "monument . . . 'encapsulates and nurtures an idea or a set of ideas' that incorporate certain values and ideals of that society."[34]

As readers will see in the forthcoming chapters, the period of monument building occurred at the end of the nineteenth century. In their article "Reconsideration of Memorials and Monuments," Modupe Labode and Kevin Levin argue that communities across the South participated in this symbol creation to connect their local residents. Chapters of the United Daughters of the Confederacy and the Ladies Memorial Association took on critical roles in the creation of the narrative of the Lost Cause and the creation of the mascots for this cause, the statues of the Confederate soldiers and officers. One critical point that Labode and Levin make is that these statues were moved to more prominent places. Instead of erecting statues in cemeteries to honor the bygone Confederate dead, now these associations oversaw the construction of these statues in civic spaces.[35] However, they also wanted to link their memories with those of other Confederate memory makers in the region who were still attempting to deal with the loss of life and property in the aftermath of the Civil War. Winberry argues that the building of these Confederate statues took on an urgency toward the end of the nineteenth century and the dawn of the twentieth because many of these Confederate veterans were dying. Women who had cared for Confederate gravesites and taken charge of southern memory decided that the statues of Lee, Forrest, Davis, and others would serve as the connective tissue that white people needed to hold on to their past.[36]

Chapter 5 marks a transition in this book, because a different group of observers begin interacting with these memorials to the Confederacy. Readers learn about the reception of the Cotton Carnival in Black neighborhoods of Memphis. Although white Memphis enjoyed the images of the carnival and the feelings of sentimentality that the parades and floats encouraged, Black Memphians looked on with dismay. They believed that the carnival did not display the true role of African Americans in slavery. In response, several prominent African American business and political leaders decided to create their own celebration of cotton, complete with their own Black king and queen. The Cotton Makers Jubilee was not meant to be the Cotton Carnival in blackface. These men and women were serious about promoting cotton and various other career opportunities that agriculture could offer the next generation. Organizers believed that by presenting Black women in gorgeous ball gowns and men in suits with crowns, they could offset the image of Black people that the Cotton Carnival organizers promoted.[37]

Chapter 6 discusses the pull between integrationist and segregationist forces occurring in the 1960s and the corresponding debate over the efficacy of the Cotton Makers Jubilee. There was a noticeable tension in this decade between those who believed that the passage of the Civil Rights Act called for the total dismantling of segregation and those who argued for exceptions on the basis of the preservation of Black traditions. For the NAACP and other organizations closely linked to the civil rights movement, the jubilee simply served as a reminder of racial struggles.

Chapter 7 highlights the Forrest statue theme once again and explains how Black activists began to reinterpret the statue throughout the latter decades of the twentieth century. Unlike the words of hope and admiration white people spoke at the statue's dedication, African Americans offered a very different perspective on Forrest's life and work. The protests of the late twentieth century against the Forrest statue, in many ways, were similar to those against the Cotton Makers Jubilee. Both groups decided that the story white southerners promoted concerning Reconstruction, the Civil War, and most importantly the experiences of the enslaved and freedmen was mostly fiction, and that they had a responsibility to respond.

The epilogue begins with a short narrative of the shooting at Mother Emanuel AME Church in 2015. It is my position that the shooting led to a swell of activity around all Confederate memorabilia. The desire to confront our Confederate past slammed into a familiar political enemy entitled white nationalism that embodied itself in the presidential campaign of Donald Trump. Just like at other points in history, those of us who choose to highlight the lives of the enslaved and their descendants have to fight through the noise of white supremacy that wants Black Americans to just get over it. "It" being the degradation and humiliation of a race of people who have struggled to eke out an existence filled with dignity and self-respect while their white brethren benefit from the obstacles placed in the way of African Americans.

The efforts of African Americans to become a part of southern history are worthy of examination because the counternarrative provides a more bounteous interpretation of American history. When African Americans develop their counternarrative to Confederate (and thereby American) history, they demonstrate the white hegemony reflected in most historical accounts. They also take ownership of this history that has controlled how people have interpreted their lives and their experiences. The winners tell the tale of how they overcame insurmountable odds, and of course they believe they were right, and in the case of neo-Confederates, in their telling, their ancestors were right even if they were wrong. This is what African American activists protesting symbols of southern heritage blatantly reveal to these flame holders. Hopefully the following chapters will enable readers to understand that southern history as they have understood it has not been inclusive, to understand the reasons why that history excluded certain groups, and to understand how to move forward in this endeavor of creating an inclusive southern history.

An article in the *United Daughters of the Confederacy* magazine told the story of how Forrest came to turn his life over to Christ. He listened to a sermon based on one of Jesus's parables found in the book of Matthew:

> Listen! A farmer went out to plant some seeds. As he scattered them across his field, some seeds fell on a footpath, and the birds came and ate them. Other seeds fell on shallow soil with underlying rock. The seeds sprouted quickly because the soil was shallow. But the plants soon wilted under the hot sun, and since they didn't have deep roots, they died. Other seeds fell among thorns that grew up and choked out the tender plants. Still other

> seeds fell on fertile soil, and they produced a crop that was thirty, sixty, and even a hundred times as much as had been planted! Anyone with ears to hear should listen and understand.[38]

Forrest listened to this sermon and concluded that he had been living his life on rocky ground and needed to make a change. Unfortunately, neo-Confederates have lived the past 150 years thinking that their ancestors planted their seeds in fertile ground. What they do not realize is that those seeds landed in shallow, rocky soil in which the narratives blossomed and gave the appearance of fecundity. This text is an attempt to make the study of southern history more productive as scholars learn more about how the narrative of African Americans is inextricably intertwined with the history of the Old South.

1

DEFINING FREEDOM IN ANTEBELLUM AND POSTBELLUM MEMPHIS

African Americans living in Memphis, Tennessee, whether enslaved or free, during the nineteenth century always looked for ways to expand what little independence they had. Alternately, white Memphians made it their duty to curtail any semblance of Black freedom at every possible turn. What ensued throughout the nineteenth and twentieth centuries was a battle between the races concerning control over the Black population. The harder Black Memphians pushed for better access to jobs, education, or political autonomy, the harder white Memphians pushed back in order to keep the African American population in its place, especially in public spaces. Black Tennesseans' push for entrée into and occupation of public space made them more than static characters in the fairy tale of southern history their white neighbors created.

White Tennesseans have had a long history of being anxious when they had to share public spaces with African Americans. As early as 1794, when Tennessee was still a part of North Carolina, legislators passed laws that provided for patrols of the streets in order to control the Black population. By 1806, when Tennessee was a state in its own right, the legislators built upon those earlier laws by requiring that each town council choose its own delegates to serve in six-man patrols. The law empowered these officers to police both the slave and free populations. Lawmakers wanted to make sure that the patrolmen targeted free people who "encouraged disorderliness among the slaves."[1] In that sense the patrols were one of the first instances in which white southerners made public space their domain. Of course, both the enslaved and free persons of color resisted the attempts to control them, and they carved out spaces where they could exercise agency.

One of the most common ways for the enslaved to demonstrate a level of independence was when they worked and lived in urban settings like Memphis. As a rule, enslaved people in west Tennessee lived on plantations, but on occasion masters hired out their slaves to work in urban areas. Among the many reasons that former slaves sought out a new life in a city like Memphis was that, as a group, urban slaves experienced more freedom than their rural counterparts. Their freedom was so visible that in 1849 one of the editors of a local newspaper, the *Memphis Daily Eagle,* chastised his readers on the dangers of having a slave population in the midst of white citizens without some form of control. Another problem plaguing the city, according to this particular editorial, was the increasing number of "free Negroes" that inhabited the city. White Memphians believed that the free Black people were a dangerous entity that threatened the stability of the city, despite the fact that they only made up about 1 percent of the total population. They considered free Black Memphians to be "immoral, unproductive, slothful, and injurious to property—particularly slave property."[2] The city officials, in the opinion of the editorial writer, did not control the behavior of slaves and their masters in terms of freedom of movement. This was especially true when masters allowed their slaves to hire out their own time. The editor believed that to allow a slave to do this made the slave unfit for his duty to serve. In his estimation, the practice "debauched the slave" and made "him a strolling agent of discontent, disorder and immorality, among the slave population."[3]

From the editor's comments it appears that the city had sections that were "'Negro' resorts" where drinking and frivolity were the orders of the day. In the editor's analysis, the problem of roaming Black people (whether slave or free) was so unmanageable that he called on all thinking citizens to present evidence before the grand jury if they found anyone in violation of city ordinances. He believed this action encouraged all parties, master or slave, to understand that the city leaders would not tolerate this behavior.[4] What this editorial indicates is that slaves in the city had a modicum of independence and access to public space. They could walk the city without supervision and they had access to Black communities where they could drink and socialize. This freedom did not go unnoticed by white Memphians, or at least the editorial staff of the newspaper.

The strong desire among white Memphians to rid the city of free "Negroes"[5] and increase control over the enslaved population grew in the mid to late 1830s. In the opening decades of the nineteenth century, the state legislature had allowed freed slaves to stay in the state as long as they had the proper papers that identified them as free persons. But by 1831, the state of Tennessee required that all emancipated slaves had to leave the state immediately upon their acquisition of freedom, and the state provided ten dollars to the Tennessee Colonization Society for every removed free person.[6] Not so coincidentally, the year 1831 was the same year of Nat Turner's rebellion in Virginia. As a result, states across the South began passing ordinances to limit the presence of free people of color. Politicians and their constituents believed that free people negatively influenced the behavior of the enslaved whether on a plantation or in an urban setting. Legislatures began to ensure that no free Black Americans could migrate to their states. They also encouraged colonization and made it more difficult for slaveowners to emancipate their slaves.[7]

In Memphis, the city council enacted even more restrictive laws concerning the movement of slaves and free people. This was due, at least in part, to an increase in the city's Black population. By the end of the decade, the city created the position of town watchman, whose job it was to arrest every slave or free person out after 10:00 p.m. Further, if an enslaved Black person did not have a pass, the council authorized city officials to inflict ten lashes on their "naked backs" and to charge slaveowners a two-dollar fine. If the watchman caught a free person out after curfew, then he was to jail him and charge a ten-dollar fine.[8]

The city's concern about the Black population grew even more by the 1860s because of a dramatic increase in the enslaved and free population in the decade between 1850 and 1860. In 1850 the slave and free Black population stood at 2,486, with free "Negroes" making up 126 of the total number; by 1860 that number grew to 3,871, with the percentage of free Black people remaining the same. In real terms this meant that the city experienced a 64 percent increase in the number of Black citizens in a relatively short period of time. For white southerners, this increase meant that they had to hold on to any control they could muster over this population. They thought themselves superior to the slave and felt it their duty to monitor and limit any behavior that allowed African Americans to express any freedom or independence. However, the fact that they had to write down regulations and punish slaves for infractions involving movement in and out of public space makes it clear that slaves and free people pushed the envelope in order to create spaces for their own independence. All of the activities city officials believed they had to limit represented a form of resistance on the part of African Americans. As they worked and lived among white Memphians, they challenged the notion that there should be limits on any of their behavior.[9] The actions of the Memphis City Council were an outlier in terms of the activities of broader southern legislatures. Author Emily West points out that in general the size of the free or enslaved population did not move politicians to act one way or another; however, there was a steady drumbeat toward more strict controls over the enslaved and free populations throughout the region.[10]

In the city of Memphis, officials took action to curb what they believed to be disruptive behavior on the part of the city's Black population. As evidenced by the editorial written in 1849, there was still a lot of work for the officials and citizens to do. In 1860 the issues with the Black population had become so disturbing to white Memphians that the paper's editors believed it important to reprint all of the local ordinances regarding slaves and free persons. This article reminded citizens that slaves could not hire out their own time without risk of fines to their owners. Editors also reminded readers that it was unlawful for interracial groups to congregate except for worship. Further, no person was to sell alcohol, property, or establish any rental agreements with slaves. And lastly, Black people had to abide by a 10:00 p.m. curfew, and any Black person from out of town had to leave Memphis before sundown.[11]

The Civil War broke out in 1861, and white Memphians' concerns regarding the Black population continued. Free and enslaved Black people (many of whom were in the city because they abandoned the plantation seeking the protection of Union soldiers after Memphis was occupied in 1862) provided an even bigger problem for white Memphians by that time. Not only did the former slaves come to the city, but they also began to work for the enemy of white southerners. Former female slaves worked as inspectors for the Union army and searched white women they suspected of smuggling goods to the Confederate soldiers. They also worked as laundresses and cooks for Union soldiers in what became contraband camps.[12] At the same time that newly free Black women took on duties in the Union army, the Tennessee legislature decided to conscript all registered free Black males between the ages of fifteen and fifty for service in the Confederate army. The Confederate legislature gave any sheriff the authority to arrest all Black males who resisted the law. This law only applied to free Black males, because the white men in the legislature believed that their slaves were loyal and would fight for their masters and mistresses.[13]

The Union army conquered the city on June 6, 1862. By the next year, federal troops occupied the state, and the free (and newly freed) Black population made decisions about what types of freedom they wanted for themselves and their families as they joined up with the contraband camps attached to the Union troops. Initially, Gen. William T. Sherman was not convinced that freedom for the slaves was a good thing, and he did not want to have anything to do with them. He soon came to realize that he needed their help to build fortifications and create transportation lines. For the freedmen, helping the Union army allowed them to participate in their freedom in a very real way and to enjoy their new status as citizens. In contrast, their presence among the federal forces, and specifically their appearance in uniform, was another point of annoyance and betrayal for white southerners.[14]

With the dawning of this new political day, freed persons decided to take advantage of all opportunities that presented themselves—in particular, those involving economic independence. One of the first ways Black Memphians decided to assert themselves in this occupied and then postwar society was to begin to sell their labor. Freed people who remained in rural areas continued to work under the labor contracts that began during the Civil War. Others traveled to Memphis in order to seek out jobs on the docks. If they remained in the country, they began to engage in sharecropping contracts with local landowners, or they occupied lands that slaveholders had abandoned. The desire of freed people to sell their labor ran into a brick wall of white southern planter resistance. While the goal of freed persons was to experience freedom, the mission of the former planter was to obtain a workforce that was as close to the slave system as possible. This meant that former slaves would often have to negotiate any salaries or benefits from the planters, who of course had formerly been slaveholders. This was a very thin rope the freed people had to walk because the planter class and law enforcement remained one and the same. If a Black worker rejected a contract, the planter could have a warrant sworn out on the worker for vagrancy. Once the police picked up a vagrant, he or she would be sent to the very plantation to work for the planter they were trying to get away from and on the planter's terms.[15]

Another benefit of freedom that the former slaves sought was education. School attendance grew after the war, and so did the aid of northern organizations and the Freedmen's Bureau. Unfortunately, white resentment and harassment also increased, but the students continued to pursue their goal of gaining literacy and more in spite of these hardships. The American Missionary Association worked to create learning institutions for young and older Black Memphians who chose to receive an education. There was one school on Beale Street, and another operated on President's Island just south of the city. Interest in these schools was so great that the missionaries had to begin evening classes to handle the demand. Another indicator for the demand for education within the Black community was their constant request for more teachers and the complaints about overcrowding in the schools.[16] It was in this area that an interesting struggle developed between the Black and white communities that reflected the larger struggle the two groups would have throughout the century.

The issue once again came down to control, specifically who controlled the education of Black Memphians. Freed people took every step they could to ensure that their children had access to education, but white missionaries and white Memphians did what they could to limit the autonomy of these Black schools. There were two types of schools in the mid-1860s for Black people: one controlled by the missionaries, and the other controlled by the Education Association, which Black Memphians funded. What followed between the parallel systems was a fight over who would be the superintendent, what type of curriculum should be taught (Black parents wanted a grammar school, as well as primary and secondary education, for their children while the missionaries only wanted grammar school and primary education), whether the teachers should be Black or white, and how much money should be spent on building and maintaining school buildings for Black children.

What had to be disheartening to freed Memphians was that they thought they could begin to control their own destinies only to discover that northerners could be just as paternalistic as white southerners. Although freed people funded their separate schools by donating ten cents a month to the general education fund of the Education Association, the Tennessee state legislature stymied their efforts when the state took over the funding of all schools. The state government charged counties with the responsibility of taxing citizens to fund their educational systems. They also told the counties across the state that to receive state funding, they had to demonstrate that they supported Black education to the same extent as white education.[17]

Memphis officials agreed to this funding arrangement, but they decided not to open schools for Black children in 1867 because the state had not lived up to its economic side of the agreement. Black schools stayed closed until the American Missionary Association raised the money for schools but only with the agreement that the city would repay the group once state funding came through. The state government and the missionary societies worked together to remove the Education Association from the equation of Black education, which caused a great deal of resentment. Further, white Memphians believed that education ruined Black people for work. They argued that educated "Negroes" would not want to work in their fields but instead would strive for something better and something more equal to opportunities white southerners benefited from.[18]

Before the official end of the Civil War, federal loyalists held a state convention to reunite Tennessee with the rest of the Union. The delegates decided to put an end to human chattel slavery by declaring any law that allowed one man to own another unconstitutional. During this session, they repudiated the state government's actions after the state seceded, and they declared the secession ordinance unconstitutional. The men in the state convention acted to restore Tennessee by meeting the requirements of Lincoln's reunification policy. However, there were Tennesseans, especially former Confederates, who believed that the actions of this group were illegitimate. No one had elected the men who made up the convention, and from the standpoint of ex-rebels they had no authority to speak for the entire state. Despite these objections, the convention members submitted their resolutions to the people for a vote, which passed overwhelmingly.[19]

While the delegates met in Nashville to restore the state to the Union, African American Tennesseans took an active role in asserting their newfound freedom. African American men wanted to make sure that the delegation granted them the right to vote. They also wanted to seek protection from the courts if former rebels attempted to interfere with that right. In a petition submitted to the committee, the freedmen of Tennessee expressed concern that their former masters would try to re-enslave them. They reiterated that they were ready for all of the rights, privileges, and responsibilities of citizenship. The men who presented the petition reminded the convention that the "colored" man had fought when the Union government needed him to fight. Therefore, if he could be trusted with weapons on the battlefield, then surely he could be trusted with the weapons of freedom, which were the vote and the right to seek legal redress in the courts.[20]

Another source of agitation between the Black and white populations of the state was the franchise bill of 1865. Once the state government reconstituted itself, the state house of representatives received a report from the Joint Judiciary Committee on Franchise. The report argued that the state government should limit the voting rights of white males who had been sympathetic to the Confederacy. The bill prohibited anyone from voting who "had served as officers—civil, diplomatic, or military in the Confederacy." Further, the bill denied the right to vote to those men who had left their posts in the United States military to offer aid to the Confederacy. Under this bill, the prohibition against white male voting was not permanent. The measure required that they be denied the right to vote for no more than fifteen years. At the end of that period, those affected by the bill had to register and take an oath of allegiance to the Union. While the state legislature passed this act, it also entertained legislation and petitions that considered granting Black men the right to vote. The ex-Confederates found the notion of Black men voting intolerable. In their opinion, leaving white men without the right to vote while granting that right to freedmen made them the slaves of Black men. In the end, the state legislature did not pass any laws that granted Black men the right to vote. At that session, however, they adopted legislation that restricted the freedom of their "colored" citizens. They made a law that prohibited Black citizens from making contracts, another that ensured Black Tennesseans could only testify against other "colored" citizens, and, lastly, a law that directed that failure to pay any fine could result in Black citizens being turned over to white southerners to work off their debts. These laws were in effect until January of 1867. At that point, the legislature passed an act that allowed people of African and Native American descent to be witnesses in court. Later that year, the legislature granted Black and Indian citizens the right to engage in contracts and litigation. They could also expect the same protections from the courts as white Tennesseans, and it was now illegal to punish the "colored" population differently than white citizens for the same crime.[21]

The year 1865 revealed that many individual Memphians took steps to stretch the boundaries of their newfound freedom. Rev. Morris Henderson, for instance, took the opportunity of Confederate defeat and Black emancipation to release himself and his congregation from the watchful eye of the all-white First Baptist Church. Henderson and his members built the Beale Street Baptist Church, and it became the first church built by ex-slaves in the mid-South.[22]

Added to these concrete pushes within the freedmen's community for an education and access to legal redress also came an "air" of freedom. After the Civil War, Black Memphians' attitudes changed toward white Memphians. They no longer felt the need to show the deference to whites that they showed under slavery. It is no surprise that this dismayed white Memphians to no end. One white person who demonstrated this anger and frustration at the results of the Civil War in Memphis was Elizabeth Avery Meriwether.

Born in 1824 in West Tennessee, Meriwether wrote about her life experiences at age ninety-two as a message to future generations. Meriwether's observations about the Civil War and Reconstruction reveal a common attitude of southerners as it related to life in the South under what she labeled "Negro" domination. Elizabeth married into a family of colonization activists who decided to free their slaves and send them to Liberia. Garrett Meriwether, Elizabeth's father-in-law, believed that he had a duty to educate his slaves and teach them how to live and work in a free society. His goal, according to Meriwether, was to have them go back to Africa and "Christianize and civilize their savage cousins." Meriwether claimed that she opposed slavery. Nonetheless, after marriage she owned a slave named "Evelyn." Meriwether decided that she would rather have a servant do the drudgery of housework than engage in the tasks herself. Minor, her husband, did not fight her on the issue, stating that if she wanted a slave it "was her affair." Regardless, she clearly believed in white supremacy. After the war she found herself stunned by writers, politicians, and editors who argued otherwise.[23]

For Meriwether, Memphis was a perfect example of all that was wrong with Reconstruction. She believed that "any stranger . . . would suppose the Blacks not the Whites, were masters in the South" if they viewed the actions of Black and white southerners in everyday situations. Much of her outrage came from the fact that she did not feel she could travel in the city with the same respect and comfort she had before the war. To illustrate this point, she recounted an incident that occurred when she returned to the city after the surrender and witnessed events that greatly "distressed and alarmed her." She saw Black soldiers "staggering" in the street. What seemed to annoy her the most was that they walked "four and five abreast [on the sidewalk] and made not the slightest effort to let white women pass." She believed that if she "had not voluntarily gotten out into the street they would have elbowed [her] off the sidewalk." To add insult to injury, she stated that freed people gave her "insolent looks" and proclaimed to her and anyone else who listened that Black and white Memphians were all equal and that she should not expect any special treatment or deference because of her color.[24]

This frustration and tension between the freed people and their former enslavers would lead to the Memphis riots of 1866. The desire of white Memphians to regain order in their society and cement their control over the Black population crested. White citizens constantly asserted their rights to political access and to be free from what they called "'Negro' rule." As early as January of 1866, white people raged against the "offensive" presence of Black soldiers in the city. The *Memphis Daily Avalanche* reported that the Black garrisons were "against the natural feelings of the white man . . . [and] against peace." The paper stated that the "colored" troops corrupted the Black population and raised their "expectations beyond reason," as they became "discontented with plain tasks of their labor." As far as white Memphians were concerned the troops were evil and a nuisance. The presence of these troops to enforce white southern cooperation was an insult in their view. The editors of the paper stated that if the commanders believed they needed troops, then why not have troops of the same race instead of the "infuriating" presence of "Negro soldiers"? In case anyone was confused as to the object of the public's vitriol, the editors made it clear that the soldier was the problem. Especially since they wore the "uniform of the conqueror" and patrolled the South with an "air of command."[25]

Just a few months later, the newspaper editors of the *Avalanche* again assailed the presence of Black troops, and they also added that the Freedmen's Bureau was equally as evil. The editors had just received word that Union officials had summarily dismissed the petition white citizens of Memphis had filed in the previous year. In this document they requested the removal of the troops. Gen. George Stoneman, the commander of the Memphis area after the war, stated that as long as white Memphians conducted themselves in a disorderly fashion, they would have to submit to the control of the Union regardless of the color of the troops. The editors fumed at the thought that they were anything but contrite with respect to the new order of the day. They also complained about the lack of civil authority exercised over the Black population. They pointed out that when the police arrested white men, they paid fines or spent time in jail. However, when officers detained Black men, the rest of the Black community came to "rescue" them from punishment.[26] The presence of Black people in public probably was not offensive to white Memphians in and of itself; it was their presence outside the expected roles as servants and instead in positions of authority that was the problem. On May 1, 1866, white Memphians exacted their revenge on the "colored" soldier and the "radical" government that had placed them in their midst. White Memphians violently attacked the free people and the institutions they established in one of the worst post–Civil War riots in United States history.[27]

Although the riots began on the first day of May, the incidents that precipitated the event occurred in late April. According to the testimony of a Memphis physician, on or about April 23, 1866, the police arrested a Black man and beat him severely. The arrest occurred in an area where a number of the Black soldiers lived. After the gruesome arrest, many among the soldiers decided that that would be the last time a police agent came into their neighborhood and committed such an act. On or about May 1, a crowd of Black citizens gathered, soldiers among them, on a street corner in south Memphis. They caused a commotion during which someone sent for the police to disperse the crowd. The police arrived and began to make their arrests. The man who had been beaten the week before was among the crowd, and he recognized the officer who had abused him. He began to call out to the rest of the crowd, and the soldiers surrounded the officer and shouted, "Club him" and "shoot him." The officer escaped their clutches, and as the police left with their prisoners, the soldiers began to fire their weapons in the air. The police, assuming that the group meant to shoot them, fired their weapons into the crowd, and a gun battle ensued. After all of the weapons were silenced, people began to exclaim that one police officer was dead.[28]

After this round of battle the police officers went back into the city to get additional guns and reinforcements to quell the crowd. When they came back to the scene, an even greater number of Black soldiers greeted them. They exchanged bullets, but neither side backed down. Witnesses heard the soldiers command the white officers to "halt" and to "drop their weapons." By sundown this second fracas left many bruised, but none were dead. Also, it was at this point that the soldiers went back into the fort, but the white officers still had revenge on their minds. What happened next was one of the bloodiest scenes the city had ever witnessed. Over the next twenty-four hours, white mobs went through Black neighborhoods and attempted to kill every "Negro" they saw. Besides wanton murders in the street committed by white police officers and their agents there was destruction of great magnitude. Mobs burned schools, homes, and churches to the ground while they stole from, beat, and raped Black citizens with impunity. By the end of the disturbance, the US House Committee in charge of investigating the riot estimated that more than $130,000 (or $2.4 million in today's dollars) worth of damage occurred to property in Memphis.[29]

After the riots cooled, the *Memphis Avalanche* editors decided to sum up what the riots meant. In their opinion the riots proved one thing: "that the Southern man will not be ruled by the 'Negro.'" The editorial went on to congratulate white Memphians on their achievement of getting their city back. The white man was in control once again, and now the city could return to the good old days for which the populace yearned. Yet again the editorial pages of the *Avalanche* laid the blame for the riots at the feet of the "colored" soldiers. The editors claimed that for months the soldiers ran the city into ruin. They claimed that soldiers constantly robbed, beat, and even killed white Memphians with no punishment in response, while the "good" and "decent" white citizens stood by and watched in horror. Never once, according to the editorial, did whites step in and defend themselves or take revenge on the soldiers. The tipping point was the gunfight that occurred on May 1. The editors surmised that "the 'Negroes' now know, to their sorrow, that it is best not to arouse the fury of the white man." Interestingly, the editorial stated that the Black persons who served in positions as drayman, hackmen, porters, or servants were not the problem for white citizens. They performed their duties, and one imagines, did not offend whites with "an air of command" in the execution of their responsibilities. One reason for these assaults may lie in the final few paragraphs of the editorial. The editor showed great excitement when the paper received word that residents of south Memphis (who were overwhelmingly African American) now sought out country homes. As a result of the riots, the Black population wanted to leave the city, and the editor thought it a fine idea. He believed that the country farmers could pay them for their work, thus relieving the city of that burden. The second reason the editor favored this move was because the former slaves "[placed] themselves beyond the ready reach and contamination of the low pimps of that 'ebony line' whose position and pay depend upon fomenting troubles between the whites and blacks."[30]

Despite these horrific assaults on their mental and physical conditions, African Americans remained optimistic about their rights as citizens of Tennessee not even a year after the riot. In February of 1867, Gen. John Eaton, with the Union army, spoke to a group of "colored" Memphians. He talked about their duties and responsibilities once the state granted them the franchise. The general praised the gathering for their continued loyalty. He told them that the fact that the slave and free "Negro" did not take up arms for Jefferson Davis proved that the group was ready to shoulder their part in making this nation great. He also noted that despite the fact that the Tennessee legislature passed their version of the Black codes, the Black population did not abandon the state or take up arms against their white neighbors. From Eaton's standpoint, the ballot had little to do with Black men being able to marry white women, as former Confederates claimed. But the ballot had everything to do with the Black man having power in his government. Eaton exhorted his listeners to continue on the path to good citizenship through memberships in loyal leagues and reminded them to stay informed by reading loyal newspapers.[31] The fact that this meeting occurred nine months after the riots demonstrates that freed people were not scared into silence by the violence they faced. They were willing to step back into public space and take their place in the newly reformed Union.

Ever since the closing years of the Civil War, Black Memphians had gathered on the Fourth of July to make a claim on the guarantees of the Constitution. Their picnics and parades throughout the city were not massive demonstrations against the injustices they suffered under slavery and Reconstruction. Their public patriotic displays were messages to the Union community that they wanted to be a part of the nation. They loved the flag and what it stood for, and more importantly the Union could always count on them to be ready to fight for federal principles. As Brian Page points out in his article "Stand by the Flag," Black Memphians decided that by embracing the holiday they believed that they proved themselves worthy of complete equality.[32] Unfortunately their efforts to demonstrate loyalty were not enough for northern politicians who forfeited freed people's rights in the name of reunion. Reconstruction ended with the election of 1876. Rutherford B. Hayes, the Republican candidate, did not have enough electoral votes to claim the presidency; Samuel Tilden, the Democratic candidate, won the popular vote, but because of a dispute over twenty electoral votes, he was one short, and he could not take the office of president either. The country faced political gridlock until the parties reached a compromise. Southern leaders (who represented the entire Democratic Party at that time) agreed to cease any challenges to Hayes if the federal government agreed to remove federal troops from the South. Politicians sacrificed African American access to the political process on the altar of national unity. The troops provided a measure of protection for newly freedmen who wished to exercise the franchise and those who wanted to run for office. After this compromise the decline of African American political activity was dramatic.[33]

White southerners set out to accomplish culturally what they could not do militarily. They redeemed themselves and their cause of southern independence. Once white southerners took control of the legislatures and retained seats in the US House of Representatives and Senate, the time came to redefine the meaning of the war. As white southerners rebuilt their society, they defined the true cause of every Confederate soldier. In this myth, southern veterans fought for freedom and independence from the tyrannical rule of an oppressive federal government.[34]

Observers noted that the ex-Confederates took every opportunity to explain that the Civil War had not been a war about southern rebellion. To the contrary, southerners who took up arms against the federal government lived up to the ideals of the founding fathers. Their commitment was not to the institution of slavery per se, but to being free from the federal government's oppression. The war was about individualism and self-rule, and they believed that this was the basis for establishing the Confederate nation. The message of men like Thomas Settle Jr., a former slave holder, was lost. In 1867 Settle stated, "The war was commenced to perpetuate slavery, but it went the other way, contrary to all the leaders of the rebellion. Therefore, slavery is forever dead." By the end of the century, southern loyalists did not mention slavery's connection to the Confederate States of America. Increasingly the cost of the desire for reunion between the two warring factions meant that African Americans, at least publicly, had to sacrifice their memories.[35]

Southern women took the opportunity to capitalize on the restoration of white power and the weakening authority of the federal government in the region. They transformed their Ladies Memorial Associations (LMA), which concerned themselves with caring for Confederate veterans and their widows, into a regional organization called the United Daughters of the Confederacy (UDC). Members of this group not only cared for Confederate veterans but vindicated their cause. These socialites did not champion the principles of the Confederacy because they needed some activities to occupy their time. The people they wanted to exonerate were their ancestors, their slaveholding high-ranking soldiers and government officials, who had caused the war in the first place.[36]

The Tennessee chapter of the UDC began in 1894 with a call from Mrs. Caroline Meriwether Goodlett to the many statewide women's auxiliaries. The women who belonged to these associations served as a support system for soldiers throughout the war. Once the battles ended, these women expressed a need to care for maimed soldiers, the widowed, and the orphans of the war. They worked to raise money, and they supported legislation that funded homes dedicated to the men they believed had fought valiantly for the most noble of causes. In recounting the history of the Tennessee Division, UDC member Annie Cody wrote that they "banded together in memory of the grandest civilization, the bravest men and the fairest women the world has ever known: for the purpose of upholding the ideals and traditions for which these men died and these women suffered, the United Daughters of the Confederacy has a wonderful heritage to guard . . . as a sacred trust and give themselves whole-heartedly to the work for what they were organized."[37] Cody went on to outline the objectives of the organization, describing them as social, educational, memorial, benevolent, and historical. The women committed to honoring the soldiers who served by taking care of the loved ones they left behind as well as those veterans who no longer could care for themselves. The UDC took on the responsibility of providing them with housing, food, and clothing. UDC members also committed to fostering love within their ranks, but it was the last mission of the UDC, namely, to "collect, teach and preserve true history," that propelled the myths of southern history into the twentieth century.[38]

In their collecting, preserving, and teaching of southern history, UDC members developed a powerful narrative that has permeated popular culture in cities like Memphis for most of the twentieth century. UDC history explained that masters did everything they could to care for their "other family," the slaves in the quarters. Many of the essays submitted to the *UDC Magazine* for publication concerning plantation life fondly discussed the music coming from the quarters, and the struggles that masters and mistresses endured on behalf of their slaves. In case any reader had any concern about the harshness of slavery, the women of the UDC readily dismissed any such argument. They reminded readers that the master was the one truly burdened because of his responsibility to care for, discipline, and provide an environment for the spiritual salvation of Black people.[39]

During the nineteenth century, when the UDC began this project to rebuild the Confederate soldier's image, Frederick Douglass served as the primary voice that exhorted African Americans not to forget the past. However, as historians such as David Blight pointed out, memory for African Americans in the postwar South was extremely painful. For freed people and their descendants to remember, they had to dredge up dehumanizing treatment at the hands of their former masters. Remembering also forced them to consider all that they had lost at the end of Reconstruction. Memory in this case could be torturous. Douglass sympathized with those who wished to forget. He stated that "forgetting was 'nature's plan of relief.'" Nonetheless, he believed it was imperative that Black Americans keep the past at the forefront of their minds because the ammunition to challenge contemporary segregation lay in their ability to remember and articulate their experiences. Therefore, Douglass not only fought against the developing narrative among white southerners concerning the reasons for the Civil War and the exact nature of slavery, but he also had to challenge leaders within the Black community as well. Men such as Alexander Crummell, a leader in the emigrationist movement, took the position that memory could be hazardous because it paralyzed the person doing the remembering and could be "dangerous in excess."[40]

The debate between these two men highlights the two tracks that civil rights activists took in the late nineteenth century. While both perspectives led to racial uplift, in a sense, one believed that memory of enslavement should serve as a mark by which the race should measure its improvement. The other, represented by Douglass, wanted to facilitate uplift by using the memory of slavery, and the Civil War, to force Americans to live up to the "civil and political rights" established in the Constitution and won for Black men and women by Black and white Union soldiers alike at the close of the war.[41]

Paul Shackel argues that "the control of a group's memory is usually a question of power." He further states that "those who are able to commemorate the past are those who have the money and political power to publicly remember a particular past." The UDC did not need to be of one accord with Black southerners about the meaning of the war. They also did not need to come to an agreement with northerners before they decided on how to recount the war because the groups that control society often dictate the official account of an event.[42] There is no doubt that the UDC was one of those groups and heavily in control of the mythmaking in the white South. Through the ritual of monument dedication, UDC members passed down their version of southern history to future generations. Most importantly, they transmitted this culture to their children, whom they charged with carrying on the torch of the "Lost Cause." These women continued their role of caretakers, but now they were the caretakers of the Confederate traditions.[43]

Northern politicians and businessmen also participated in this effort to promote the ideology of the Lost Cause. One such example is the uproar among southern elites about the purchase and removal of Libby Prison located in Richmond, Virginia, in 1888. The men who bought and reconstructed the prison in Chicago tried to assuage southern outrage by stating that their museum was about fairness and propagating the reasons for the war from both the northern and southern points of view. Despite the developers' reassurances, both northerners and southerners remained concerned about the refabrication of this dreaded facility. For those northerners who wanted to focus on reconciling the sections, the prison would reignite hatred between the two regions. For white southerners, the Libby Prison relocation was about protecting southern history from the commercialism of northern industry. In essence, southerners saw these developers as creating a tourist trap at the expense of their ancestors.[44]

UDC members committed themselves to the "vindication of Confederate men," as well as recording "the sacrifices of Confederate women, and the [exoneration] of the South." This organization set the standard for communities across the South to meet in order to be included in the movement to cleanse the region of its past. The UDC felt challenged by the North because they believed that non-southerners who wrote accounts of the war approached the subject with a bias "against the South," so it was the duty of the members to turn this perspective around. As women and as mothers they were the keepers of the flame, and they taught their children about the past and what they determined to be the truth of southern history, so the importance of the UDC's education objective cannot be overstated. The daughters did not write about the military battles. They left that to the men. But what they did write about was the peaceful antebellum plantation life with contented and obedient slaves. They argued that slavery was tough for the masters because they had to govern and provide for such an ignorant population, and that the public should be grateful for the slave owners' contributions because they ably taught this unfortunate people about Christianity. Therefore, they performed mission work as their religion commanded them to do. UDC members also wrote extensively about what they perceived to be the magnificent character of men like Robert E. Lee and other Confederate generals. The UDC even discussed Reconstruction, the horrible impact of "'Negro' rule" in the South, and how organizations like the Ku Klux Klan had to restore the rightful order of white supremacy.[45]

In the legacy of the war, as perpetuated by defeated southerners, slavery was a peripheral concern instead of the one central cause for the war. This aspect of the southern mystique is very tricky. While the issue of slavery was supposedly a secondary (some contemporary Confederate loyalists will even argue tertiary) cause for the war, the issue of the role of African Americans within a postbellum South was a primary concern for white southerners. This sentiment is especially apparent in the comments of contemporary observers and Memphis newspapers. Another issue that the southern loyalists ignored was the active role that African Americans played in obtaining their freedom. To undermine this role, UDC members asserted that moral outrage or a sense of duty to a cause greater than themselves was not the motivation for the United States government. According to southern enthusiasts, the US government and its agents were no more than busybodies interfering with southern traditions.[46] Frederick Douglass saw these narratives forming during the latter part of the nineteenth century and could only look on in despair. The southern white public assaulted post-Reconstruction African Americans in every sense of the word. Their intent was to reclaim the valor and glory of their ancestors. Douglass and other civil rights leaders had to deal with not only the cultural assaults but the legal ones as well.[47] From Douglass's standpoint, the promise of the Civil War's legacy was slipping through the hands of those who held that promise so dear. Despite the verdict on the battlefield concerning the status of African Americans, white southerners took control of every level of social, political, and economic life. They also reinterpreted the meaning of the war so that US citizens' attention never really focused on the conditions of former slaves. This refocusing served to absolve white Americans of any responsibility toward these newly freed citizens. Civil rights leaders struggled with an appropriate response to America's forgetting. And this is where freedmen and -women have remained throughout the twentieth and twenty-first centuries, fighting and pushing to create and be included in the southern narrative.

Whether enslaved or freed from slavery, African Americans occupying public space was a problem for white Memphians since the early nineteenth century. White Memphians were not concerned with the reason for their presence. Black people might have been working, receiving an education, or just creating their own communities, but their presence in the public arenas without being under the direct supervision of white Memphians was a political act. Their mere presence in Memphis society was a constant reminder that the social order had changed in a fundamental way. By the end of the nineteenth century, southern state legislatures had instituted restrictions on Black movement in public spaces, but that did not push African

Americans into the shadows of Memphis society. As the second chapter will demonstrate, there was one group in particular that continued to have a public presence much to the chagrin of white (as well as some Black) residents of the city. The chapter will highlight the various intraracial struggles concerning public space and answer the questions surrounding how different classes challenged the white status quo that wanted to restrict their participation in the public spaces of Memphis.

2

THE CHALLENGES OF FREEDOM

As the nineteenth century came to a close, Confederate memories became embedded in the fabric of southern society. While Frederick Douglass fought to retain the true meaning of the Civil War, many of his contemporaries did not make the same connections between the development of this philosophy and the attitudes that ferociously worked to thwart African American progress. Many late nineteenth-century Black leaders, including those in Memphis, believed in racial uplift. They felt that when Black citizens proved themselves, the American dream would be within their reach. In particular, there were two groups who advocated for this position: assimilationists and accommodationists. When these groups discussed their racial philosophies, they directed their criticisms toward a third group of Black citizens made up of migrants and working-class people. Members of this group came to urban areas like Memphis from neighboring rural communities to have access to better economic opportunities.

The group of African Americans who believed that Black people needed to use the method of assimilation to achieve racial equality were also part of W. E. B Du Bois's "talented tenth." This group maintained that their values were American values and that they should not endure any kind of treatment that was demeaning in public spaces. They believed that they could fit in with white society if they were just given an opportunity. On the other hand, the accommodationists (many of whom aligned themselves with Booker T. Washington) believed that the way to achieve racial equality was not to protest or to sue. Accommodation simply meant that Black people needed to accept the racial order and learn how to survive—and then thrive—within the racial caste system. From their perspective, the majority of Black citizens needed to accept their need for morality, literacy, and occupational training. After they acquired these things, white Americans would grant them the awesome responsibility of governing and working with them.[1]

The third group was made up of the poorer classes of African Americans. Many of them were rural people who migrated to the city, and they were unwilling to submit to the social prescriptions of either the assimilationists or accommodationists. As noted in the last chapter, Memphis saw a dramatic increase in Black migrants beginning in 1862, after the fall of Memphis to Union forces. Not only did these migrants pose a problem for the Irish working class, who saw the migrants as invading their neighborhoods and encroaching on their job opportunities, but they also proved to be a problem for Black Memphians whose families had lived in the city for generations. No one schooled the migrants in the ways of racial etiquette, and they tended to think that the war gave them more freedom, not less. These were the people who made it difficult for the more established Memphians to insert themselves into the middle-class lifestyle they desired.[2]

The hostilities among the African American communities became so great that established Black Memphians decided to petition the Freedmen's Bureau to ship all migrants back to the Mississippi and Arkansas countryside after the 1866 riots. As in other southern cities, migrants came to Memphis to take advantage of the new opportunities that they believed freedom and urban life offered them. What they found once they arrived was that they were not welcomed by any group. The established African Americans felt that the newcomers pushed race relations back with such unacceptable behavior as drinking or loitering. In his work on the Black middle and upper class, E. Franklin Frazier asserts that loitering was not a minor issue for the educated classes of any race. Loitering, whether it was in public saloons or even at card games, was detrimental to the spirit and uplift of the Black race. Free time and idleness led to vice, and it was the job of educators and pastors to stamp out this injurious behavior. Black Memphians, who had lived in the city for generations, believed that this new group of migrants disturbed the relatively comfortable peace that Black people had established in Memphis society. White Memphians also felt overwhelmed by Black migrants constantly streaming in from the countryside.[3]

This chapter explores differing meanings of freedom among the classes of African Americans living in Memphis. The middle and upper classes often shared the racist assumptions of white people regarding the poorer classes of Black Americans. They believed that Black men raped white women and subsequently found themselves lynched for their criminal behavior.[4] The Black industrial and political leaders of the city did not always agree upon how to solve the problems of the working class. Some believed that the state had a responsibility to teach young people about values as well as basic educational skills. Others maintained that the church and the home provided the best opportunity for Black Memphians to pull themselves out of poverty and become productive members of society.[5]

Working-class African Americans living in Memphis believed that the results of the Civil War meant freedom. They often had physical altercations with white citizens about the type of treatment they received in the public sphere. By the 1890s, streetcars became sites of racial contests to determine which race would remain dominant and control the activities of Black Memphians. The physical and verbal confrontations among working-class Black and white people frustrated the wealthier classes of Black Memphians as they tried to integrate into white middle-class society. Any accomplishments they made in education or industry were overshadowed when they opened the newspapers and read about Black criminal behavior. To offset these negative images of Black Memphians a woman named Ida B. Wells partnered with local businessmen to form the publication entitled *Memphis Free Speech and Headlight*. As editor of the newspaper, Wells believed that "the condition of the masses gave large excuse for the humiliations and proscriptions under which we [Black people] labored, that when wealth, education and character became more general among us, the cause being removed the effect would cease, and justice be accorded to all alike. I shared the general belief that good newspapers entering regularly the homes of our people in every state could do more to bring about this result than any agency."[6] In effect, Wells chose to foster uplift through her newspaper. She stressed character building and morality in order to stave off lynching.

The issue that propelled Wells into the international spotlight was lynching. In 1892, three of her friends, Thomas Moss, Calvin McDowell, and Henry Stewart, opened the People's Grocery Store. Besides selling food and various household items, this business served as a beacon in the community of Black people living in south Memphis. Black Memphians regularly gathered in the store because it was a place they could be proud of as it demonstrated the ability of Black people to be economically independent if given the chance. Unfortunately, the business drew the attention of a competitor grocery store—a store that was owned by a white man who dominated Black trade on the southside of Memphis. The white owner was not pleased with losing customers to the People's Grocery, so he set out to have the store declared a nuisance. When plainclothes deputies showed up to serve a warrant to shut the store down, they were met with armed Black men who were intent on defending the store. A shootout occurred, and the white men were injured and taken to the hospital. McDowell, Moss, and Stewart, along with the rest of the armed Black men, were arrested and taken to jail. Even though the deputies recovered, the local newspapers had created sensational stories about the event and encouraged revenge. In response to this tense atmosphere, a white mob entered the jail and took hold of the three men. They took the captives away from the jail and executed them.[7]

This lynching devastated the Black community, and it struck Ida B. Wells particularly hard. The three men were personal friends of hers, and she was even the godmother to Thomas Moss's young daughter. It was at this point that Wells began an exhaustive investigation into the causes of lynching throughout the South. Initially, Wells accepted the most common reasons that the lynch mobs gave for lynching: Black men raped white women. However, in examining the lynching of the People's Grocery Store owners she knew that these men were among the finest in terms of character and comportment and could not be rapists. For Wells, there had to be something else driving these mobs. She began to understand that no matter the Black person's station in life, he or she was vulnerable to the lynch mob.[8]

As a result of her investigations, Wells began to focus on the status of Black women. White men had long considered Black women promiscuous, and thought that this supposed promiscuity encouraged Black men to engage in sexual abandon. To reverse these negative perceptions, Wells and other members of the assimilationist class began a plan to uplift their most "unfortunate" sisters. By uplifting Black women, Black families would become stronger and a source for a moral center for the Black community. Wells and other leaders in the Black women's club movement believed that by uplifting Black women, those same women would be shielded from sexual violence perpetuated by white men.[9]

Another assimilationist in the Memphis upper middle class who thought she had a duty to uplift the "less fortunate" members of her race was Julia Hooks. Born Julia Britton, Hooks's free parents raised her in Kentucky. She was a prodigy and was trained in classical music at an early age. She pursued music at Berea College until she graduated in 1870 and moved to Greenville, Mississippi, to marry Sam Werles. Werles died in one of the frequent yellow fever epidemics, and she then moved to Memphis in 1876, where she married Charles Hooks four years later. The Hookses spent their lives working to improve the welfare of working-class African Americans who migrated to Memphis after the war.[10]

Julia Hooks's life's work was to educate and inspire all members of the Black community to commit to the values of education and hard work. What is most important to this analysis is that she was a woman whose life provides a great example of the class divisions within the African American community. Hooks was a woman of great respect in Memphis. Her work as an activist often addressed issues of crime, education, and values training within the Black community. After the death of her first husband, she settled in Memphis at the invitation of Benjamin Kellogg Sampson, principal of the Clay Street School, who called on her to teach. Hooks stepped into a school system that was very divided. There was the racial division throughout the system, and the school where she taught in particular had a lot of internal division as well. As noted in the previous chapter, there was tension between the Black-funded Education Association and the Black school system run by the state but operating under missionary officials. This tension came to a boiling point at the Clay Street School, where J. H. Barnum was principal. Barnum and one of the teachers at the school, Mrs. S. H. Thompson, became involved in a power struggle. Thompson was no stranger to the school board, as she requested a raise in 1871 based on what she believed were her vast qualifications, but the school board promptly denied her request. She proved to be a very competent teacher; she also knew how to do Barnum's job better than he did. When these two giants struggled, they pulled the entire community into the affair. The situation came to an end when, in a secret meeting, the pro-Barnum forces on the school board fired Thompson.

Many Black people in Memphis sided with Thompson partly because of Barnum's association with the American Missionary Association, whom they blamed for the deterioration of their children's school facilities. Another reason they may have sided with Thompson is that they saw the white-led school board and American Missionary Association, once again, trying to usurp the authority of competent Black people who had a genuine interest in educating Black children.[11]

This conflict marked the first time Hooks came face to face with the inadequacies of the Black school system. There were not enough desks, and the material the school board required her to use was out of date. What also disturbed her was the attitude of the teachers who worked at the school. They continued to tell her to "be patient" and explained that if she pushed too hard, she would never get what she needed. Hooks was not satisfied with this response but found herself having to endure in the unequal system. After working in the Memphis City Schools as a teacher and later as a principal, she opened a school in her home in 1892. Her desire to create this school came from her experiences within the public school system.[12]

Julia Hooks believed that Black families and communities needed to focus on character building for Black children. If their character improved, then all Black citizens would not have to continue to suffer daily physical and mental insults. Her concern was not just with poorer classes being able to assimilate into the dominant society; she also held a belief that as long as poor Black people acted inappropriately, she and others like her would always face obstacles accessing the finer aspects of Memphis society. Hooks served as a schoolteacher for most of her adult life, and she viewed the classroom as the place where children had the best chance to learn how to become better citizens. In her 1896 essay, "Duty of the Hour," she explained her focus on character building. If Black citizens wanted to "avert dangers and troubles" in everyday life they needed people like her to teach them appropriate public behavior. She believed that mothers loved their children, but they lacked preparation for the seriousness of child rearing. Hooks surmised that in the "slums . . . where abject ignorance, careless indifference and depravity hold sway surely no character building that will benefit the child, home, or State can be looked for there."[13]

From Hooks's perspective, the state needed to take a more active role in making sure that Black parents produced Black children that benefited society. Therefore, she advocated a two-prong program. First, the state needed to require that every child get an education. Second, to support Black children directly, the legislature should funnel tax money into Black school systems to pay for their education. She concluded that "it is the duty of the State to see that her subjects grow up with noble characters. It is her fault, and she alone must bear the blame for every vicious act, for every diabolical crime done and perpetrated within her borders if she neglect this duty." Hooks believed that the state neglected its duty to educate and train its youngest citizens for productive lives in society; however, when they became adults, the state did not hesitate to "crowd her jails and [fill] up her prisons" when these same people took the wrong path. Education was not just a venue for children to learn of foreign wars and great explorers. For Hooks, education was about learning how to love and respect oneself as well as your neighbor. Once again, the state had a responsibility to see that this was done.[14]

Because Hooks believed that the state did not fulfill its responsibility, she concluded that news reports about the causes of lynching were accurate. At least that was her response to a survey evaluating the accuracy of the Memphis newspapers on the causes of lynchings. She argued that Black men did "not respect the virtue of their own women as they should [and] their conduct [needed] improvement." The Women's Loyal League presented the survey to Hooks in order to spark interest in their club. Based in New York City, the membership of this organization comprised prominent African American women who set up franchises throughout the nation. In 1894, they chose to send the survey to Hooks because they believed her to be a leader in her community. Hooks was to fill the survey out and return it to the New York office. After Hooks made these statements about lynching, she went on to declare that there was not enough race pride among the Black people of Memphis. She believed that there was "too much disunion, too much prejudice [and] so little confidence in each other." Despite these assessments of the Black community, Hooks informed the league that race relations were "decidedly friendly."[15]

Despite Hooks's assessment in 1894, she understood how important it was for Black women like herself to take a stand for the dignity of Black people and Black women in particular. She was a woman of action who was willing to court arrest for her beliefs. In March 1881, authorities arrested Julia Hooks for not obeying the segregation ordinances in a local theater. She and her companion Louise sat in a section of the theater that Black patrons used the previous year. On this occasion, white people filled the section, and Hooks and her friend were the only two Black people among them. An usher approached the women and asked them to leave. When Hooks refused, he returned with two policemen who asked her to relinquish the seats. Again, she refused, much to Louise's dismay and embarrassment. The policemen escorted them out of the section, out of the theater, and issued both a ticket for disorderly conduct and disobeying the segregation ordinances. When she and Louise went to court the next day, Louise apologized profusely for her behavior and told the judge, "We were wrong, I know that your honor. This will never happen again."[16] Hooks was furious with Louise for legitimizing the unjust law. But soon she had a new theater companion to "make trouble" with—a woman by the name of Ida B. Wells. The two of them spent a lot of time being moved from section to section in theaters but neither was arrested.[17]

Each Black leader in Memphis had her own method of addressing segregation and discrimination. Julia Hooks took a head-on approach to defying laws that she believed were unfair. She also worked within the school system to alter policies and create a true learning environment for Black children. She was not the only member of the Memphis Black elite to assert themselves in an effort to create a better Memphis. T. O. Fuller was another associate of that privileged class who chose to challenge the racial status quo in his own way. Fuller was born in Franklinton, North Carolina, in October 1867 and raised by both of his parents. His father, J. Henderson Fuller, worked on and off the plantation while enslaved in order to purchase himself and his wife from their masters. Henderson Fuller was an educated man who bought property after the Civil War so he and his wife would have a decent place to raise their children. He was a man of influence within his community, as evidenced by his service as a delegate to the North Carolina constitutional convention. He was also a magistrate at the end of the war and during Reconstruction.[18]

T. O. Fuller's parents raised him in a very pious home where they disciplined their children and expected them to become educated. He attended private school at the age of five and received very high grades throughout his primary and secondary education. He attended Shaw University from 1886 to 1890, and he decided to become a minister. Fuller was a man who valued the input and cooperation of white southerners. From an early time, he viewed them not as obstacles but as partners in the growth and development of the Black population. He spoke quite fondly of Dr. Thomas E. Skinner, who was one of his professors at Shaw. Skinner had owned slaves before the war, but in Fuller's words he was "now engaged to emancipate the minds of the descendants of former slaves from the thralldom of ignorance. Grander men seldom walked the earth than Dr. Thomas E. Skinner."[19] Fuller followed in Skinner's footsteps as he traveled throughout the state setting up schools. He even assisted in the construction of the buildings where he conducted classes.[20]

Fuller also committed himself to preparation. He refused to take positions at larger churches because he believed that he was not ready to lead big congregations. Instead, he worked for pastors without pay in order to gain experience. He believed that venturing out too early would lead to inevitable failure. He even worked for principals and pastors for free because he valued the experience, and he believed that if he did a good job, he would undoubtedly be rewarded. Fuller eventually pastored his own church in 1892 in Franklinton, North Carolina. He also served as principal of the church's Black grade school and girls training school. In 1898, Fuller was elected to the state legislature from Warrenton, North Carolina. As a delegate he believed that it was not his duty to "demand" anything, but rather to "gently and earnestly plead for a continuance of friendly relations" between the races. Fuller and Hooks both believed that the home held an important place in the progress of the race.[21]

Fuller's term in the North Carolina senate was tumultuous at times. The speaker did not appoint him to any committees because the white members ran their campaigns on the specter of "'Negro' Domination." Fuller said that he heard white members in the halls of the state legislature say things like "Umph! Here is a 'Negro' in the Senate—Never mind we'll fix that within the next two years." One incident he recalled speaks directly to his racial philosophy. He began to hear people antagonizing and "cat calling" him from the floor of the Senate. One day he approached the offenders with a question. He asked them, "Can you tell me where I can find the records of the geological survey?" One responded, "The ge-log-icle Surnade?" Fuller repeated, "No, the geological survey." One of the men said, "No," and another one added that Fuller was "educated." Fuller stated that at the end of the exchange he "walked back to [his] seat leaving some looking wise, some 'otherwise' and a few consulting their pocket dictionaries." He ended the story by stating that he had "no further annoyance" from anyone in the chamber.[22] The message to his readers is clear: he demonstrated himself to be competent enough to be in the senate and after that he had no more problems.

After his term in the senate ended in 1900, Fuller returned to Shiloh, his home church in Warrenton, NC, to continue to pastor. During this period, a group from Memphis asked him to visit the city and interview for a job as pastor of a group from First Baptist Church on Beale Street. This group had split from the larger congregation because of what Fuller called "philosophical differences." Fuller enjoyed his time in Memphis, and he accepted the group's offer to pastor St. Paul, the new church that they planned to build on Frazier Avenue. Fuller arrived in Memphis a short time after his interview sermon, and the first thing he decided to do was raise money for the new building. The plans not only contained the design for the church, but they also included a building for a new school. Even though the church did not have the money for a school, Fuller decided to teach courses on civil government and theology. The students in his class were pastors who also served churches in Memphis and the surrounding area. He taught some of the classes at the church, and others he taught at the Howe Institute. Fuller believed he had a duty to educate as many people as possible, especially if they considered themselves to be part of the clergy. He surmised that the only way to keep the members of any congregation satisfied was to have well-planned and fact-based sermons.[23]

Fuller was tireless in his commitment to education. While he directed the funding and building of the new church and school on Frazier Avenue, he became the president of the Howe Institute in 1902. According to Fuller, northern missionaries had founded the institute to "make the Negro fit for the world." Once again, he had to put his fundraising skills to work; however, the Baptist Association in Tennessee severely hindered his efforts at keeping the school funded and finding qualified personnel due to its restrictions regarding members of secret societies. These societies had long been a nuisance to the church leaders in Memphis mainly because after emancipation both groups competed for money and members among the same constituency. The secret societies gained enormous popularity as they supported Republican candidates, hosted political debates, and paid for elaborate public funerals for their members. Through regulations the Baptist Association also prohibited member churches from raising money through festivals or other outings. Because of these restrictions, Fuller had a very difficult time garnering wide support for the institute.[24]

Despite these obstacles, Fuller managed to increase enrollment, and he immediately started Bible study courses for men and women. He trained the women in domestic science and taught men the fundamentals of farming and industrial education. The men could go out into the community and train under professionals already in the field. The women were not allowed to be employed outside of the school. One imagines that the school implemented this policy in order to protect the womanhood of the female students. Jacqueline Jones asserts in her book *American Work: Four Centuries of Black and White Labor* that Black leaders were convinced that the Black race would continue to be degraded as long as their women were humiliated by being employed in domestic service. Domestic laborers, whether Black or white, faced long hours and very difficult work; however, Black domestic servants would never develop the same political voice that their white counterparts would eventually enjoy.[25] Therefore these women were trapped in work that both Black and white people saw as degrading, and they would shoulder the blame for the race not being able to move forward as these women had to forgo education and self-improvement in order to support their families.

Despite Hooks's desire to educate Black children on citizenship and Fuller's desire to protect his female and male students from the slings and arrows of segregation and its byproducts, public accommodations in the Jim Crow era remained battlegrounds. The tension was between African Americans, who sought equality, and white southerners, who sought to reinforce a sense of superiority over Black people. This arena is where the actions of migrants become readily apparent and the fact that their goals differed from those of urban Blacks and white southerners is evident. Streetcars were often the sites for racial conflict, as white and Black southerners came into close contact in these public spaces every day. Historian Leon Litwack observes that the streetcars were often the first places where African Americans had to deal with their legal inferiority. Young people also had to confront the embarrassment and anger of their parents and guardians in relationship to segregation on streetcars when they looked to them for an explanation. Moreover, the conflict was exacerbated because after a long period of a malleable approach to segregation, authorities took a more aggressive approach to enforcing the rules of Jim Crow. One explanation for their increased vigilance, according to Litwack, was the belief among white politicians that the younger generation did not know its place. The law had to step in and make clear that the place of Black southerners was behind that of white southerners. Before the 1900s, Memphians practiced de facto segregation, in that the Black and white population took the initiative to segregate themselves from each other. This caused problems because neither the streetcar companies, nor city ordinances, offered any concrete rules concerning the process of segregation on the cars. Therefore, many confrontations among passengers, and between the conductors and passengers, occurred over where to draw the line to separate white and Black patrons.[26]

At the dawn of the twentieth century, lawmakers approved legislation that governed race and space on the streetcars. One of the reasons for this change was because local Memphis business leaders no longer owned the streetcars. Just as in other southern cities, large northern conglomerates bought out local companies. Because the streetcar companies in the South were no longer owned by local entrepreneurs, legislators were able to pass Jim Crow laws with ease—albeit slowly. One reason for this pace was that business leaders pressured them to act slowly. Some of them wanted to demonstrate how the city had advanced economically and socially from a slave-based society. That also meant that they wanted to remove themselves, at least on the surface, from the images and attitudes of a slave society. At the same time that industry leaders wanted to portray this modern image, they also had to confront a bitter southern population that wanted to re-establish an antebellum way of life based in part on the mythmaking efforts of groups like the UDC.[27]

The streetcars were a racial battleground in the early part of the twentieth century, especially as white and Black Memphians tried to adjust to the new legal restrictions passed down by the state legislature. All classes and races of people used the streetcars every day, and the situation offers an interesting perspective on the rules of segregation. Streetcars were special places of contestation because Black and white southerners were in such close proximity. A number of white citizens submitted complaints to the streetcar company about what they believed was offensive behavior. For example, an editorial written to the *Commercial Appeal* in 1903 stated that "there can be no doubt that many of the 'Negroes' who travel on streetcars are very offensive to the white passengers." The writer went on to say that because white Memphians made up the majority of the streetcar railway's patronage, the company should be diligent in its efforts to make them comfortable. Unfortunately, white citizens of Memphis learned quickly that there was no way to effectively control African Americans or their behavior. White Memphians looked for the deference that freed people had showed to their parents.[28]

In 1903, A. K. Hancock drafted the first successful piece of legislation regarding segregation on streetcars. The bill, which maintained that under no circumstances were the races to interact, became state law two years later. This first attempt at a streetcar segregation law is noteworthy not only because of its implementation seven years after the *Plessy v. Ferguson* decision, but also because the law only applied to counties with a population of 150,000 or more. The only county with that size population was Shelby County, and the only city affected by the measure was Memphis. The Memphis Street Railway Company (MSRC) was slow to implement the changes the law required because as its vice president, F. G. Jones, stated, the company had to acquire more than two hundred screens to put inside heavily used cars.[29]

In March 1905, the legislature enacted a version of the Hancock law that applied segregation to the entire state. Another change was that this version of the law did not require streetcar companies to provide partitions to separate the races. The MSRC implemented the provisions of the Hancock law in July 1905, and the monthly statistical report for the company noted the following: "The Jim Crow law went into effect July 5th and was put into operation with a great deal less trouble than was anticipated. It was necessary to make comparatively few arrests to persons refusing to comply with the provisions of the law. A very decided falling off in the 'Negro' travel has been noticed. This however was expected and will no doubt entirely disappear in three or four months. The traveling public is well pleased with the law, and we believe it will be found advantageous to the company, and give the public general satisfaction."[30]

Across the South there were formal and well-documented boycotts in response to similar legislation. In cities such as Savannah, Georgia, Mobile, Alabama, and Jacksonville, Florida, African Americans banded together to avoid having to comply with Jim Crow measures on the streetcars. In many instances, this resistance involved citizens forming their own hack companies, or, as in cities like Nashville, the development of Black-owned trolley car companies. In one rare instance of coverage of African American activism against the law in Memphis, the *Commercial Appeal* reported that a meeting of African Americans occurred at a Dr. Shelby's office on January 23, 1903. The group met to determine the best method of protesting to defeat the passage of the Jim Crow law. The men at this meeting were professionals from the business community as well as ministers from local churches. Though the men in attendance did not advocate for some type of formal and public protest against the streetcar company, the gathering was reason enough for the *Commercial Appeal* editors to take notice. In the end, the group's major accomplishment was to draft a "memorial" that outlined the prayers of the members to stop the passage of this law.[31]

Just two years later T. O. Fuller, who had become a prominent minister in his own right, took a different position with regard to compliance with the law. Fuller's opposition to any kind of protest was born out of a sincere belief that open agitation was truly detrimental to the racial harmony he tried to achieve in Memphis. Instead of direct confrontation or drafting of statements, Fuller encouraged the entrepreneurial capabilities of the Black community. He argued that "fifty cents apiece would equip a splendid transportation company to convey our lovely wives and children from place to place and remove them from the jeers, taunts, and insults of street car conductors."[32]

The MSRC court cases reveal the constant battle that occurred between citizens concerning the issue of Black obedience to racial segregation. One such example was that of W. C. and Mary Smith, who successfully sued the MSRC due to treatment that they suffered at the hands of one of the conductors. On March 27, 1907, the couple met at a downtown coffee shop. After she and her husband left, they went to catch the streetcar at Main and Beale Streets. Before they could safely board the vehicle, the conductor started the streetcar. Mr. Smith pushed his wife up on the platform and ran alongside the car. Mrs. Smith turned to the conductor and said, "Looks like you might stop the car until people get on . . . I am no man, and I am afflicted now by this Company from a collision, and the careless way you handles cars." In court she testified that the conductor responded, "Shut-up, if you can't get on the car, stay off you goddamned Black bitch, you." Mrs. Smith became indignant and responded, "You got no right to call me that," and the conductor responded by slapping her in the face.[33]

By this time Mr. Smith entered the streetcar, and his wife told him not to say anything. The couple sat down in their seats; however, this was not the end of the altercation. When the conductor came around to collect the fares, he stopped at their seat and asked, "What is that you said to me?" Mary Smith repeated what she said before, and he then told her to "shut-up," or he would "break her face." Her husband responded, "You hit her once, and if you hit her again, I will be compelled to fight you." The conductor asked W. C. Smith, "What you got to do with it?" Whereupon W. C. Smith replied, "Because that is my wife . . . if you hit her, I will be compelled to fight you."[34]

The conductor then left the Smiths alone until the streetcar reached their stop. The conductor ran down the aisle and talked to the motorman and then ran back up the aisle. At that point, many witnesses testified that they saw a gun in his pocket. Others on the streetcar protected the Smiths, standing close and walking on each other's heels when they exited the car so that the conductor would not be able to get a clear shot at Mr. or Mrs. Smith. Fortunately for them, all that occurred was that the conductor exited the car and waved his gun in the air. The Smiths believed that the conductor's behavior was unacceptable, and they filed a lawsuit. At the trial Mrs. Smith's attorney asked her to "tell the jury whether or not [she was] mortified and ashamed [to be struck] there before the people that was on the car?" She replied, "Why, certainly; it made me feel ashamed to be hit in public like that. I never was struck in my life before, outside my arm."[35] Unlike the accommodationists, the Smiths decided that the best method for them to handle this situation was to sue. They had, however, little support from upper-class Blacks like Fuller and Hooks, who would have taken issue with Mary Smith arguing with the conductor, thereby setting off the incident in the first place.

The local newspaper holds a plethora of information with regard to the daily racial contestations on the streetcars. On May 23, 1910, the *Commercial Appeal* reported that John McGowan slashed J. V. Hugney across the face after a fight broke out on a streetcar. Hugney was the conductor on the car, and he had asked McGowan and his traveling companion to move out of some seats reserved for white patrons. The two men would not move, and that is when the altercation occurred between the men and the conductor. Reportedly, McGowan cut the conductor in the face before he and his cohort exited the car through the rear window.[36]

Another example of working-class Black resistance covered in the newspaper occurred in 1916 when Black resident John Knox had a fight with a white man over a seat on a car. According to the *Commercial Appeal,* an intoxicated Knox began to curse the white man. This prompted several other white men to come to the back of the car and demand that Knox stop using abusive language. By this time, the conductor was aware of the commotion and decided to step in. Unfortunately, his presence escalated the situation. According to witnesses, upon his entrance into the portion of the car where Knox and the white men were arguing, Knox began shooting. A bullet grazed the vest of the conductor, who promptly pulled out his own weapon and shot Knox approximately five times. Not only was the conductor firing his weapon, but also the men who chastised Knox for cursing fired shots. Knox escaped despite the extensive injuries he received in the streetcar battle. He hid behind a woodshed before the police found him. The newspaper did not report that the police charged any of the white men involved in the shooting with anything.[37]

These interactions on the streetcars provided perfect object lessons for people in the elite classes who believed that character building was the key to racial equality. For accommodationists, the real problem with racial harmony was that there were too many Black citizens unwilling to work to achieve the respect of the white community. Those who resisted were overly concerned with being treated fairly while at the same time they did not value appropriate (read middle-class) behavior on city streets. T. O. Fuller, for example, stated in his biography that Black people should "shun anarchy, intimidation, and riot . . . not until in his own community, the 'Negro' makes himself felt as a strong, substantial, reliable, industrial factor will he have much weight in the political affairs of the state and nation." This was not an uncommon assessment by middle-class and elite African Americans. Even Julia Hooks made mention of the "lack of respect" Black men showed toward their own race, let alone white Memphians. The ones who needed to prove themselves were the members of the Black working class. Boycotting the streetcar company seemed inappropriate to Fuller because on some level he understood why white passengers did not want to sit with Black passengers.[38]

Against the backdrop of these incidents, it is no wonder that wealthier and more educated African Americans focused on racial uplift instead of the damaging impacts of the United Daughters of the Confederacy's narrative of southern history. Indeed, many did not disagree with the underlying racist assumptions (namely, Black inferiority) that drove Lost Cause ideology, except when applied to the Black middle class. They accepted that, on the whole, the Black race was ignorant and ill-prepared for the duties of citizenship. Frankly, how could they argue the point when they opened the newspapers and saw instances of violence, crime, and depravity in low-income Black neighborhoods? For upper- and middle-class Black people, character building was the order of the day; Black people had a responsibility to turn their race around. In the meantime, they urged avoiding agitation, and they minimized white racism as a powerful obstacle to Black progress. Instead, people like Fuller reasoned that it was the Black population itself that stood in the way of their own destiny with their continued protests and general bad behavior. He took this position after he considered that Black men and women had not done the necessary groundwork to enter decent society. Fuller was not alone in holding these views. Leaders like Mary Church Terrell, who recognized the brutality of white southern oppression, nevertheless made it clear that members of the National Association of Colored Women, or NACW, had a duty to raise up their "less favored and more ignorant sisters." Her concern was how others perceived Black women. She concluded that Black women's reputations would generally not improve if society "[would] always judge the womanhood of the race through the masses of our women."[39]

The working classes, however, did not allow middle- or upper-class values to weigh heavily on their decision-making. In point of fact, they resented the implication that the treatment they suffered was due to their own inadequacies and not the result of intractable racism. They used whatever means possible to assert their rights as full-fledged citizens of the United States and the city of Memphis. Whether through lawsuits or violence, men and women on the MSRC trolley cars used the public space to lay claim to dignity and self-respect. Just like the Black Memphians who marched in those Fourth of July celebrations at the turn of the century, African Americans continued to push for fair treatment from the legal system and from entities to which they paid money to receive service.[40]

The struggles that the Black elites as well as the Black working class and migrant communities faced continued throughout the twentieth century. While an observer can certainly respect the efforts of the accommodationists and the assimilationists, one result of their work was a fractured African American community that had, in the words of Julia Hooks herself, little trust between elements of it. In the end the wealthier classes strove to be part of white society, and that inclination would always skew their position on the migrants who came from the Tennessee, Arkansas, and Mississippi countryside with little to no education or money. It was an impossible feat for the bourgeoisie to tear down the working class while at the same time maintaining that they wanted to help them. The poorer classes recognized that the ideology of the wealthier classes had little to do with helping them and more to do with improving the status of the Black middle class and the elites.

In the end, however, the status of the Black middle class did not improve with an increase in education and financial standing. Ida Wells became an internationally known activist against lynching because her three friends who owned the People's Grocery were murdered when they posed an economic threat to a competing white-owned grocery store. Wells referred to these three men as three of the best Black citizens the city had to offer. They were in no way humiliated or degraded, as Wells had assumed of all Black lynching victims. Instead, these men had lifted themselves out of ignorance and poverty, so Wells believed that white Memphians begrudged them for it. The less ignorant and poor Black people became, the more unwanted attention they received from resentful whites. To combat this challenge, Wells began to encourage all Black people who could to leave the city and migrate to the West. So many Black people left that local white business leaders came to her and requested that she use her newspaper to encourage Black workers and consumers to stay in the city. She did no such thing, but she did praise Black Memphians for leaving and, with respect to those who stayed, for continuing to boycott the trolley cars in response to lynching.[41]

One of the more astonishing aspects of this perpetual struggle was that, as a group, African Americans living in Memphis never acquiesced to second-class citizenship. Despite the legal and social setbacks after the Civil War and Reconstruction, they did not stop believing that they deserved a fair share of the freedom that all US citizens enjoyed. The same spaces that

Black Memphians used to claim their rights under the Constitution were the same spaces that white residents used to deny them access to freedom. They were also the same spaces that they used to declare white superiority. One of the significant acts declaring white domination of public space in twentieth-century Memphis occurred in 1905, when the city dedicated a monument to Nathan Bedford Forrest.

3

BUILDING THE LEGACY OF NATHAN BEDFORD FORREST

Reportedly, on his deathbed, Robert E. Lee charged every southerner to "Remember it is your duty to see that the true history of the South is presented to future generations."[1] Heeding the call, former Confederates and their descendants decided to create their own narrative concerning slavery and the Civil War. One way in which the women of the South accomplished this formidable task was through monument building and dedication. One of the first monuments they set their sights on was one honoring the person they believed to be the greatest hero of the southern cause: Lee himself. Lee's monument dedication and unveiling in Richmond, Virginia, in 1890 provided the template for all other unveiling ceremonies in the South. Regiments from across the former Confederacy arrived in Richmond with all the fanfare of marching bands and flags. Besides the very elaborate parade, there was a fireworks display scheduled for later that evening and a grand feast at the end of the day. The *Richmond Dispatch* put out a special edition that included a visual depiction of Lee that editors called "the best portrait of General Lee ever printed in a newspaper."[2] The editors also extolled the solemnity of the occasion. Various articles commented on how the veterans would come to the city and embrace those they had fought with and remember how much they sacrificed for their cause. One article also talked about the display of all colors (Federal, state, and Confederate) and how northerners were upset that these celebrants chose to display the Confederate flag.

The article noted that the only response Virginians had to this controversy was to put up more flags.[3]

Close to one hundred thousand people gathered in Richmond on May 29, 1890, to celebrate the unveiling of the Robert E. Lee statue. The people began arriving at 7:00 a.m. for the 6:00 p.m. ceremony. Commentators remarked that seeing the reaction of the crowd to the big reveal was as if "the object of their admiration had reappeared in flesh and blood." Of the one hundred thousand, more than fifteen thousand were veterans (representing all the old Confederate states) who had come to show their respect. The day was marked by pomp and circumstance as Governor Philip W. McKinney as well as state and military dignitaries all lined up to praise and honor Virginia's favorite son. McKinney was the perfect person to open the ceremonies as he held two titles: in addition to being governor, he was chairman of the Lee Monument Association. The governor remarked that it was "with no disloyalty in our hearts to the Government under which we live and with no desire to awaken or perpetuate old animosities, we come with sacred memory for our cause which is lost, with a love and admiration of our dear ones who have fallen which is unconquerable and eternal."[4]

McKinney went on to pay homage to each Confederate state and its representatives, and he was sure to introduce Varina Davis (wife of deceased Confederate president Jefferson Davis) and Lee's classmate and lifelong friend Gen. Joseph E. Johnston to the cheers of the adoring crowd. The drama of the statue's unveiling was unmistakable in the pages of the *Richmond Dispatch* where the reporter noted that General Johnston took the rope that held the veil together. He then "walked twenty steps and then looked up to the veil. He hesitated a moment. The quivering of his hands was perceptible. Every eye in the great throng was fixed upon the veil. It parted at the top and General Lee's head appeared in sight." At the sight of the general's bronze likeness, the crowd roared. Women threw their handkerchiefs into the air, while the men did likewise with their hats, and muskets and cannons provided the soundtrack for the occasion. Everyone was in great awe of the figure before them.[5]

When city leaders revealed the Lee statue, they were participating in the memory making of the Old South. The hot war ended with the surrender at Appomattox, but for more than 150 years, Confederate sympathizers have engaged in a cold war to claim ownership of southern history. The gathering of white southerners to celebrate Confederate "heroes" was very important to the development of the Lost Cause and the white-supremacist ideology to which it is inextricably linked. Through ladies' memorial associations the women of Virginia worked tirelessly to make sure that people never forgot the sacrifices of Confederate soldiers. These women protected their men in death and carved out a place in public life where they could have a voice in politics. Just after the war, ex-Confederate soldiers allowed women to steer this movement because they believed that northern officials would not view women's activities with concern or seriousness. They did not want to deal with Union troops coming back into the South because Republicans feared another rebellion. Women took the lead in the monument-building campaign as well as in the spreading of narratives that put their veterans in a favorable light.[6]

The United Daughters of the Confederacy painted a picture of Lee that was enduring and refined. In this account, he conducted himself as a gentleman during war and took on a leadership role during Reconstruction. It is this leadership role that set him apart from other Confederate generals like Stonewall Jackson, Joseph E. Johnston, and even the former president of the Confederate States of America, Jefferson Davis. What also distinguished him from his contemporaries is that he showed great prowess and strategic genius on the battlefield especially against a better equipped and more populated Union army.[7]

To an outside observer, the work of these women and their male supporters in describing the noble characteristics of General Lee may look innocuous, but that would be a mistake. It was the monument-building campaign and their dedications that strengthened white supremacy and silenced the voices of the freed people whose enslavement before the war was the cause of the war's conflict. Indeed, according to these historical revisionists, antebellum Black people had been quite happy as servants to their benevolent masters. For the Confederate sympathizers, the inability of the freed people to handle the responsibilities of independence was evident given the supposed collapse of southern society during Reconstruction. So, the memories they made were white memories that celebrated the supremacy of white civilization. These memories were not based on historical fact, but on the social necessity of the post–Civil War era to unite all white Americans under one umbrella.[8]

Alternatively, there was a vocal uneasiness among political observers around the country about these celebrations. While all of Virginia was in a mode of reflection and celebration, much of the rest of the country watched the display with dismay. Sen. John Ingalls from Kansas addressed a crowd on the former battlefield of Gettysburg, Pennsylvania, only a few days after the Lee celebration. He reminded his audience of the importance of Gettysburg and how more than two million Union men broke the "wave of rebellion." He also stated that the day's observers would not recognize the United States if the Confederate soldiers had been successful in their rebellion. All that would have remained would have been "petty nationalities, discordant and belligerent."[9] Ingalls believed that he needed to reiterate that the greatness of the republic was at stake on this hallowed ground. The accomplishments of the Founding Fathers would have been for naught had General Lee's forces defeated Union forces.[10]

Ingalls told the crowd that even if the Union had lost, the values that soldiers fought for, such as the concept "that all men might be free," were worth holding on to, and he would have continued to push for the reunification of America. He did not see the same dedication to the principles of the United States in the ceremonies that were held in Richmond. He believed that the only thing the people devoted to the celebration regretted was the fact that they lost, and not the fact that they caused so much death and destruction. He recognized the prewar contributions of Lee to the US army, but he expressed his disappointment that Lee had turned down the opportunity to command the Union troops in order to take "the leadership of the most causeless rebellion since the devil rebelled against the sanctity of Heaven."[11] In Ingalls's mind, if the southerners were right then everything the soldiers had fought and died for was wrong.

He was indignant that organizers chose May 29, 1890, for the celebration as this was the week when US officials honored the sacrifices of Union soldiers in the Civil War, and he was also offended at the attempts of the former Confederates and their ideological descendants at appropriating the goals of men like George Washington. Washington stood for the republic, and in Ingalls's estimation southerners placed Confederate flags in the first president's hand. He believed it was necessary to "rebuke" southern loyalists because it was "sacrilege of the vilest type" to equate the actions of Lee and Davis with those of Grant and Lincoln.[12]

In another article, "Heathen Rage," the *Richmond Dispatch* reprinted a telegram sent to the paper from Boston. The telegram contained an article from the *Transcript* newspaper that proclaimed that southerners were busy honoring the Lost Cause and not Robert E. Lee. The article also relayed the attitude that some northerners had that the ceremonies were an attempt to "[inflame] in the hearts of the rising generation the heresies of secession."[13] There was particular disdain for the fact that southerners waved Confederate flags and that a northern manufacturer was responsible for producing most of the flags at the celebration. Also, a few days later the *Richmond Dispatch* reprinted a speech given by Union Gen. Daniel Sickles in celebration of Memorial Day. In his remarks he commented on the sight of Confederate flags waving proudly in Virginia: "I yield to none in the sentiments of fraternity and charity that actuate you and our country. I am unmoved by any rancor or asperity or hatred towards the men we met in battle. But I am an American like you—a soldier—and I love my flag. For Americans there should be but one flag—the flag of Bunker Hill, Yorktown, and New Orleans and the flag of Washington—and that flag alone should be permitted in this country to be honored."[14]

In the decades following the end of the Civil War, Confederate loyalists made every effort to control the history of that conflict so that it could be transmitted to future generations. One key aspect of that effort was their elevation of the Confederate battle flag and the construction of monuments to fallen heroes erected in city parks and cemeteries across the South. Memorializing a figure or a time period is fraught with complications. On the one hand, people can use memorials to transmit group values and also to move beyond a traumatic event. Memorialization allows a group to recommit to a shared identity that will help prevent the group from executing the same mistakes of the past. Conversely, memorials can be the focus of inconsistent truths, outright myths, and inner conflict in the individual and the larger community with which one identifies. Further, monuments can also become weapons in a community to further divide its members as the "memorializers" use the monument to separate themselves from other groups, relitigate racial grievances, or lay claim to the status of victim.[15] In Memphis, the erection of the statue of Gen. Nathan Bedford Forrest in 1905 sought to solidify a group of southerners and transmit a particular narrative about the Civil War and its heroes. Controlling history was particularly important to the participants especially at that moment of great historical, social, and economic change.

Memphis increasingly became a part of the New South movement due to its increased dependence on manufacturing and distribution. The city was a very prosperous and productive port because of its prime location on the Mississippi River. Memphis was a town comprising citizens determined to have all of the twentieth-century flair of any other modern city. This money from new industry gave rise to the symbols of twentieth-century prosperity: the skyscraper and the electric streetcar.[16] While the modern observer may conclude that all of these changes meant progress, Memphians viewed them with ambivalence if not outright skepticism. Like their Virginian counterparts (from chapter one) at the end of the nineteenth century who protested the removal of Libby Prison from Richmond, Memphians who treasured the Lost Cause had an antipathy toward modernization and the idea of a New South.[17]

Throughout the South, white pastors warned their parishioners that the region was in a very vulnerable state after the Civil War. Southerners felt that northern ideas and northern investments in commercial and industrial concerns posed an encroaching threat. Modernization frightened people in the South because modernization meant change. Pastors told their parishioners that it was their duty to uphold the Confederate tradition and the values that made the South unique; otherwise, the war had no meaning. Even though southerners lost on the battlefield they still fought the war for hearts and minds. The war for the Lost Cause of honor, chivalry, and individualism continued. Instead of embracing the materialistic values of the North, southerners challenged one another to retain the economic simplicity of their ancestors, which enabled them to remain true to the supposed moral code that their ancestors fought and died to maintain.[18]

The development of a more technologically advanced and commercialized New South troubled the citizens of the Bluff City. This transition mystified and concerned those southerners who attempted to establish their communities as places of prosperity and forward thinking, while at the same time they tried to hold on to the moonlight-and-magnolia days of the antebellum past.[19] The building and dedication of monuments to Confederate heroes was part of the ritual of the Lost Cause. In doing so, community leaders cemented the traditions of white supremacy embodied in the statues and the rituals that surrounded them at their dedications and ever afterward.[20]

Ryan Andrew Newson gives insight as to why this anxiety over modernity is relevant. He points out that these monuments are not really about the past, but they are a commentary on where people are when their communities erect the statue. To the twenty-first-century observer, it would seem that white southerners at the turn of the last century had a firm hand on all levers of society. By 1900 Jim Crow was the law of the land, and the increased numbers of lynchings of Black people and white insurrections occurred in the South with little to no punishment from the federal government. The angst of the white southerner is quite puzzling in the face of these demonstrable facts. At any rate, these statues crop up across the South because white southerners felt their cultural foundations shifting. From the New South to the everchanging rules around race, these southerners needed something that they could hold on to, something that allowed them to remember a time when there were no questions about their status as the heads of society.[21]

The Confederate hero honored in the city of Memphis in May of 1905 was Nathan Bedford Forrest. Historians and military strategists have all documented the prowess of Forrest on the nation's battlefields. He was able to overcome and outsmart many of his northern counterparts, and his actions only increased his postwar esteem among southern loyalists. His victories against the Yankees soothed Confederate sympathizers who still felt the pains of the results of the Civil War. The southern identity was about winning and honor, and the redeemers found those qualities in Forrest.[22] Nothing is as simple as it seems, though. Many aspects of Forrest's life conflict with notions of nobility and integrity in victory.

By far, Forrest's most notorious confrontation with Union soldiers took place at Fort Pillow just north of the city of Memphis. Forrest and his men encountered the Fort Pillow garrison after a long fight at Fort Anderson in Paducah, Kentucky. It was at this fort that Forrest and his men encountered the one man they despised the most—the Black Union soldier. Forrest's men determined to kill every Black soldier in the fort. The battle at Fort Anderson was fierce, but Union soldiers were able to prevent the Confederate forces from taking over the stronghold. This was due in large part to the bravery of the "colored" soldiers. While his soldiers came away from the Kentucky fight with a lot of goods from the local stores before they burned them to the ground, Forrest did not achieve the goal he desired, which was to capture the fort. The fact that he did not succeed in Kentucky set him on a mission to capture the river post Fort Pillow in Memphis. Forrest later claimed that the reason he attacked the fort was because local women and men came to him and told him of the outrages that the Black soldiers had committed against the population. However, he only circulated this story after the media began to report that his soldiers initiated a massacre at the fort.[23]

Forrest decided to move on Fort Pillow on April 12, 1864. Initially, the officers at the fort wanted to stave off direct confrontation with Forrest. Their scouts had already informed them of the Confederates' movements, and the Union officers sent for reinforcements, which they believed were en route. The Union officers scrambled for a way to literally hold down the fort, so they decided to enter into a truce with Forrest's unit. During this time, the Union soldiers took a break from their fighting, but Forrest's cavalrymen decided to take the opportunity to move themselves into a better position. While the truce was in effect, Forrest sent a message to Major William Bradford demanding his complete surrender, and if the major decided to fight the consequences were solely his. Bradford refused, perhaps because he could not ascertain what Forrest planned to do with the Black soldiers after surrender. Forrest had a reputation for capturing Black troops and enslaving them, and Bradford had no guarantee that Forrest intended to do anything different in this situation.[24]

Forrest became quite angry and frustrated with the major's refusal to admit defeat. When his last request for capitulation was met with a rebuff, the general decided to commit to a full-on attack. Motivated by the knowledge of who occupied the fort, Forrest's men needed little encouragement to take on the battle. Forrest commanded them to have all their guns loaded and to attack at the sound of the bugle. The Confederates had to cross a waterway and climb up the side of an embankment to get to the fort. Their commander informed them that the sharpshooters were ready to take out any Union soldier that attempted to attack them while they were out in the open. The ease with which the Confederates entered the fort most likely stunned them. Immediately they were successful, but instead of just subduing the soldiers, they opted for total annihilation. Soldier after soldier recounted the viciousness with which the southern cavalry took on their work, still attacking after the Union soldiers surrendered. Forrest's men saved their worst for the Black soldiers, as they slaughtered them mercilessly.[25]

When accounts about the massacre at Fort Pillow began to circulate, the federal government launched two investigations into the matter in 1864. The federal staff interviewed all types of army personnel, as well as civilians, to uncover the truth of the events that occurred at Fort Pillow. The Joint Committee on the Conduct of War interviewed those who saw the carnage and reported back to President Lincoln that they could confirm the charges made thus far. The investigators lay most of the blame on Forrest for the bloodshed that occurred, and they did not fault the Union soldiers for wanting to hold the fort. Upon reading the report, officials within Lincoln's cabinet wanted to take out their vengeance on captured Confederate soldiers. This was not a popular opinion, but there was a consensus that Forrest should be charged with treason. Lincoln took all of this under advisement as the committee decided to compile a report and distribute it nationwide. In response to the Congressional investigation, Lincoln decided to create a type of decree demanding that Confederate troops treat Black soldiers within the "rules of war." If they did not, they faced the retaliation of the federal government. No one ever saw this declaration because Lincoln never officially released the document. As would become the pattern throughout the end of the nineteenth century, and well into the twentieth, white violence against Black citizens went unpunished.[26]

Forrest and his men moved on from Memphis and continued to have small victories across the South, but as many have pointed out the power of the northern soldiers would be too overwhelming for the Confederacy to succeed. Long before Forrest's surrender, he understood that the Confederacy had lost its battle for independence. In the aftermath of Lee's surrender at Appomattox on April 9, 1865, Confederate politicians drew up plans to gather all the troops that had yet to surrender in order to launch a counterattack against the Union. Forrest gave them a dose of reality. He told the politicians that the Union troops outnumbered the Confederate soldiers by at least ten to one, and there was no way that he would subject his troops to that kind of slaughter. Forrest's commanding officer, Lt. Gen. Richard Taylor, surrendered to Union Maj. Gen. E. R. S. Canby on May 4, 1865. From that point Forrest made his way to Gainesville, Alabama where he surrendered. Like many of his fellow warriors, Forrest remained wistful about not only the current state of Confederate affairs but also what the future held. He even had thoughts of just heading straight to Mexico to live out the rest of his life. In the end he recognized that he had a duty to be with his men when they surrendered whether it was humiliating or not. In a farewell note to his officers, Forrest reminded them that now was the time to mend the country and not hold on to grudges with opponents the southern soldiers fought so vehemently against. He challenged them to be "manly" in all of their future duties so that they commanded respect from their families and their nation.[27]

Although the Civil War had ended, Forrest continued to fight for the principles that led him to battle in the first place. He found the Reconstruction government of Tennessee to be hostile to former Confederates. He believed that the governor of Tennessee, Parson Brownlow, and his agents allowed carpetbaggers and "Negroes" to have a free hand in southern society. This meant to him that white men and women would be attacked daily with no assistance from civil authorities. Forrest believed that the Union officials created this situation because they wanted to punish the South for the war. Former Confederate soldiers and officers could only look on the deteriorating region with despair, and this is what led them to create a fraternal society on December 24, 1865, in Pulaski, Tennessee. This organization was supposed to be a place where former rebels could gather in a safe environment and recall the days of the war. What soon happened, however, is that these same men became the enforcers of the former social hierarchy that had tried to put everyone in their proper place.[28]

The men decided not only to get together to tell old war stories but also to cheer up their wives and daughters. They began to ride around in costume and even dress up their horses in white sheets with masks. While this may have had a lighthearted effect on the women of their community, they discovered that their night rides in costume terrorized Black people, and this pleased them greatly. The group, named the Ku Klux Klan, decided to use these rides as a form of intimidation of freed men and women and gain back the control they believed they lost after the war. At Loyal League meetings, where freed people regularly gathered, the Klan showed up in white sheets with lit torches to frighten them. They wanted freed people to stop talking about rights and economic justice. They wanted them back in the fields and submitting to white southerners as they had in the time of slavery.[29]

For decades southern historians recounted the period between 1865 and 1877 as one in which supposedly illiterate and ignorant Black men ruthlessly ruled over accomplished white men. Not only did southern aristocrats have to deal with Black men they considered ignorant, but they also confronted a vengeful Congress that wanted to punish the South. According to this version, general public sentiment disapproved of the Radical Republicans' agenda. Interestingly enough, the misgovernment was not blamed entirely on the African American population. Historians such as Col. Winfield Jones suggested that it was the "evil" carpetbaggers who operated this tyranny over the white southern population, while the unschooled "Negroes" acted as their pawns.[30] It was in the midst of this supposed chaos and lawlessness that the KKK formed. As Jones explains: "It is difficult to imagine the dark superstition and universal ignorance of the Negro race in the South during slavery times and for years afterward. The Ku Kluxers seemed to the ignorant Negroes to have some connection with their beliefs of various kinds in the powers of Satan, and the tales spread until soon it was difficult to induce any Negro to leave his home after dark . . . the Ku Klux . . . had no intention of terrorizing the Negro population . . . [however they soon realized] that a power had been placed in their hands that could be used to keep the recently freed Negroes peaceful and law abiding and they were not slow to take advantage of this fact."[31] According to this benign description, the Klan was some kind of degenerate fraternity making prank calls on communities throughout the South instead of the domestic terrorist organization that persecuted Black people in the region. For recent historians, this sanitized description of the Klan's humble beginnings is quite off the mark. Although most scholars agree that the KKK started out as a type of social club for nostalgic, small-town former Confederates, these same scholars tend to disagree when they attempt to determine how this organization took the turn that it did. Allen Trelease in his book *White Terror* contends that lawlessness was rampant within Tennessee after the war. The formation of the Klan was to create "a club . . . of regulators, self-dedicated to the curbing of lawlessness and Unionism, and above all to keeping the Negro in his place." Richard Tucker, who wrote *The Dragon and the Cross,* claims that while the group had simple beginnings, when these men faced freedmen, whom they considered belligerent, their mission changed drastically.[32]

What seemed to distress white southerners the most about Reconstruction was that the federal government allowed former slaves to vote while it disfranchised the beloved and valiant white men of the South.[33] In this retelling, the white citizens of the South endured the political dominance of ignorant "Negro" men at the point of Yankee bayonets, and they found that to be intolerable. The freed people showed no discipline, and there needed to be sober-minded men and women to create order and reestablish the hierarchy that had existed before the war. One champion of the white southerners' cause was Nathan Bedford Forrest.

Forrest heard about this group of ex-Confederates and decided to travel to Nashville to join. His former artillery chief, John Morton, gave him the oath, and he went to the Maxwell House Hotel to be officially inducted. That very same day the members decided to make him the leader of the Klan and gave him the title of imperial wizard. Forrest felt the need to join the organization not just because of Brownlow but also because he claimed to receive more than one hundred letters daily detailing outrages committed against white southerners. He claimed, in an investigation of the Klan before the Joint Select Committee of Congress, that he was compelled to fight for the South because northerners and freed people put the region in jeopardy with their corruption. He claimed that the organization was formed only for self-protection against the state militias that the governor sent out to terrorize former Confederates.[34]

In the estimation of white southerners, the Klan was an organization designed to right the wrongs of freedom for slaves. In an interview Forrest gave in August of 1868 he stated that he "loved the old government of 1861[and] the old constitution yet. I think it is the best government in the world, if administered as it was before the war. I do not hate it; I am opposing now only the radical revolutionists who are trying to destroy it."[35] These so-called radical revolutionists were those who attempted to enforce the Thirteenth, Fourteenth, and Fifteenth Amendments to the US Constitution. They were the men and women who had the audacity to teach freed people that they were the equals of white southerners and deserved more of the economic wealth of the region. Something had to be done to thwart them, and Forrest and other elite southern men were the ones to do it.

Forrest concluded his interview by stating that Tennessee Reconstruction governor Parson Brownlow made organizations like the Ku Klux Klan necessary. Forrest indicated that at the point that Brownlow called out the militia he declared war on the white Tennessean. The former general stated that the governor had "already issued his proclamation directing them [militia] to shoot down the Ku-Klux wherever they find them, and he calls all southern men Ku Klux." Forrest believed that the militia would "molest" and "commit outrages" upon the white citizenry. Under these conditions, it was the job of all Ku Klux Klan members to act in order to protect their way of life and halt the lawlessness that accompanied the government of the radicals.[36] He pointed out that the organization was all over the South and that its membership numbers reached about 550,000. Forrest believed that the Klan was a "protective political military organization" whose goal was the protection of former Confederates from the Union army and any Loyal Leagues. Forrest noted that once the organization became functional and found some success it became political in nature and loyal to the Democratic Party.[37]

Just like the incident at Fort Pillow in Lost Cause storytelling, the Klan apparently became something that Forrest could not control. Unlike the original membership, which he characterized as sober-minded men who thought like him and shared his outlook, the Klan had become overrun with men he thought to be quarrelsome and hard drinkers. These men used violence to get the point across that white supremacy would rule the South once more, and Forrest claimed to be outraged at the atrocities committed in the name of the Klan. To combat this, he decided to disband the Klan. However, his proclamation did not actually call for the organization to be dissolved. What he indicated was that all participants could not wear masks any longer. They had to be seen and identifiable so that if there was violence perpetrated on persons or property it would be easier to stop the behavior.[38]

Forrest's fight against what he considered the excesses of Reconstruction continued throughout the rest of his life. He finally came to see success with the election of 1876, when federal troops left the South and order, for white southerners anyway, was restored. Forrest did not spend his final years of life consumed with the Klan and its activities. He turned his attention to money-making pursuits, such as his interest in the railroad. He was always very practical and in a way the Klan could be seen as a means to an end for him. He needed things to return to the way they were before the war. He needed access to financing, a pliable labor force, and land. The Republican government of Tennessee briefly frustrated all of these things for him. The Klan was a unique way for him to clean out the state of hostile freed people and subversive Unionists. Forrest's life ended in 1877, and fittingly the men he rose to glory with during the war surrounded him at the time of his death. Jefferson Davis was at his bedside for a while and then another faithful comrade and fellow Klan member, Minor Meriwether, attended him until he passed away at about 7:00 p.m. on October 29.[39]

The journey of the Forrest monument began more than ten years after his death. Community leaders and former Confederate soldiers gathered together to create some type of memorial to honor the general. A committee of three men—Mr. James Beasley, Col. W. F. Taylor, and Mr. W. W. Schoolfield—began to request donations and pledges in the amount of fifty-five dollars, and they were successful initially. When the contributions began to taper off in the mid-1890s, they suspended their activities. The efforts to immortalize Nathan Forrest began to take shape once again in the city of Memphis when the committee of three united with Mr. W. S. Hansel. The committee selected Hansel because of his proven fundraising abilities in the effort to establish the Robert E. Lee memorial in New Orleans. Money raised for the Forrest monument came from a variety of sources. Former Confederate soldiers charged admission for drills with other veterans with the monies received going to the project. Also, by the turn of the century, women became an even more important part of the effort, as they formed an auxiliary organization to the Forrest Dedication Committee and raised close to $3,000.[40] Further, at the dedication ceremony Sen. T. B. Turley honored: "The loyalty and affection of those women of Memphis and of Tennessee who knew him in his lifetime . . . [and] their children and their children's children. . . . And largely from his old comrades and from their sons and their sons' sons."[41]

The Forrest statue dedication ceremony had all the necessary elements to be a success. There were an untold number of veterans at the service. Speakers who knew Forrest had more than enough material to pull from to speak of his bravery. Lastly, there was an effort to reconcile the soldiers from the North and South into one large alliance that fought for abiding American principles. Veterans and civilians referred to Forrest as a "prophet" of "dauntless courage" and someone who remained "faithful to the claims of law and order." George Gordon spoke to Forrest's commitment to civility and above all fairness. Gordon told the crowd about a career criminal named Able whom the police accused of murder. When the citizens of Memphis found out that the police had arrested Able, they did not want to wait for the court system; they decided to lynch him. The crowd went to the jail to take charge of the prisoner and that is where Nathan Bedford Forrest emerged as the voice of reason. He addressed the crowd and told them to disperse. He understood their impatience with lawlessness in the city, and he told them that they could voice their opinions at a meeting the following day. When citizens came together again the next day at the Exchange Building to meet with city leaders, the gathering became uncontrollable. They assaulted a guard and took Able to the Navy Yard. Once there they placed a rope around his neck and demanded that the hanging commence, but the lynching came to an abrupt halt. Forrest rode in and took out his knife to cut the rope from around Able's neck. He then grabbed the prisoner up with his other hand and put him on his horse to take him back to jail. The crowd numbered more than one thousand outside the jail, and they demanded that the jailers hand over the prisoner. Forrest told the crowd, "I will kill the first man who approaches this door!" According to Gordon, "the mob quailed, the clamor ceased, the crowd dispersed, order was restored and law maintained—all by the intrepidity, the imperious will, and the dauntless courage of a single man."[42]

Yet another element in the dedication ceremony was the effort of participants to place all Civil War soldiers under the same umbrella of American exceptionalism. This element is analyzed in Adam Domby's *The False Cause,* where he explains that these dedication ceremonies were about uniting white Americans around white history. Following the war, many in both the North and the South wanted to focus on reconciliation between the two sections. At the Forrest dedication, for instance, Colonel Stanton, a Union soldier, gave a speech that lent credibility to Forrest's legacy and the efforts of southerners to define their own version of ante- and postbellum history. Stanton described Forrest's bravery as "without limit" and he also stated that "his resources seemed to be endless, and his decisions, like Napoleon's were instantaneous; he was aggressive, masterful, resolute and self-reliant in the most perilous emergency; he was comprehensive in his grasp of every situation, supremely confident in himself and in his men."[43]

It is difficult to believe that during the war Stanton considered Forrest an enemy. Stanton went on to discuss the wondrous accomplishments of the men who served with Forrest and how they were prominent members of every community in which they lived. The men who had served with Forrest now served in all facets of state, local, and federal government. These men ensured that the values that Forrest fought for never died but lived on. For historians, the tension comes from the realization that Forrest's values were exactly what the Union had fought against. In Stanton's speech it is not clear whether any of the Union's values were worthy in the first place. According to Stanton the soldiers fighting under the Confederate flag committed themselves to upholding "the honor and credit of our nation," just as the men who fought under the stars and stripes. He told the former Confederate soldiers who were in attendance that they had every right to "honor and cherish" their compatriots whether living or dead. He also told them that they should have "a feeling of affection for the old stars and bars which they so often followed through smoke and flame of battle."[44]

During his eulogy, John A. Wyeth focused on the scripture that states, "a prophet is not without honor save in his own country." Wyeth noted that Forrest's presence and ability did not go unnoticed by General Sherman on the battlefield. Wyeth claimed that Sherman made the proclamation that he could "cut the Confederacy in two" if the Union forces just "[kept] Forrest away" from him. Wyeth could easily point to the respect that the northern forces had for Forrest. He could also point to a statement by Jefferson Davis to demonstrate how Forrest's comrades in southern leadership did not respect him enough. Wyeth asserted that Jefferson Davis never acknowledged the general's genius, and this was due to the elitist attitude of the other officers of the Confederate army. Forrest did not formally train in any military school, but he seemed to adapt to the battlefield as if he had been born to serve. In his closing remarks, Wyeth claimed that on the battlefield Forrest was a man of calm and rapid reasoning, which he needed especially when his forces came under attack. Wyeth concluded, "It is to the honor of Memphis, of Tennessee, and of the South, and to the honor of all admirers of this great American soldier, whether of the North or of the South, that there should be erected to him there this fitting memorial."[45] This view arises from the desire by whites in both the North and South to reconcile and reunite the country for the future. They moved to resolve the bitter conflict by focusing on the honor and courage of soldiers rather than on issues and causes that divided them. This effort to reunite the country came at the expense of African Americans, who believed that the war was about their freedom. This idea was shoved aside by these old soldiers as Colonel Stanton's closing remarks made clear.[46] Under a section of his speech entitled "What the war meant," Stanton stated the following: "It will be the verdict of history for all time that the soldiers of the South and the soldiers of the North both fought for what they believed was right; both were inspired by convictions of duty; they were of kindred blood and they fought with the same Anglo-Saxon valor."[47] In these few sentences Stanton put all the soldiers into one large society. They were no longer two warring factions: all Anglo-Saxon men were brothers.[48]

Rev. D. C. Kelley, who had served with Forrest throughout his career, gave the benediction at the dedication service. He told the audience that General Forrest did not need this monument to prove he was a great soldier. He concluded that the people present at the monument needed to "prove themselves worthy to have been his comrades and co-patriots." This statement implies that for Memphians and southerners to continue to prove themselves worthy, they needed to fight to preserve what they believed Forrest's work and statue meant. As Sen. T. B. Turley stated in his address at the memorial the "principles of the cause for which Forrest fought are not dead, and they will live as long as there is a drop of Anglo-Saxon blood on the face of the earth."[49]

In addition to the wonderful feelings of camaraderie, accomplishment, and nostalgia expressed at the Forrest Monument dedication, observers also expressed feelings of sadness. On the same day that the *News-Scimitar* informed Memphians that the statue represented a "lesson in courage and faith," it also commented that the people gathered around the monument felt a collective loss. The strength and honor immortalized in the bronze and marble figure left many with the "sense of mutability and decline of today."[50] The *Commercial Appeal* reported, "New men and new ideas and new interests are thrusting aside the broken fragments of the past. The shadows darken about the survivors of Forrest. A little later and these survivors will become shadows themselves, but the great bronze statue of General Forrest will stand for all time to come a vindication of a nation's hero; a tribute to a great man's greater achievements . . . a record of an epoch in the experience of a generation."[51] If Memphians needed to remind themselves of the meaning of the war all they needed to do was travel down Union Avenue in Memphis. The statue stood as a reminder of what white southerners valued.[52]

The day after the ceremony, the editor of the *Commercial Appeal* wrote that the statue became a permanent part of the city's history on the day of its dedication. He added that the statue would be a "perpetual reminder of [the Confederate soldier] and one of their greatest leaders." The editor believed that the Christian values that the mid-South community held were, at their essence, contrary to the goals of war. However, he stated that the monument and the man it honored interested the public because the study of the "art" of war was a "valuable asset." In his words, "there is a never-ending struggle, in which the fittest survive." Forrest was the personification of these values, and the city's celebrations of the man and his accomplishments were appropriate in his opinion. Although there were several references to the horrors of war and the desire that the region live in peace, the editor supported the right of citizens to honor the general and his many accomplishments. From his perspective this was true especially when one took into account that the "passions of the war have subsided and sectional animosity has grown pale." He also wrote that "it is better for a nation to be warlike, for its citizens to fight, and to aspire to military glory than to sink into ignoble sloth and to become enervated with vice and sin." In the end, for the editor, the ceremony and the statue represented "one of the proudest triumphs of Peace . . . [because it was] a lasting token of a reunited country."[53]

Overall, organizers worked diligently to fine tune Forrest's image so that the rough edges of his temper and disposition became smooth and palatable. They excused his participation in the horrific activities of the Klan by dressing his actions up in chivalry and in the guise of protecting Tennesseans from lawlessness. Observers could look upon Forrest as a "civic hero," a man who used his negative qualities in furtherance of the southern way of life. The statue not only depicted a new beginning for the city of Memphis, but it also meant that its citizens had a permanent connection to their past. The editors at the *Commercial Appeal* commented that the experience of standing before the statue left them in awe of what it represented.[54]

Together, Robert E. Lee and Nathan Bedford Forrest represent the paradoxical nature of southern identity. Lee was the refined general with a formal education and a devotion to Christianity since his early years. He conducted himself with dignity and honor in battle. General Forrest represented white grievance and what happens when that grievance takes it revenge against a world that is telling southerners that their way of life is wrong.[55] The building of the monument and the ceremony surrounding the unveiling were all part of an effort to form an account of the war that encouraged southerners to remember their past. For those living in Memphis, the past the organizers wanted citizens to remember was not the one filled with financial ruin after the war nor the numerous yellow fever epidemics that decimated the city's population. The organizers wanted the white people of Memphis to focus on values like bravery and heroism. The statue of Forrest embodied what the southern armies fought for even if they were not victorious. The ceremony also furthered the UDC's goal of inspiring white people to continue to hold on to southern traditions. Southerners established an official history of events in which they heralded the participants in the war as valiant heroes. Afterwards they found it easy to champion the cause of the Old South without fear of northerners calling them unpatriotic or, in the later twentieth century, racist. According to the new narrative created and dispersed by the UDC, the war was about ideas, ideas that the South shared with the rest of the nation. Their cause was just and they should be honored.[56]

The dedication of the Forrest monument, as well as other giants of the Confederacy, should be considered within context. The ceremonies and the drive to rebuild the Confederacy did not reflect an accurate description of the past as much as they revealed the state of contemporary society.[57] Commemorations were an opportunity for every member of the white community to come together to honor the Old South. They wanted to reminisce about the nation that never existed in fact but lived on through the stories of their parents and grandparents. Children attended these ceremonies and the elders told them of the greatness of the Confederacy. Elders encouraged them to feel proud about what their ancestors had accomplished. Furthermore, southern youth learned that although these statues were immovable and inanimate, they brought them to life by carrying on the values that the statues embodied. Not only did they have a right to feel proud; they had a duty to tell the stories and push the agenda of the Old South into the twentieth century.[58]

In the year 1905, when the city held the dedication to the Forrest statue, the racial philosophy of the city of Memphis became increasingly conservative, and the battle for public space more intense. The reason white southerners fought so hard to establish their dominant position was because from insolent behavior on streetcars to not accepting a "coloreds only" section in the theaters, Black Memphians pushed back in whatever venues they could to fight for equality.[59] This is relevant because while these monuments were about the Confederate descendants' desire to push a particular agenda concerning the meaning of the war these monuments also represented what group controlled public space. White Memphians explored additional ways in which they could control public space. In the next chapter readers will discover that parades and festivals had a significant impact on how white Memphians viewed their role in the Depression-era South as well as the role of their ancestors in the Civil War. These people did not erect physical monuments but they did build on the tradition of public memory of the Lost Cause.

4

THE GREATEST PARTY IN THE SOUTH

The mythology of the Lost Cause continued to captivate and motivate the white citizens of Memphis over the early decades of the twentieth century, strengthened no doubt by the perceived threats of modern society and the aspirations of African Americans in Memphis. By the 1920s, city officials no longer built monuments to lost heroes. White-supremacist ideology was often more subtle in its communication to the larger community, but the messages remained the same: Black people could not escape their history and should remain second-class citizens. One example of how white southerners communicated this message within the context of popular culture was through the Cotton Carnival, which began in March 1931. Local media touted the event as the rival of Mardi Gras in New Orleans. Organizers meant for this party to not only promote cotton and its many uses, but also to give the community a much-needed lift during the Great Depression.

For most of the country, the Great Depression began in 1929 with the crash of the stock market. For Memphians, economic wreckage began at the end of World War I when the supply of cotton far exceeded the demand for the crop domestically and abroad. The population of Memphis began to explode when farmers' unproductive land forced them to leave the countryside and find other means of support in this urban center. This increased population taxed the resources of the city.[1] Because of the influx of migrants, Memphis represented, in the words of historian Roger Biles, "a strange paradox—a city modern in physical aspect but rural in background, rural in prejudice, and rural in habit."[2] Memphis, like most southern cities, found itself caught between the "magic" of yesteryear and the uncertainty of the future.

These new Memphians devoted themselves to the Lost Cause and carried other cultural baggage with them, including a commitment to white supremacy and a willingness to commit violence to maintain the practice.[3] These migrant farmers remained financially invested in the cotton crop in one way or another. Therefore, the development of the Cotton Carnival by business leaders was a positive step because they had a ready-made audience within the white Memphis population. Memphis represented the same type of paradox that was evident in many urban areas across the South. While people saw increased industrialization and technological advancement, these same people wanted to hold on to those things that made the South unique in their minds. They wanted to hold on to the image of valiant soldiers fighting for a Lost Cause that lived on in their hearts. Industrial progressive men like Henry Grady, the editor of the *Atlanta Journal and Constitution,* became a bridge between the memories of an agricultural juggernaut and the promise of a profitable industrial future. Unfortunately, the memories of the plantation South weighed heavily on contemporary Memphians, so much so that the differences between the Old and New South were hardly noticeable.[4]

Across the South, leaders debated the usefulness of southern farmers holding on to what seemed to be a dying agrarian system. They wondered aloud how or if the South should change its way of life to meet the new challenges that industry presented. For most Memphians the answer to these questions was a resounding "no!" They said "no" to industrialism, change, and any kind of federal government influence that told them to live otherwise. The Cotton Carnival was another piece of this conversation concerning modernization of the South. The region was in major flux demographically and economically. Southerners regularly relied on the land and personal initiative in order to live the best life possible, but they faced the knowledge and reality of a dying agrarian system. The debate between the two forces crystallized in 1932, when debaters met at the University of Tennessee in Knoxville to argue for or against the following resolution: "That the best interests of the South demand an emphasis on industrialism rather than on agrarianism."[5]

Proponents of industrialism believed that the time was right for northern manufacturers to look to the region for expansion. Of course, northern corporations had been relocating to the South since the early 1920s. One of the main reasons for this move was the fact that businesses could keep wages low due to the inexpensive cost of living, and owners did not have to deal with unions. This became more of an issue at the beginning of the twentieth century as the South showed promise as a competitor in the textile industries.[6]

The South also offered industries opportunities to build and expand without fear of congestion. When millowners built in these small communities, the local government offered a guarantee that accommodating the new industry was the sole focus of the local people. In the South labor was in plentiful supply. News articles declared that the workers showed marked hostility toward unions. As one article explained: "The southern worker is hard to organize because coming from rural sections as he does, he brings with him a marked individualism, bred of having performed most of his work alone or with the aid of his family."[7] This same trade magazine also pointed out that the workers were accustomed to "low living standards" and "limited opportunity"; therefore, they would not be as rigorous in their demands of management as opposed to northern workers.[8]

To support their argument, the debaters at the University of Tennessee who supported the resolution pointed to the millions of acres of uncultivated land in the South that could be used for construction. They also believed that with the abundant number of natural resources, southern manufacturers could not only produce more raw materials but also finished goods as well. Instead of factories being the source of poverty and unemployment, as the debaters who were against the resolution argued, the pro-industrialists believed that the South's wealth lay in creating more industry. They saw the developing factories as a way in which farmers who had to leave the land could reestablish themselves within the community.[9]

Those who wanted to hold on to their agrarian roots saw nothing beneficial in the industrial way of life. To southerners, the industrialists' motivation was pure profit and their marked indifference to whether or not they made their living honestly. For many southerners, holding on to agrarianism was a way to retain a connection with the essence of southern civilization, which was individualism, and that correlated with the founding principles of the nation. Industry further compromised individualism because the federal government demanded compliance with its regulations.[10] Agrarian holdouts tended to believe that corporate leaders lost the value of the individual among their ledgers and profits because the very nature of the industrial system "[cheapened] . . . human life." Also, they believed that the social costs of industry were great as the "factory [tended] to substitute the church as the community center."[11] Therefore, instead of securing a regional future for the traditional values of faith, self-sufficiency, and autonomy, the industrial system would transform the region into one made up of people who only thought about profits. These industrialists neglected the God-given natural resources that sustained agrarian forefathers for generations. The proponents of agrarianism believed that despite the fluctuations in the market price of cotton, and other money crops, that this system still promoted "independence and self-reliance." Farming was the heritage of the southerner, and many believed that this was where the most money and effort should be placed in order to bolster the southern economy.[12]

One issue that concerned both industrialists and agriculturalists was the ever-increasing presence of the federal government in local affairs. In Memphis, New Deal dollars were a significant part of the local economy, and with these dollars there was anxiety among political leaders concerning the racial status quo. The efforts of government officials in the Roosevelt administration to ease racial tensions throughout the country caused many southern leaders great concern. They believed these same outsiders would interfere with the well-established racial hierarchy. Former Memphis Mayor E. H. Crump was elected to the United States House of Representatives in 1931. He corresponded with Tennessee Sen. Kenneth McKellar on this very issue: "The Negro question is looming big in this part of the country. . . . The Roosevelts dug up the Negro question. . . . There was a big dinner, social equality—Negroes and whites—at the Roosevelt Hotel in New York last Thursday, honoring Walter White, a Negro leader."[13] The reason for Crump's concern with the close relationship between White (who was an investigator for the National Association for the Advancement of Colored People and an executive at the head the organization for years) and the Roosevelt administration was because he believed that he would be put in an awkward position. In the letter he stated that he supported Roosevelt but made it clear that he did not want the federal government to interfere with fifty years of Jim Crow rule in the South.[14] It is the stubbornness represented in Crump's letter that has continually crippled the South in terms of development and led President Roosevelt to declare that "the nation's No. 1 economic problem" is the South.[15]

Crump's conflicted view of Roosevelt was not isolated. Southern Democrats decided that Roosevelt was the best representative for their party despite the fact that Roosevelt did not have many southerners in his cabinet. During the hard times of the Great Depression, these southern representatives (and their constituents) were more than thrilled to be on the receiving end of the federal government's largesse. Further, southern Democrats might not have had direct executive influence, but they did have legislative power after 1932, when the Democrats won the majority in both the House and the Senate. Because Democrats continued to win seats in the legislative branch, especially the Senate, southern Democrats would form a powerful voting bloc. Initially, Roosevelt could use this power to his agenda's advantage. In his first hundred days he moved a significant number of measures through both houses of Congress with little resistance, even from conservative southern Democrats.[16]

One of the many issues that Roosevelt would face, as far as southern representatives were concerned, was the challenge that New Deal agencies created for local authorities. The people these agencies served came to appreciate the policies of the New Deal as well as the benefits. Their reliance on federal initiatives meant that they were less likely to remain loyal to the local power brokers in their cities and states. The wall between the president and the legislative branch grew even higher after the 1936 election. From this year until 1944, Roosevelt would continue to win reelection with an overwhelming number of popular votes from every region of the nation, but most importantly he won without needing any electoral votes from the South.[17]

Compounding the issue of federal interference with local power brokers was the ever-present issue of the racial hierarchy in the South. Not only did Roosevelt, at least on the surface, give powerful positions to Black Americans within his cabinet, but also programs like the Civil Works Administration (CWA) provided employment opportunities to even the most rural African Americans at wages that were double what they would make in the fields of landowners. As was the case with the various New Deal policies, local leaders had a good deal of control over how they would implement these initiatives. In the case of the CWA, southern politicians were able to remove farmworkers from the program so that they would be available to the planters for agricultural labor.[18] Despite this workaround to keep local power brokers supplied with desperate and therefore cheap labor, southerners like

Georgia Gov. Eugene Talmadge were already looking to oust Roosevelt by 1936. Talmadge held a convention where he invited Democrats who were committed to the Jeffersonian ideal of individualism, but a top issue of concern was the Roosevelt's friendliness with members of the Black community. The Confederate flag–draped dais even welcomed speakers like Thomas Dixon, who had authored the novel *The Clansman* at the turn of the century, and spoke about the dangers of Roosevelt's intrusions into the authority of the state and the dangerous rise of the National Association for the Advancement of Colored People.[19]

In addition to the issues surrounding states' rights and the racial hierarchy, southern leaders were skeptical about the technological advances brought on by increased industrialization in the thirties. John and Mack Rust invented a machine that could pick cotton, and they demonstrated the machine's ability on a farm in Mississippi. Despite a few problems, all observers were pleased with the machine, but there was panic among southern legislators. Rep. E. H. Crump, who had never made a speech from the House floor up to this point, spoke violently against the invention. In this same speech he suggested that Congress "legislate this machine and others like it out of existence." The human cost was the issue that concerned others. The South suffered tremendously during the Depression. Citizens faced certain unemployment if this machine became popular. This prospect terrified legislators because of their present inability to meet the needs of their constituents. Representative Crump also warned that if farmers used the machine, it would leave "Southern 'Negroes' [with] nothing to do and millions of them will be idle." Also, southerners were concerned with losing the sentimental value of cotton-picking time in the city of Memphis. As one observer, James Bealle, wrote: "Memphis is the scene of the largest mass migration of city 'Negroes' toward the cotton fields at picking time. Queues of 'Negroes'—hundreds of them—gather at the Arkansas bridge just before dawn late in August, when the cotton is ready for picking. Men, women, and children join the growing crowd, waiting for trucks to carry them to the cotton fields. There are noisy farewells in the denim-clad army; now and then you hear a burly Black amoor [*sic*] speak sharply to the dice."[20] The author on some level seemed to be lamenting the loss of this romantic and time-honored tradition. Furthermore, the author noted that the majority of the Black people picked cotton for extra money because many of them worked full-time jobs in the city. Their only purpose for returning to Arkansas, according to Bealle, was to help their families. Bealle believed that lawmakers had no reason to fear the cotton-picking machine. The cost alone made the machine unattainable for most farmers. And the fears that Crump had of idle "Negroes" was unnecessary. He believed that stating Black people depended on cotton picking for survival was the equivalent of stating that a white-collar employee depended on his Christmas bonus to make ends meet.[21]

Crump and Sen. Kenneth McKellar, who was also the chairperson of the Appropriations Committee, garnered much needed financing for the people of Tennessee.[22] It was this federal government influence that transformed the makeup of the city's social, political, and economic relationships. Because Memphis, as well as other southern cities, became closely engaged in the workings of the federal government it could no longer operate solely based on antiquated ideas about racial harmony and the social order.[23]

This struggle between the agriculturalist and industrialist reveals that the Cotton Carnival was part of a larger conversation in the South. Memphis leaders faced the daunting task of promoting the fruits of the agrarian system in the face of the looming industrial revolution that was surfacing across the South. In the book *I'll Take My Stand* (which was published the year the Cotton Carnival began), twelve southern authors talked extensively about the benefits of agrarian life. These authors argued that southerners should reject industrialization and commit to the supposedly less-complicated society of the Jeffersonian era.[24]

On average, southerners committed to this one-crop economy even though leading economic indicators suggested that this system was a detriment to the region. Social and economic commentators who observed this commitment noted that cotton "had been king only to those who owned and traded [the crop]; to the masses who tilled it . . . [it] has always been a tyrant." One such observer, Alva Taylor, noted that the one-crop system "inevitably begets poverty and a low standard of living for the actual tillers of the soil."[25] Taylor pointed out that not only were growers of cotton victims of market forces that determined prices, but they also neglected to grow food for consumption. Local businesses imported more than $2 billion worth of supplies such as food and fertilizer. These items were imported into the South from other areas of the country before the Depression even took hold. The states that produced items such as cheese and milk made more money than all ten cotton states combined.[26] Taylor's solution to the difficulty southerners faced was for them to abandon the plantation and the tenant system. She offered three solutions to the economic setbacks of tillers and planters. First, she believed that individual farmers needed to be able to own their own land at reduced mortgage rates. Second, the farmers should then be able to get loans for the materials needed to plant their crops. Third, she believed that all expert scientific information should be shared with the farmers so that they could "diversify" and focus on "subsistence homesteading."[27]

The 1932 debate that occurred in Knoxville at the University of Tennessee highlighted the major philosophical struggle of the Depression years in the mid-South. While many believed that the future lay in industrial development, there were those who wanted to hold on to the past, a mythical past in which every man owned his own land and plow, at a time when labor, by enslaved Black men and women, was unpaid and southern states exercised great power in national affairs. Even in cases when farmers joined unions, such as the Southern Tenant Farmers' Union, many members believed the goal was to use the organization's activism to gain possession of their own land. They wanted to be landowners themselves despite the admonitions of the STFU's leaders about the dangers of capitalism.[28] The coming of industry meant the coming of change. Further, the presence of the federal government disrupted the small fiefdoms with its regulations about how to treat workers and that was something the ancestors of southern powerbrokers fought a war to prevent. Also, the continued development of industry meant that men and women had to adjust to wage labor, including the potential for layoffs. Many southerners feared this loss of control. When they worked the land for themselves, they controlled how long they worked, how much they planted, and where and when their families worked. Under the new industrial system, all of that would inevitably change, and the fact that they never really had control in the first place was a stunning realization.

The Cotton Carnival can be described as a "nativistic movement," meaning organizers claimed that they wanted to rejuvenate the local economy.[29] To a great extent this was true in Memphis, but the carnival promotors also designed the event as a way to challenge the diversification of the economy and the shifting southern way of life. With the uncertainty of the stock market, bank closings, and the dismal price of cotton, observers clearly understood that white Memphians needed "a sense of place."[30] Throughout the Depression, mid-southerners demonstrated a desire to hold on to their agrarian past. They wanted to remember the great days when the leaders were not city Babbits but country gentlemen, a place where they could remember the power that cotton once brought the region. However, as author Rodger Brown points out, in order to do that Memphians had to "conjure up images of a lost paradise that never existed."[31] The Cotton Carnival was a place to forget all the unpleasantness of the present. In 1932, when the city hosted its second carnival, a reporter for the *Commercial Appeal* wrote: "The word, 'depression' became obsolete for the moment and other disconcerting problems of the day were taboo as subjects of conversation. It was a night for making merry and the carnival spirit reigned in all its glory."[32] But this glory came with a price. White Memphians relied upon the myth of the Lost Cause as a basis of their identity as southerners. At a time when Black people competed for jobs with whites in a very restrictive economy, this nostalgic gaze at the good old days had great appeal for whites.

Anthropologists Ralph Linton and A. Irving Hallowell supply a framework with which to understand nativistic movements. Linton and Hallowell conducted their study in the middle of the last century, but they provide some useful concepts to describe the Cotton Carnival. The researchers divide nativistic celebrations into two categories, revivalistic and perpetuative. When a festival is revivalistic, the organizers and participants are looking to resuscitate bygone rituals. A perpetuative nativist is looking to magnify certain cultural phenomena in the present. This type of nativist has no use for assimilation into the present culture, as they are committed to the continuation of elements in their own culture.[33] While Linton and Hallowell have several subcategories of both of these types of nativistic celebrations, the one that most closely matches the Cotton Carnival is the one labeled "rational revivalistic." In this concept the nativist movement has more to do with the participants' perceived decline of their society. The celebration is designed to remind the crowds of how great the community once was despite the troubles they are currently living through.[34] This is very similar to the beginnings of the Cotton Carnival as organizers promoted the event as a way to shake off the blues of the Depression by commemorating the city's agrarian past.[35]

The roots of the festival began in January 1931. The Memphis Chamber of Commerce faced a shortfall in annual contributions from local firms. Board members A. Arthur Halle, Frank Grout, president of Colonial Bakery, and Walter Acroyd, general manager of Sears and Roebuck, met with Herbert Jennings, manager of Loew theaters. In the meeting, they discussed the chamber's financial shortfalls. As the men continued to discuss the financial situation of the city, Jennings suggested that they stimulate the economy by promoting cotton.[36]

The men discussed the matter further and their concept grew. They talked about placing cotton exhibits in the lobbies of the theaters and cotton clothing in store windows. They also proposed having parades and decorating the entire city with cotton bales. As they became more excited about the idea, they decided to call Everett Cook, the newly elected president of the cotton exchange. Cook joined them, and they all continued to build on Jennings's idea. The goals of the Cotton Carnival were to increase cotton usage throughout the mid-South and the nation and to inform the world that Memphis, despite the depth and breadth of the Depression, still thrived.[37]

In a 1952 essay, where he recounts the history of the Cotton Carnival, Arthur Halle reminds Memphians that the city was not new to celebrations such as this one. He invited readers to reminisce with him as he discussed the Memphis Mardi Gras, which the city had held in the nineteenth century. One of the most important connections that he made between the two festivals was that both Mardi Gras and the Cotton Carnival started under much the same conditions. He stated that "both of them made their appearance during periods of depression, both of them came in a time of uncertainty and re-adjustment, and both had for their object the creating of a feeling of unity and cooperation in the Mid South."[38] Halle argued that the impact the Memphis Mardi Gras had on the psyche of Memphis could not be overstated. He believed that Memphis was "probably harder hit by Reconstruction than any other Southern city . . . the culture and luxury of the plantation was gone, and people had to adjust themselves to an entirely new system of labor." In Halle's estimation, Reconstruction-era Memphis had also been a powderkeg of racial tension because of the four thousand Black soldiers stationed at Fort Pickering. He explained that riots occurred daily. As if that was not enough stress, he stated that "an actual feeling of hate had grown up within the city between the older more aristocratic families and those who even remotely cooperated with the 'foreign' administration." With all of this social chaos, the Memphis Mardi Gras had come to life on February 13, 1872. During the first year of the Memphis Mardi Gras no one knew what to expect. Many merchants had not prepared for the masses of people who descended upon the Bluff City from across the South.[39]

The first celebration revealed that citizens from Tennessee, Arkansas, and Mississippi were in attendance as party organizers sent out invitations that requested the presence of delegations from mid-South towns. Alcohol played a major part in the nineteenth-century celebration. The sheriff let all partygoers know that there would not "be any fines for 'too much spirits'"; however, if the police discovered weapons the offenders would be "severely dealt with."[40] Mardi Gras was a huge festival where partygoers shed all social constraints, and the city became a free-for-all in terms of the debauchery displayed. For the partygoers the "dark and gloomy days of reconstruction [were] at least temporarily forgotten."[41] However, with the growth of the Protestant church in Memphis, Mardi Gras celebrations became less appealing to the increasingly conservative population. The local newspaper, which had previously been the event's most enthusiastic supporter, became its most vociferous critic at the beginning of the twentieth century. By 1903, no bawdy celebrations took place in the streets during Mardi Gras. There was only one masked ball at the Lyceum, and it was attended by society's elite. The Cotton Carnival represented a new direction for Memphis celebrations because the organizers learned from the mistakes of Mardi Gras. It was professionally organized and carefully controlled by its founders.[42]

Halle made an important connection between the spirits of the citizens of Memphis at the end of the previous century and the morale of Memphians during the 1930s. In both cases organizers committed themselves to bringing some fun and gaiety back into the lives of Memphians. Oftentimes these feelings of revelry came at the expense of African Americans. The theme the first year of the Cotton Carnival was "the Old South," and it featured "Southern belles and gallant Southern gentlemen. Black women, dressed as mammies, perched on bales of cotton aboard the floats or greeted passers-by on street corners. Teams of Black men, along with horses and mules, pulled the floats through the streets as thousands of eager spectators packed shoulder-to-shoulder to cheer them on."[43]

Carnival organizers displayed their homage to the antebellum period, which they believed featured the mid-South at the height of culture. In the parade there were eighty-five floats "garbed in perfect accuracy, and harmony." The reporter for the *Commercial Appeal* also noted that "many of the floats were well calculated to stir old memories." The reporter observed that mules and horses pulled all of the floats and to participants and observers, this was a welcome change "from the motorized parade of recent years." The weeklong activities included numerous parades and balls. The event organizers kicked off the event with a decorated barge landing of the preselected king and queen of the carnival. The king was typically an established businessman, and the queen was a coed. The carnival not only demonstrated the usefulness of cotton but also highlighted the mid-South as being just as cultured as any other area of the country. Organizers infused the opening ball with an Old South atmosphere as the volunteers decorated the 19th Century Club, the scene of the ball, in an antebellum style. The musicians dressed as cotton pickers, and, as a reporter who described the party pointed out, "A regal note was developed in the midst of the plantation scene by high backed chairs draped with ermine and placed on a terrace of velvety grass just below the stage proper." It is from this vantage point that the king and queen observed dancing guests at the carnival.[44]

Carnival organizers also wanted the entire white citizenry to be a part of this celebration. This was not to be an exclusive event as so many of the events at Mardi Gras had been. According to these leaders, the carnival "was going to promote business for everybody and should not be used by any one special group as a promotion, even though some of the proceeds might be channeled to the Carnival for its operation. In other words, the Carnival was going to be for ALL the stores, for ALL the people, for ALL kinds of professions and businesses, and for the City as a whole regardless of the size of the business, the social standing, wealth, prestige, family background or anything else that would tend to make anyone feel that he or she would not be invited, expected, and welcome to participate in the Carnival."[45] Despite the inclusive message, country clubs put on many balls and banquets where participants needed tickets in order to attend. Many of the tickets cost a dollar, but men and women who wanted to attend needed to factor in the cost of the dresses and tuxedoes. Therefore, many of these events were out of reach for the average white family; African Americans, of course, were excluded from balls and banquets. The events that were open to the public at large were the barge landing, street dancing, foot races. For the children, the pet parade was a big hit.[46]

The Cotton Carnival realized its primary goal of producing more cotton-minded citizens. Merchandisers were asked to display only clothes made of cotton, but there were few available. At the time cotton was not the fabric of choice for buyers or makers of new fashions. Memphis buyers began to go around the country and seek out these cotton dresses. When they could not find them, they began to purchase cotton material. When the larger fashion community began to notice these purchases, they became aware of a new trend on the horizon. They also began buying cotton fabric as well. Soon in every store from coast to coast, consumers could purchase quality cotton garments. Maintaining the rule to wear only cotton was a struggle for carnival royalty. For example, Queen Mollie Darnell in 1935 wore white satin with rhinestones and a blue-and-silver-trimmed silk dress. This caused a stir in the press that stimulated efforts to provide cotton gowns. By 1936, the carnival program reported that due to the work of entrepreneurs, Memphis stores stocked plenty of cotton evening gowns and men's summer suits of very high quality. Apparently, shoppers did not have this option just a few years earlier.[47]

The carnival took a hiatus during World War II, but upon the event's return in 1946 organizers added a special addition to the festivities: they selected a young woman to serve as the ambassador for cotton. The winning Maid of Cotton was a young white woman who competed with other young women for the honor of representing the carnival throughout the world. After selection the Maid of Cotton traveled to New York City, where she modeled various fashions created from cotton fabrics. She then traveled internationally to model the clothes and meet with dignitaries in various countries to talk about the carnival and the utility of cotton. While the Maid of Cotton traveled, she often gave interviews detailing her tour and discussing the interesting new people she met along the way.[48]

The point of the carnival was to remind all southerners of the vital role that cotton would play in the South's economic future. To that end the organizers promoted the event as "A Party with a Purpose." They wanted to remind participants that they were not involved in festival planning for their own self-aggrandizement but for the community's common good. Unlike Mardi Gras, the focus of carnival emphasized the existing social order and disavowed the lawlessness that was so much a part of the nineteenth-century celebration. Instead, the Cotton Carnival was a glamorous affair in which young women showed off their beautiful jewelry and gowns and in which young men introduced themselves as the new leaders of the city.[49]

Just as the Forrest statue dedication served to forge a uniquely white identity, so too did the Cotton Carnival. The festivities surrounding the carnival allowed white Memphis to live in the long-past era of wealthy planters, engaging southern belles, and an adoring public that relied on the benevolence of these elites to further the southern way of life. The organizers wanted to cure the malaise brought on by the slow economy, but it also seems as if they wanted to remove the angst white Memphians felt about the changing economy and racial order. The celebration of cotton allowed white people from all strata of society to cling to the one thing that they believed gave them standing in the ever-changing world: their whiteness.[50]

One last important aspect of the Cotton Carnival is the way in which the celebration highlighted the beliefs of white and Black Memphians concerning the Lost Cause. The carnival represented the perpetual struggle between the desire of a people to hold on to a memory and the contemporary fundamentals that force change. During the first and successive years of the carnival, Black people had very limited participation. Their only purpose was to serve white partygoers. Black women dressed as mammies and greeted arrivals, and the men were workhorses. During that first year, the *Commercial Appeal* reported that "feminine beauty and the lore of the Negro race" were two themes extremely popular with the designers of the floats" for the parade.[51] Most of the floats had a historical theme as most were Confederate and Civil War–styled floats. Of all the stereotypes of enslaved Black women, the mammy figure was the most beloved for white southerners. She represented the faithful and dutiful slave who cooked, nursed, and cleaned up after the master's family. Her presence at the carnival provided a significant amount of the connective tissue that these white partygoers needed to frame the events before them.[52]

The cotton celebration represented a time and place when African Americans were not a threat to white southerners' reality despite the fact that African Americans pursued economic justice and political rights. It represented the construction of historical memory in stark detail. During this time, African Americans took part in the push for fair wages through union organizing, and they also left the farms that they and their ancestors had cultivated for centuries. They left the plantations and headed for the city in search of a new and better life; however, once they arrived, they faced job discrimination since unemployed white southerners were the first choice of employers. There was also the issue of the New Deal and the rules and regulations that came along with the aid programs. On the surface at least, these programs required that African Americans get a portion of the money the federal government offered to municipalities across the South.[53] All of these factors were significant in creating anxiety within the white community. The more African Americans pushed for their fair share of rights and opportunities the more resistant to change the white population became, and the more susceptible they were to the sentimental feelings that drove the Lost Cause. Instead of dealing with African Americans as equals, or even seeing them as human beings, white Memphians chose to remember them as they believed they had been. In reality, what they remembered were stereotypes that their ancestors had created over time to solidify the racist foundations that gave birth to Jim Crow.

Psychological theory that has social and political dimensions may offer some insight into how this dynamic works. From an early age, an individual goes through a process of splitting. This is when a person has to reconcile the positive and negative features of the character of other individuals, particularly those they love. Eventually, children become adults and learn that they do not have to see the object of their affection as either wholly good or wholly bad. They can see an individual's behavior as sometimes positive or negative and realize that those contradictions are normal, and they are able to make peace with them. This did not happen for white southerners in general nor for white Memphians in particular. For white Memphians, freed people and their twentieth-century descendants became frozen caricatures from the days of slavery, and so they became conflicted when their caricature did not match their current situation. This mismatch produced something scholar Mary Caputi labeled "melancholic depression." Caputi defines this depression as one that people experience because they have lost a "love object" that was key to understanding themselves.[54] The love object in this case is the social order of the Old South. Since white Memphians could not have that society back, they clung to the only access to it they could have: nostalgia. What complicates this issue even more is that white Memphians in the 1930s were relying on the recollections of the ante- and postbellum stories of their parents and grandparents so that they were not sad about something that they had lost themselves, but were sad about the myth of what they lost as seen through the eyes of their relatives and community leaders.

The carnival, therefore, was about more than selling cotton; it was also about selling an idea. By the 1930s, advertisers and producers of consumer products became quite adept at freezing African Americans in their antebellum roles as hapless, obtuse slaves. Typically, this act of confining the image of African Americans took the form of Black collectibles. Collectibles were everyday items purchased by consumers that depicted Black people in a very stereotypical manner. From cookie jars that were shaped like an obese female slave (think Aunt Jemima) to the tightly packed "Niggerhair Chewing Tobacco," Americans had a variety of ways in which to comfort themselves with nonthreatening images of African Americans.[55] The depictions of Black people at the carnival as characters from the days of slavery were also collectibles. These men and women formed living products for white men and women to consume at the carnival.[56]

The Black Memphis population made up the second group of consumers at the carnival. They took in the sights and sounds of the carnival and observed all the enthusiasm shown by their white neighbors. But in all this excitement there was uneasiness, interestingly enough the discomfort was first expressed through the voice of a child. Members of the Black community would respond to this discomfort by forming their own carnival to exhibit the history they wanted to tell.

5

DEFINING BLACKNESS AND FEMININITY THROUGH THE COTTON MAKERS JUBILEE

The African American population of the mid-South saw a dramatic decrease in their standard of living during the Great Depression. The proposition that Black men and women needed some type of economic relief is not a major revelation. Throughout the early part of the twentieth century, African Americans suffered from major economic depression long before stockbrokers allegedly jumped out of New York City skyscrapers. The New Deal offered African American and white workers some ways to alleviate the hardships of the Depression. However, leaders in charge of these programs did not fight hard enough to distribute this money equitably. Reports from New Deal workers reveal that they were satisfied with the inequity because most Black households contained at least two working adults, a husband and a wife, while most white households only had one gainfully employed man to support the household. Further, they believed that even with the unequal fund distribution, Black families still fared a lot better than they did without any aid at all.[1]

It was under increased federal government activity that the Cotton Carnival took the mid-South by storm. While white revelers enjoyed the show, Black observers began to question their role in the carnival as well as their place in the economic structure of the city. Black Memphians saw the devastating images in the carnival and decided to form their own festival. They planned an event that did not play up the stereotypical roles of Black men and women during slavery but one that told a more complete story about the work of their ancestors in the cotton fields of the mid-South. They came up with the Cotton Makers Jubilee, and the event was more than just the Cotton Carnival with Black people in the starring roles. Not only were Black Memphians attempting to establish their own identity separate and apart from white Memphis, but also the jubilee was a challenge to determine who would control the image of Black citizens. While organizers may not have been able to directly counter the carnival's images, the jubilee stood as an alternative to what they believed was a warped version of history that either turned them into caricatures or made them invisible.

Organizers celebrated the accomplishments of Black scholars and leaders in the city. Like many organizers of the Cotton Carnival, they also believed that the way to economic freedom for most Black people was with their hands. They did not believe that studying the liberal arts in college was particularly useful if the graduate could only be employed as a janitor upon graduation. For the jubilee organizers, fieldwork was not something Black men and women should spurn. As the programs pointed out, they believed that the vast majority of Black Memphians should turn to the fields to find economic independence.[2]

During World War I, the nation had witnessed a dramatic increase in the population of African Americans living and working in the northern centers of manufacturing. Due to the buildup of troops in Europe, many white men joined the military and left their jobs, and Black men and women moved North to fill those vacated positions. Once the war was over, white men began to retake the jobs they had given up during the war, but Black southerners did not move back down South. Because they decided to stay in the North, they were often subject to the same labor issues white workers dealt with in the manufacturing sector. During the 1920s, industries steadily closed up shop in the North and moved to the South. Northern entrepreneurs did this to pay lower wages and minimize union interference. Though the northern industries had more skilled jobs, the laborers who filled these positions were white not Black. White workers even took over the unskilled or semiskilled jobs that Black workers dominated during the war. That meant that Black workers continued to be excluded from factory work except for what contemporaries referred to as the "meaner sort" of jobs.[3] Furthermore, because of the National Recovery Act (NRA) codes and the introduction of a minimum wage for all workers, industry managers believed that there was no benefit to hiring African American workers any longer. If all workers received the same wages, the managers preferred an all-white workforce.[4]

The situation for urban southern African Americans was not as bleak as that for rural Black people. They secured some benefits, even if they were hardly comparable to their white counterparts. From housing to jobs to recreation, African Americans faced exclusion and substandard facilities.[5] Black men and women who gained employment in the fledgling industries of the South received lower pay than white workers for the jobs they performed. There was little that they could do to correct the situation as their presence in unions was minimal.[6] The designers of the New Deal had knowledge of the inequitable treatment that Black people received under the actual implementation of the programs they created. In a letter to the editor of *Survey* magazine, one of their readers named Marion Conover complained about this inequity. He wrote in response to another article published in the magazine written by Lisbeth Parrott, who worked as a New Deal official in North Carolina. The New Deal worker stated that when Raleigh officials called for local workers, their request "was answered by hundreds of job seekers. . . . White labor was paid two dollars a day and 'colored' one dollar and a half for the five days work per week."[7] Conover wanted to know "How a Negro laborer with a dependent family could exist on fifty cents less per day than a white laborer?" Parrott responded to Conover by stating, "The Negro in the South generally has a lower standard of living than the white man, regrettable as this may be. As a result, it seems reasonable to assume that $1.50 per day would come as near meeting the Negro's minimum demands as $2 would the white man's. . . . It was felt that this differential was equitable by reason of the fact that there are few families of the colored workers which fail to have a wife or daughter employed in the white home. From these homes foodstuffs are carried to the colored homes every night."[8] Since white families commonly only had one breadwinner—a man—the program organizer felt that it was perfectly reasonable to expect that the economic burden on white workers would be greater. In her concise statement, Parrott explained the situation of the Black worker during the Great Depression. All administrators of relief programs made the assumption that the "colored" standard of living was not that high, and if it was it should not be—thus discrimination was acceptable.[9]

For those African Americans who lived in rural areas and worked as sharecroppers or tenant farmers, every day presented the possibility of eviction. Landlords pocketed the money they received from programs like the Agricultural Adjustment Administration (AAA) instead of using it for its intended purpose of upkeep and maintenance of their tenants. There was aid for rural Black workers, and in some instances the aid unintentionally offered many tenants a better way of life. Esther Douty, a caseworker for the Federal Emergency Relief Act, noted that "while standards are still wretchedly low, they are better than many of these Negroes knew during the prosperity era."[10] Douty made this conclusion based on the fact that sharecroppers ate hot biscuits "on the most ordinary of days." She also commented that because of a canning campaign, farmers had a varied diet that included vegetables. A major point that Douty made in her report was that because of the federal government, power dynamics changed significantly between the landowners and the tenants they supposedly managed. She noted that "the most fundamental change has come from the fact that FERA has given a measure of independence to a group tied for generations to the white landlord by the urgent need of food and shelter."[11] The aid that the New Deal agencies provided to Black and white farmers allowed them to break the cycle of poverty in which many landlords had trapped them. The landlord was not the only provider anymore because the federal government could provide some relief. If the farmers recognized this, then the landlords did as well, and frankly landowners resented what they believed was Washington intruding into their affairs. The caseworker stated that one landowner told her, "The niggers ain't worth a damn any more. Ever since federal relief and especially the CWA came in, you can't hire a nigger to do anything for you—the men nor the women neither. High wages is ruin' 'em."[12]

At the same time that they disliked what they perceived as federal government intrusion into their affairs, landowners shrewdly took advantage of FERA benefits.[13] The caseworker reported that the landowners began to refuse to provide food for their workers. Once again, the money they received for the tenants' upkeep, they pilfered for themselves. They told the tenants that if they wanted to eat, they should go to the welfare agency; landholders argued that they paid a lot in taxes and should not have to take on the entire burden of feeding tenants. This benefited the landlords in another way as well. Landowners told the sharecroppers that since they received food from welfare services, they could work off their past debts to the landlord. No longer would they get their supplies from the landlord and continue to get deeper in debt. Douty appears to have been a sympathetic caseworker. She stated that the present situation meant more farmers on relief, and she noted that the new economic arrangements did "ruin" the "colored" farmer. She concluded that "relatively high wages are undoubtedly ruining the 'colored' folk-ruining them for a quiet acceptance of sub-subsistence pay, ruining them for months of labor with only debt at the end of the year."[14]

In the cities, the struggles of Black Americans took on a new shape. For African American Memphians, the political landscape of the city changed significantly in the 1930s. The National Association for the Advancement of Colored People (NAACP), founded in 1909, was a very influential organization on the forefront of fighting for equal rights for all Americans.[15] The NAACP became a lot more active in its efforts to register people to vote, and its members continued to fight for justice for African American citizens. In the opening decades of the twentieth century, Black Memphians voted, but the E. H. Crump political machine often diluted their vote. Machine operatives encouraged Black voters to fill out their ballots for certain candidates. They also gave them liquor and a ride to the polls to secure their votes. The Depression changed much of that activity, but not necessarily for the better. Because of the New Deal and Boss Crump's political power, Republican power brokers within the Black community were ineffectual. Crump had the money and control over federal projects, and he did not need any of their help. Men like Dr. J. E. Walker attempted to secure a solid Black Democratic electorate separate from Crump and his machine. But according to Dr. Walker, this effort was only met with physical and mental intimidation by Crump. He used the local police to attack dissidents and used the local newspapers to assault organizers' character.[16]

The Cotton Carnival began against this backdrop of political absolutism, increased migration, and a steady commitment by white southerners to control the Black population in the mid-South. In 1935, a Black dentist named Dr. R. Q. Venson attended the Cotton Carnival with his family. As they stood at the corner of Wellington and Union Avenues, they were in awe of the beauty and pageantry of the affair. Dr. Venson put his nephew, Quincy, on his shoulders so that the five-year-old could watch the parade with an unobstructed view. Once the parade was over, Venson and his wife, Ethyl, asked the little boy if he enjoyed the parade. The child answered with an emphatic "No." Stunned by his response, the couple inquired about the child's distress. He went on to tell them that he did not like the fact that "all of the "Negroes were horses." Quincy saw that the Black men pulled the floats, and he equated that with being an animal. He was not pleased that servitude was the only position for Black people in the carnival.[17]

The Vensons went down to Beale Street after the parade. Ethyl Venson remembered that there was a huge sign in big letters that read "Gates of Ham." In an interview with Sanders Williams, a University of Memphis graduate student studying oral history collection and preservation, Mrs. Venson stated that Beale Street was the site of a midway the carnival organizers reserved for "colored" people. At the site they could sell goods and spend money as they pleased. For Venson this seemed to be the first time that she or her husband gave any thought to the role of "colored" people in this celebration. Ethyl Venson said that she and her husband could not sleep very well that night because they were thinking about the remarks of the child and the sign that greeted them on Beale. It was at this point that Dr. Venson decided to talk to the organizers of the carnival about having "some kind of dignified role" for "Negroes" in the carnival.[18]

Dr. Venson's meeting with carnival organizers did not go very well. As Mrs. Venson stated, "that was 1935," and no white person gave any serious thought to having some dignified role for Black people in the carnival. Although the other organizers crudely rebuffed Dr. Venson, A. Arthur Halle showed interest in Venson's idea and told him that he should start a separate event for "colored" people.[19]

Dr. Venson planned on doing that very thing all along, and he enlisted the help of his wife in his efforts to organize the community. Jubilee organizers received support from the moneyed African American class in Memphis. The jubilee received sizable donations from prominent Black businessmen like Dr. J. E. Walker and Robert Church Jr. They also received a substantial amount of money from the men who had served with Dr. Venson in World War I. Dr. Venson commanded a unit in the American Legion, and the men who served with them had just received bonuses from the federal government. They used the money to help get the Cotton Makers Jubilee off the ground. Mrs. Venson stated that the jubilee treasurer repaid the men in later years, without any interest being added. This funding was greatly appreciated since the carnival organizers forbade Venson or anyone else associated with the jubilee from going to white-owned businesses for sponsorship of their endeavor.[20]

Members of the executive committee for the Cotton Makers Jubilee wrote that they had several motives for starting this venture. Like the white community, they wanted to promote cotton. The committee members viewed cotton as an important asset to the "colored" community because the crop formed the basis for economic prosperity. In turn that money allowed for the business and social development on Beale Street. Since the organizers recognized the significance of cotton, they believed it was their duty to help promote and sell the product worldwide. The second reason the organizers gave for the initiation of the jubilee was that they believed that Black Memphians had a duty to promote the city as one of opportunity and good will. But their primary objective in putting on a separate carnival was their desire "to obtain for the 'colored' residents of the Mid-South, the cotton country . . . the favorable publicity, without which, no group can adequately present that side of its collective personality, which the world will respect and admire."[21] The work of the organizers set the stage for Black Memphians to claim the streets of Memphis as their own. This type of activism, as James Cobb points out, enabled organizers to tell their own stories about the South and how the Black community fit into the building of the wealth and culture of the region in general and the city in particular.[22]

The jubilee was about public relations, specifically about relaying to the general public that slaves were important to the development of cotton. Jubilee organizers wanted to demonstrate to a larger audience what they believed the descendants of slaves already knew. Their goal was to show the world that "colored" people played an important role in the cultivation of cotton and that it was their work that truly built the fortunes of many within the Memphis business community.[23] Another significant point they made was that African Americans were more than "mammies" and "pickaninnies," despite what the carnival organizers and participants put on display. African Americans made a bold stand. Instead of men and women being paid to act out the stereotypical roles of slaves that saturated the consciousness of white Memphians, they could now be kings and queens. They were cotton royalty. In their eyes, Black people occupied the space they should have had all along.

For Venson, being a founder of the jubilee was a natural extension of his upbringing and the lessons his father taught him. Venson recalled that his father was a very religious man who had served as a deacon in the church. He often told his son that he should demonstrate "individual responsibility for the betterment of the community in which [he lived]." The senior Venson promoted education even though he was never trained in any formal way. Venson's father taught him the value of community service, which he practiced in every community in which he lived in.[24]

Venson made it clear that the jubilee was an important stand-alone event. In producing the jubilee, Venson believed that "the Directors [wanted] to avoid the description of 'clowning.'"[25] In Venson's estimation, the Cotton Carnival was an important event, and the Cotton Makers Jubilee was not intended to be a "sun-down interpretation" of the carnival. The organizers were determined to be serious-minded in their promotion of cotton and the historical role that Black people had in the cultivation of the product. The gathering still featured entertainment, and music and dancing were important parts of the jubilee. Organizers also provided historical sketches of the many African Americans who worked to create the Memphis sound.[26]

The program also included the selection of a king and queen. Traditionally ticket sales determined the winner. Not only did the money raised establish the king and queen, but the fundraising also put money back into jubilee coffers. Since the event's inception, participants and observers complained about this system of selection. They believed that this method of fundraising "cheapened the annual affair [because] it had the featured personages of the occasion indulge in a muck-racking ticket-selling contest." The organizers decided to yield to the community's desire for a ceremony that reflected the dignity of the occasion, so in 1941, instead of selling tickets, the people chose the winners by popular vote. The selection committee still examined the character, social standing, and personality of all contestants. Once the committee deemed a man or woman suitable to hold the office, they placed the person's name on the ballot. The actual voting took place at a talent contest held in Memphis, and it included participants from surrounding areas as well. Nat Williams, one of the original organizers of the jubilee, named the ceremony "The Jubilect." Everyone involved with the new addition to the jubilee only had positive feedback for the organizing committee. Unfortunately, the 1941 program indicated that while the event was a success, the money collected at the ceremony did not create a financial surplus.[27]

By 1958, Jubilee officials again shifted their criteria for choosing royalty. Male business and political leaders organized a new club entitled "The Kings Club" to choose appropriate candidates for a king. Memphis's African American elite comprised the membership of this club. Members included businessmen, civic leaders, and politicians from the Tri-State area. Every member of the club paid an annual fee, and they sponsored at least one new member into the club every year. This not only allowed the organization to create longevity, but it also created a steady stream of new income. There was a committee selected from within the club to choose the candidate for king, and this committee sifted through potential applicants and made its selections.[28] Once the committee chose a set of individuals, the applicants became eligible to be selected for the office of king. A different committee selected the women who became eligible to be queen. Hopeful candidates submitted applications to the committee that revealed their marital status, club memberships, what community honors they received, their education, and their weight. If the committee deemed their applications acceptable, these women could compete for the crown. From that point the men and women attended the Jubilect, where the selection of the king and queen took place. All women wore beautiful, full-length gowns adorned with rhinestone accessories, while the men wore nicely tailored business suits.[29]

The jubilee was about image and who controlled the image of Black people. Throughout the history of the jubilee, the original founders included essays in the yearly program. They often spoke of the significance of the image the participants in the jubilee displayed. Phrases like "it was important for . . . the 'Negro' to portray himself in a positive light," or "It [the jubilee] affords us an opportunity to portray our better side" peppered the programs from the 1930s through the 1970s.[30]

What the men on the executive committee hoped was that through their efforts they could transform the way in which white Memphis, and white America, perceived the Black community. They also believed that their mission of transformation was greater than the limits of the mid-South. They wanted the jubilee to be a jewel in the crown of all African Americans. These men set an example of the marvelous work that the group could do through their own ingenuity. Dr. Venson believed that the jubilee was not just about celebrating cotton; he believed that the celebration was a matter of citizenship. He stated: "For the first time, realizing the great possibilities for the development of all phases of citizenship by a community, I pledged myself to make an effort to have the 'Negro' citizens of Memphis identified in this great enterprise. And upon this determination, together with the fact that it is impossible to exclude the 'Negro' from cotton, I submitted to you [the Cotton Carnival Association], a request to enter the 1936 Cotton Carnival."[31]

At first Dr. Venson just wanted the Cotton Carnival to allow "colored" participation in the parade. Venson desired to create "the greatest presentation of its kind in the world" and to point out to all of Memphis, and to the mid-South and beyond, that "the Negro is an entirely more important personage in the Memphis scene than a mere menial to be presented as a clown and mountebank." Venson concluded that the onus of providing the world with a more positive image of the "colored" community was on the "Negro." Once the "Negro" presented himself as respectable and "deserving of dignity," Venson believed that there was no reason why any Black person would not be accepted into society.[32]

The jubilee organizers' philosophy clearly developed from the concept of "racial uplift," which had been the bailiwick of African American leaders since emancipation. Uplift is a fascinating theory that affluent and educated African Americans developed in the latter part of the nineteenth century; it still has a foothold in African American society close to 150 years later. The subscribers to this belief held that the reason white institutions denied African Americans full citizenship benefits was because African Americans had not proven themselves worthy of equal participation in the American dream.[33] The ideology fit well into the tenets of accommodation as articulated by Booker T. Washington. In 1895, he delivered his famous "Atlanta Exposition Address." In this speech, Washington declared his belief that there was an inextricable link between the destiny of Black people and that of white southerners. He exhorted all southerners to "cast down their buckets" in the South and recognize the links that both groups shared. Black people worked in the fields, nursed white children, and held the hands of their former masters and mistresses when they laid on their deathbeds. In Washington's opinion, white southerners should look to labor with Black workers and not look to immigrants to meet their labor requirements. Furthermore, Washington concluded that once Black laborers took advantage of economic opportunities, they would enable themselves to develop into upright American citizens. For Washington the desire for social and political access that many other Black leaders called for was premature. He stated: "The wisest among my race understand that the agitation of questions of social equality is the extremist folly, and that progress in the enjoyment of all the privileges that will come to us must be the result of severe and constant struggle rather than of artificial forcing. . . . It is important and right that all privileges of the law be ours, but it is vastly more important that we be prepared for the exercise of those privileges. The opportunity to earn a dollar in a factory just now is worth infinitely more than the opportunity to spend a dollar in an opera house."[34]

Washington was a firm believer in industrial education for the freed people and their descendants. He believed that a liberal arts education was impractical for most Black people because the land was where most of them achieved financial success. In another speech he gave entitled "The Fruits of Industrial Training," he talked about how the education of Black people was not a top priority for Black politicians and the press since emancipation. He stated, "The appointment of one Negro postmaster at a third or fourth rate post office will be given wider publicity through the daily press than the founding of a school, or some important discovery in science."[35] Washington leaned into the philosophy of the northern missionary in running schools in the South. He believed that Black students needed to be taught thrift, industry, and piety, and he stressed those values in his Sunday evening lectures to his students at Tuskegee. The "Negro" student was to be separate from the "Negro" masses, according to Washington, in their speech, dress, and behavior.[36]

Washington believed that it was time to give the spotlight to industrial education, since the political power of Black people had diminished at the end of Reconstruction. He actually referred to Reconstruction as a time filled with "unwise" and "unfortunate" decisions. One can only guess that he meant that the venturing of Black men into politics, while unfit to hold such offices, caused much of the racial strife associated with the period. While the contemporary Black leaders believed that the majority of white southerners opposed liberal arts education for Black southerners, Washington did not find that to be true. He told his audience that every white person who approached him inquired about the classical languages taught at Tuskegee Institute, and Washington thought most white southerners believed in higher education for Black people. However, what Washington noticed was that industrial education became the vehicle where interracial cooperation in Black education held the most promise. Further, in his mind, what was the purpose of learning about visual art, music, and literature if a person could not afford to indulge in enjoying them?[37]

Washington noted that many freed people seemed to believe that the term *freedom* meant "freedom from work with their hands." He stated that they did not understand the difference between work and being worked. From the white southerners' perspective, Washington believed that they wanted to teach freed people the dignity and honor of working with their hands because this work provided the people with the best avenues for success. He also believed that white people assisted in industrial education because "they saw at once that intelligence coupled with skill would add wealth to the community and to the state, in which both races would have an added share."[38] But readers should not be misled by this soft-sell speech Washington gave at the beginning of the century. He definitely made industrial education and work sound appealing to both Black and white southerners, but very often he did this at the expense of those elites who sought out a liberal arts education. There were plenty of instances where Washington discussed the follies of those Black people who shunned the dignity of labor with their hands. He indicated that they were people who learned useless things like Greek and proper syntax and now lived in squalor, or they opted for the profession of teaching or ministry because they believed those professions offered easy money.[39]

R. Q. Venson reflected this same view in an essay, first released in the 1941 program, but organizers thought the piece was important enough to release it at least three times after that year's celebration. Venson began his commentary by asking:

> Where is the spirit and the type of Negro who founded Tuskegee and other Institutions of training in America? [Where are] the Negroes who organized banks, bought farms and built homes? . . . whose record for honesty made it unnecessary to require bonds or securities for loans and advancements . . .

> whose respect for law and order made it unprofitable to build large institutions for the incarceration of his criminals? . . . whose clean living and keen appreciation of good health made him physically immune from many of the diseases which today have caused his alarming death rate? What have become of those family altars presided over by the mothers and fathers who gave their children information and guidance in the proper ways of life?[40]

Venson answered his own question by stating that "these conditions have been replaced by disillusionment, dishonesty, foreclosure, unemployment, loss of self-respect, pride, disease and death." Venson, in a somewhat stunning essay, sets up a class dynamic to the jubilee. He talked extensively about the educated Black men and women who were part of a "bumper crop of proper-phrasing, smart talking, overstuffed jellyfish. Who talk of rights and their living without being willing to pay the price." He believed that much of the education that "colored people received" was impractical to their daily lives because in his words "it [education] is teaching the Negro daily to be a White man while he is in school . . . it teaches him for the Bank president's chair and then speedily places a mop and bucket in his hand."[41]

Venson supposed that the education that "colored" citizens received in the thirties only reinforced the misguided notions he believed some of their ancestors had in slavery. He believed that "education [was] buttressed by the traditions of a not so distant past . . . when impressionable Black slaves . . . favored slaves, if you please . . . the ones who were fortunate enough to be worked in the Big House . . . gazed in admiring awe upon the ways of their White aristocratic masters, and mimiced [sic] them . . . mimiced them so much so until today, no minority group surpasses the Negro in the role of play acting." The close association some Black men and women had with white people fostered "arrogance" and pretentiousness. These people, Venson continued, were "ten cent millionaires . . ." who grew fat "and crusty over the mere fat crumbs that fall from the table of the mighty . . . and who coin such phrases as 'Po White Trash,' and 'Field Nigger,' as contemptuous descriptions of their fellows, who, in their Fool's Paradise, they deem their inferiors."[42]

He called these people the "pseudo Negro elite," whose celebrated writers have all of America thinking that "colored" people were just "Bigger Thomases of Native son [*sic*] extraction, choking and dying in frustration like cornered rats." Conversely, he asserted that these "Negroes" often disparaged the hard-working "colored" farmers, and they kept filling their heads with propaganda about education when the workers should have been focused on the land. More specifically they should have been focused on cotton. Venson called on all Black Memphians to support the "Back-to-the-Soil Movement." He believed that it was in working the soil that Black people could be self-supporting and could enjoy real gains instead of the superficial ones provided by education. This is where the jubilee becomes even more important to the "colored" community. Venson explained that the jubilee dramatized "the Negro's contribution to the agricultural South."[43]

There is clearly a tension in Venson's statement between himself and prominent leaders who questioned his desire to create such a celebration in the first place. From early on, the jubilee faced financial trouble because many Black organizations with monetary resources thought the celebration of cotton was counterintuitive.[44] Like Washington, Venson believed firmly that for most Black southerners their fortunes lay in the land and not the hallowed halls of some university. Furthermore, as Washington had pointed out in his address more than forty years before the advent of the jubilee: "Those who once opposed this [industrial and domestic training], see now that while the Negro youth who becomes skilled in agriculture and a successful farmer may not be able himself to pass through a purely literary college, he is laying the foundation for his children and grandchildren to do it if desirable."[45] From Venson's perspective in the late 1930s and early 1940s, uplift was about protest and accommodation. He and the other organizers protested their portrayal in the carnival, but for them one of the primary goals was to be accepted by white society. As stated previously, to present the positive side of the race without which there could be no advancement or respect.

To reiterate in more detail, the event's purpose was twofold. First, there was a concerted effort by its organizers to encourage the promotion of cotton. In the jubilee's charter, point three stated that purpose this way: "To assist and promote all agricultural, livestock, mechanical, commercial and industrial arts and trades, and other worthy endeavors of a similar character." The charter also stated that its purpose was to "[form] a liaison with the white Cotton Association, with the design of showing the Negro's sense of 'one-ness' with the Carnival Association's desire to give Memphis favorable publicity over the nation and the world, and to increase the consumption of cotton, the 'backbone' of the Mid-South economy in which Negroes, as well as white people, live and seek to prosper."[46]

Clifton Satterfield, who served as the secretary-treasurer of the Cotton Makers Jubilee, echoed this sentiment in a 1949 essay. He stated: "If we do no more than to give Memphis the praise it deserves for its growth and advancement; if we do no more than give cotton the place it holds on the scale of economic security, if we do no more than to present, for development, youthful talent for use in the advancement of a better citizenship, a greater America, a united fellowship, and a more progressive civilization, I believe you will agree that it deserves the whole hearted support of the citizens."[47] Presenting an alternate image of Black people and their work during slavery was Venson's second purpose. The jubilee was a form of protest against the racism of the carnival, even as it simultaneously was an accommodation to the racial proscriptions of Memphis, and this can be a confusing point to grasp. There was a tension in uplift philosophy: the ideology discussed how the better side of the race could be displayed, but it also highlighted the "savagery" that supposedly existed within the race to demonstrate how far the group had come. Uplift was, and still is, a class-based movement that cannot document progress without further polarizing the differing economic and social classes within the Black community.

Carnival organizers contented themselves with their yearly cotton celebration with no inclusion of Black people. There was a type of disconnect between what they said they celebrated and what they actually honored at the Cotton Carnival. Most white southerners had the Old South myth firmly planted in their minds. They looked fondly on the time when the white man was king of all he surveyed, and the "darkeys" happily picked cotton and sang in the fields. Nat Williams remembered the mammies on the stools and the Black men as mules, and he stated these bandana-wearing men and women sat on bales of cotton "singing almost forgotten spirituals."[48] And that quite simply is the point. Uplift was about one class of African Americans being able to point to their progress by demonstrating how far they had come since the days of the plantation. The Cotton Carnival was the return of the plantation in full force, and the affair shoved into Black Memphians' faces that by white southerners' estimation, they had not come very far at all. Even if they made significant progress up to that point, white southerners decided not to recognize the fact. They retreated comfortably into the myths that they constructed and learned about the old plantation "Negro."

Venson faced considerable opposition because he meddled with the myth. He wanted to highlight the hard-working Black men and women who toiled in the fields to make cotton a premier crop. Venson wanted to enhance the status and prestige of Memphis "colored people," and that objective ran counter to the myth. The organizers believed that the portrayal of African Americans in the carnival conflicted with the reality of the position and ambitions of contemporary Black citizens. They believed that the Black community had made progress that carnival organizers refused to display.[49]

According to Ethyl Venson, she and her husband gathered support from the larger Black community through appeals to businessmen and women. They also managed to convince the schools to participate in building the floats for the parade. Another experience Venson recounted foretold of future celebrations of the jubilee. The jubilee committee worked overtime to convince the teachers to become involved in the project. Venson stated that their attitude was that "it [cotton] has not done anything for us and we don't want to get our children involved in this." Further in an interview, she stated that "little by little, we were able to get people to come in with us. But it was a struggle. And it has continued to be a struggle through these fifty years." The community, for the most part, supported the jubilee, and many of the people worked on the committees planning and carrying off the event without being paid.[50]

The first year of the jubilee was a success in Venson's estimation. The parade was successful in part because of its uniqueness. Venson claimed that no one had ever heard of a festivity organized and operated by an all-Black committee. Furthermore, no one had ever seen a parade that celebrated Black people's participation in the production of cotton.[51] Venson remembered all of Memphis showing excitement about the new event. She also recalled what she considered to be a very funny incident when reporters who had come to town initially to cover the Cotton Carnival got wind of a second celebration. She stated, "[*Time* magazine] and [*Life* magazine] had sent representatives here to do the Cotton Carnival. Well, these writers became interested in what was happening on Beale Street. . . . The Carnival was looking for these important writers. . . . Here they were down on Beale Street and [interviewing] the Black King and Queen."[52] The reporters interviewed Ethyl

Venson at the Palace Theater because they could not fit their equipment into her small apartment, but for her the extra effort was worth it, because both magazines mentioned the jubilee.[53]

While reinforcing the connection African Americans had to the land, the jubilee organizers engaged in their own mythmaking. In 1948 George W. Lee served as president of the jubilee, and he wrote a separate piece for a brochure entitled "Cabin in the Cotton." In this work he reaffirmed the jubilee's aim to be a stand-alone event. He stated that the jubilee presented an "illuminating picture of a civilization within a civilization, far from being a purely dependent growth, parasitically clinging to the White man's culture. The 'Negro' is here displayed as developing a culture of his own."[54] Lee goes on to praise the work of the sharecropper, the tenant farmer, and Dr. Venson. Lee believed that Venson and the organizers of the jubilee presented a more accurate picture of the work of the rural "Negro." According to Lee, the organizers respected the cotton farmers, who worked six days of the week and who "hitched their mules to the plows and moved slowly up and down row after row, pushing their plow shares deep into brown earth. . . . Sometimes they sang. Often they would lift their faces, dripping with sweat and look up at the sun, as if pleading with it to have mercy on them, but at all times their movements were in perfect rhythm because when the songs died on their lips, they echoed in their hearts. It was their way of taking the pain from their labors."[55]

Lee noted that the workers valued religion, and they rejoiced on Sunday morning by singing to the Lord to "wash them whiter than snow."[56] He went on to talk about the vibrant social life of sharecroppers, who enjoyed cheap whiskey, smoking, and close dancing on Saturday night. The idyllic picture that Lee constructed was much different than the observations made by New Deal workers during the thirties. Part of the reason for this disparity is that in his description Lee built a philosophical foundation for the jubilee. He argued that individuals should respect the fields and its workers. He painted a romantic portrait of rural life so that he could legitimize the jubilee organizers' efforts to celebrate a crop associated with the subjugation of millions of Black Americans, and on its simplest level Lee's account of farm life was just good public relations. He attempted to adjust the kaleidoscope of social change and justice with the harsh realities of an intransigent South. Due to poverty and racial discrimination, not all deserving Black students attended college; therefore, the cotton fields offered them an alternative. Possibly, Lee wanted to create a social climate that honored the achievements of the "race" but did not ridicule the field-workers or their lifestyles since most Black families still relied on the land for their survival.[57]

Organizers sought to develop this new perspective on cotton and the honor of working with the hands in order to market to the people who never grew up with the pain of cotton and slavery. Jubilee supporters wanted to reach into the high schools to children just starting on the journey to adulthood. Their goal was to communicate with children beginning to think about a life for themselves that was separate from that of their parents. Jubilee organizers developed the ZoZo Club not only to encourage participation in the jubilee but also to develop a sense of pride among high school–aged Memphians about rural southern living. Four Memphis high schools (Melrose, Douglas, Hamilton, and Booker T. Washington) provided the setting for the ZoZo Club. In order for students to be selected for the club, they had to meet certain qualifications. First, young men and women needed to have acceptable grades. Second, they had to possess good public relations skills. They had to develop their own project that showcased cotton, and then they had to sell the idea to the larger community. Third, they had to be well-behaved, involved in community service, and congenial so that they could work with other members of the group. ZoZo Club members had a code of conduct to follow once they became members. The club's rules required all ZoZo members to always be courteous, to be "curious about the world of tomorrow," and to watch the "scientific developments in today's world." Finally, the guidelines reminded members that "science and worldly materials will always be secondary to our moral and spiritual values."[58] As James Cobb points out, African Americans from the South believed that they were as much a part of the community as white people.[59] The ZoZo club could be seen as an effort to anchor their presence even more in Memphis as well as providing a fruitful garden from which future generations would extend their ties to the land and the commodity.

Jubilee organizers believed that the cotton industry was an integral part of these young peoples' lives and teaching them about the different avenues available to them through agriculture was an important job for all involved. Erma Clanton, who served as chairman of the ZoZo clubs in 1952, stated that "if our boys and girls can gain knowledge about cotton . . . its vast potentialities . . . it is my earnest belief that they like the commodity itself, will move into some of the facets of the industry which will bring fruitful returns." Jubilee leaders judged the clubs, which they founded in the early forties, a success by the end of the decade. They based their opinion on the positive response they received from participants and their advisors who came from among the high school faculty. ZoZo Clubs encouraged young people to get involved in civic activities, and they provided a much-needed mechanism to develop future talent needed to continue the jubilee.[60]

Another method organizers used to get children involved in the programs of the jubilee was an essay contest. The coordinator of the public school system directed this contest, and only children enrolled in elementary school could participate. Organizers provided a theme for the essays so that the students could reveal "the individual's reaction to the influences of cotton in his own environments, and his observances and studies of the South's white gold, cotton." A committee judged these essays, and they announced the winner during the juvenile portion of the jubilee. This feature of the event was in no way an afterthought.[61]

The organizers believed that by reaching out to Black youth, they could influence them at a turning point in their lives. Jubilee organizers charged group leaders with an important responsibility because, as Ethyl Venson concluded, "This period in the lives of those young people are the purest, sweetest, and most exciting that they will ever experience. Paradoxically . . . this period . . . can be the most dangerous and the most difficult period that they will ever encounter."[62] Venson believed that it was important for the youth to know that the leaders cared about them. They focused on working tirelessly to assist them during the jubilee. In order to further the larger goals of the jubilee, adult volunteers held seminars on comportment, like proper manners, personal hygiene, and good behavior.[63]

Yet another development jubilee organizers initiated was the Spirit of Cotton. Committee members selected a young coed about two months before the actual festivities began, at a ceremony entitled "The Jubilect." In her discussion of the event, Ethyl Venson stated that the "Negro" in America had for years "huddled over cotton . . . the 'Negro' dutifully nurtured this crop until it blossomed into full maturity."[64] She then went on to discuss how the National Cotton Council of America as part of the Cotton Carnival sent a young white female as an ambassador around the nation to promote cotton and talk about Memphis as a prosperous city with many economic opportunities. They called this ambassador the "Maid of Cotton," and from the standpoint of Cotton Makers Jubilee officials, her representation of the city was not impressive. Because while she publicized the greatest party in the South, the people who were at the center of cotton production, the ones who "nursed the infant cotton industry with the blood of [their] back, and sometimes [their] life . . . [was] still neglected, burlesqued, or completely forgotten."[65]

The Spirit of Cotton was an alternative to the carnival's ambassador. Ethyl Venson readily recognized that this exclusion served to create a "deep, festering spirit of resentment among "'Negroes.'" Instead of being powerless to fight their much-maligned images throughout the world the jubilee organizers came up with a solution that challenged the narrative white southerners created. Venson stated that this "spirit [of resentment] grew from a whispered protest into a strong, vibrant personality with a beautiful voice eager to sing of the Negro's contribution to King Cotton's power. It is this 'Spirit of Cotton' which today tours selective cities in the United States singing, I, too, make Cotton. Behold how lovely I am!"[66]

The importance of the Spirit of Cotton as a form of protest cannot be overstated. For centuries white people considered white womanhood to be the essence of civilization. White men met any threat to the sanctity of white womanhood with a visceral response. This sanctity was not limited to wealthy white southern women because any white woman who lacked wealth or privilege in southern society could make herself a part of this protected class by railing about the threat of Black male bestial sexuality. Conversely the Black woman has never enjoyed the same place of sanctity in the minds of white southerners. In their minds, the fact that mixed-race children existed was all the proof they needed to support the position that Black women lacked morals. In this myth, white men were supposedly unwilling victims of the sexual prowess of Black women.[67] These themes about Black womanhood are not at all uncommon. In *From Mammy to Miss America,* K. Sue Jewell argues that the popular images of Black women can be traced back to slavery and those images on the whole are negative. She also maintains that whether the image is of an overly sexualized Jezebel or of the ever-devoted mammy both were in direct contrast to the image of the idealized white female.[68] These stereotypes of Black women made the implementation of the Spirit of Cotton all the more important.

Typically, the individual chosen to wear this heavy crown was a coed, but she could be as young as a senior in high school. Invitations for participation went out all over the city of Memphis and throughout the region. The selection committee required applicants to be single, at least five feet tall, no more than 125 pounds, of good moral standing, and in good health. The Spirit of Cotton made "personal appearances on radio, television, and before interested civic and social groups [and] she must . . . travel for the Memphis Cotton Makers' Jubilee, Inc., as an emissary of Cotton Fashions and good-will."[69]

The selection process began before the actual talent contest at the annual Jubilect. All contestants arrived in town at least two days prior to the event, and they endured a strict public-appearance schedule. The judges used this time to evaluate them on their poise, character, and attitude. The judges factored every one of their movements—from their walk, to their grasp of the English language, and even down to how they handled their silverware—into their final scores. Three persons who did not reside in the towns where the contestants lived and a fourth member, who did not vote, composed the selection committee. The nonvoting member served as the coordinator and liaison between the judges and the larger jubilee committee. Judges evaluated the contestants based on three categories: beauty, worth a possible 20 points, personality, worth 40 points, and talent, worth 40 points. Once they chose a winner, she traveled to selected cities throughout the United States "to publicize Memphis, as having the largest inland cotton market in the world. To publicize cotton as the nation's greatest fiber and to prove to the nation that cotton can be worn for any occasion and in any season of the year. To publicize the upcoming celebration—the Memphis Cotton Maker's Jubilee and to extend to the nation an invitation to attend this year's celebration."[70] She also carried a scroll with her, on which she gathered signatures from the residents of the hosting city, who wrote positive messages about her appearances and their impression of her overall mission. The successful Spirit of Cotton was the young lady who not only promoted the jubilee but also succeeded in presenting a "glorified image of Negro womanhood."[71]

The selection committee chose Dorothy Jean Lewis as the Spirit of Cotton in 1948. Lewis was a freshman at Lemoyne College, where she trained for a career in the performing arts. She was already an outstanding ballet dancer, and she had a talent in the dramatic arts as well. Lewis flew to Hollywood,

California, and once there she traveled by chauffeured limousine. She was ecstatic with her schedule, especially when she had opportunities to meet celebrities like actor Clark Gable. What turned out to be the highlight for Lewis was the day a photographer took her picture in a gown worn by Lena Horne in the movie *Till the Clouds Roll By*. The owners of the gown allowed her to wear the garment for the shoot, and they also loaned the gown to her for the upcoming jubilee festivities. Lewis completed her final photo shoot in her all-cotton wardrobe in the home of singer and actor Ethel Waters.[72]

Lewis also visited Los Angeles city hall and took pictures with the mayor and several city councilmen who signed her scroll with a pen used by the governor. The Los Angeles city council also honored the delegation from Memphis with the state seal of California.[73] The frenzy surrounding the Spirit of Cotton rose to what we might call rock-star status in today's terms. Bobbie Jackson, who was the Spirit of Cotton in 1949, traveled to Chicago. She kept repeating, as the plane taxied down the runway, "It just can't be true, this is a dream, I know." As the plane came to a stop, the flight attendant asked Jackson to wait to exit the plane because the press were waiting at the end of the runway to photograph her. Press ranging from the *Chicago Defender* to the *New York Age* sent photographers to cover the event.[74]

By 1956, praise for the Spirit of Cotton contest came from all parts of the South. Presidents of Black colleges and universities readily wrote the jubilee committee to express their great enthusiasm for the event. They credited the contest with creating an environment in which young women "[gained] a broader vision of their own possibilities" as they learned to develop an "appreciation for the finer things in life."[75] Dr. R. W. E. Jones, president of Grambling College, noted that the goals of the jubilee—to teach young women the value of "moral soundness, intellectual attainments, and social graces"—were in line with the goals of his institution and declared that he was more than happy to support the efforts of the jubilee. Two college presidents, Dr. Lawrence Davis from Arkansas AM&N College, and Dr. C. V. Troup of Fort Valley State College, lauded the organizers of the jubilee for their efforts to develop a finer womanhood among young Black women.[76]

The Spirit of Cotton contest offers historians fertile ground for investigating life in Memphis and the South during the forties. The contest also offers an avenue in which to discuss the ideas of womanhood, which a certain class of African American women wished to attain. Further, by examining the jubilee celebration and the contest in particular, one can easily see how the narrative constructed by organizers really confronted white southerners' notions about the Old South. In her work *A Voice from the South,* Anna Julia Cooper made one of the most thought-provoking and empowering declarations when she stated: "Only the BLACK WOMAN can say when and where I enter, in the quiet, undisputed dignity of my womanhood, without violence and without suing or special patronage, then and there the whole *Negro race enters with me.*"[77] In this one compound sentence, Cooper encompassed the struggle of Black women for the majority of the twentieth century. The race would not make any significant progress toward equality until all of America held the women of the race in the highest esteem. Since the end of slavery, Black women battled the images perpetuated by the plantation myth, which consisted of African American women being either jezebels or mammies. Of course, the focus of this text is on the mammy myth and its importance to the foundations of the Cotton Makers Jubilee. Since the end of Reconstruction, Black women were bound to their slave status, at least in the mind of Confederates and their descendants. As a group, white southerners participated in ideological hegemony, controlling the production of ideas with the placement of mammies and pickaninnies throughout the carnival festivities.[78]

The negative historical images of African American women were the very thing that women like Cooper, Mary Church Terrell, and many other clubwomen fought against throughout the early decades of the twentieth century. Black clubwomen engaged in the practices of uplift by taking on social, political, and economic issues confronting many within the African American community. The average clubwoman was a southern married woman; however, they had low fertility rates. A distinct majority of this group of very well educated women chose to participate in careers outside the home—despite the fact that they had married men who could support them. In order to appropriately address the issues of their less-fortunate sisters, these women used the feminine qualities of virtuousness, serenity, and gentleness to tackle these racialized, gender-specific stereotypes. They found these stereotypes harmful and unfair to the situation of poor women. Feeling unjustly burdened by these stereotypes, these women decided to act. For them the issue was a matter of survival for the race, and improvement of their quality of life, because their status would never improve if they could not break away from these images as a group.[79]

By the dawn of the 1930s, the Black middle class found the temptress stereotype to be a pressing issue. Blues music attracted poor Black women, and the lyrics not only touted the desire of Black women for their men, but also articulated the sexual prowess of Black women. In general, the blues represented the type of culture that clubwomen and social reformers wanted to steer the Black population away from. Much of the music was countercultural, and the artists made music that boldly challenged the social mores of the day. Historian R. A. Lawson, in *Jim Crow's Counterculture,* describes the type of environment that blues music inhabited. From smoky clubs that offered liquor and cocaine to risqué lyrics, listeners were able to escape the harshness of everyday life. This new standard set by female blues artists was unacceptable to clubwomen and other women in the middle class. Embracing the blues philosophy put them right back in the sexual trap that their ancestors struggled against during slavery. Blues music served as an affirmation of the white population's ideas of African American women, so they had to "model . . . prideful morality." Their focus remained on racial uplift, health, and education.[80]

Since Memphis was the home of the blues, R. Q. and Ethyl Venson dealt with those same images of Black women as sexually promiscuous. They made their life's work one in which they presented more positive images for Black men and women. They wanted to develop role models that the young people could look up to. By initiating the jubilee, the Vensons took control to some degree of the images that the larger Memphis public observed. This point is very important because the carnival acted as a form of mass media that essentially allowed those persons who oversaw private capital to continue to transmit images of African Americans that attributed "their depressed socioeconomic status to individual and cultural deficiencies."[81] More importantly the portrayal of Black women as mammies was also a method that white southerners used to negate the mere possibility that Black women were more than workhorses or reproductive machines. If mammy's dark skin was not enough her rotund figure was ample evidence that she was outside the sphere of womanhood that white women constructed and maintained for nearly a century. During the Cotton Carnival the presence of mammy offered many white men and women some level of comfort. She reminded them of the acceptable and comfortable way in which African

Americans belonged in the white world, which was to be submissive and even humorous, but never threatening.[82]

One of the purposes of the Cotton Makers Jubilee was to wrest control of the image of Black Memphians away from whites who organized the Cotton Carnival. This effort specifically allows readers to think about how an image becomes ingrained in the minds of those who see it and fossilize it into the consciousness of generations. The Vensons were not social scientists, but their recognition of the impact that the Cotton Carnival's images of Black people had on their nephew spurred them to action. Stunned by his comment about the positions of servitude that African Americans occupied in this white affair, they designed an event to reverse the effects those subservient roles had on not only young people but also the larger Memphis community. Organizers displayed "the best side of the race" through essay contests, talent shows, and finally the selection of a young woman as Spirit of Cotton.[83] Their efforts were part of the larger struggle of the Black middle class to point out that as a race African Americans had evolved. They had evolved to the point where they could have kings and queens and even have contests for children where they could be crowned Little Master and Miss Gold. By demonstrating their cultural sophistication, Black Memphians felt that they could squelch the offensive images that the carnival promoted.

By the time of the Cotton Makers Jubilee, Black Memphians had spent more than one hundred years trying to push their way into a life filled with equality and opportunity. Yes, the organizers knew they were Black, their parents and/or grandparents had been enslaved, but they also knew the promises of this nation. They believed they should be treated as full citizens, and the images at the Cotton Carnival frustrated their efforts. This concept is not new. At the opening of the twentieth century W. E. B. Du Bois wrote about the double consciousness endured by Black Americans. In 1930s Memphis, the double consciousness was a reality that Black citizens dealt with every day. In his article entitled "The Dialectic of Double-Consciousness in Black American Freedom Celebrations, 1808–1863," William Gravely points out that African Americans had a long tradition of creating celebrations that showed their commitment to the idea of freedom. These celebrations began before the Civil War, but they fell on significant days to the freed populations. January 1 was a popular date because the international slave trade was supposed to end on January 1, 1808. A few communities in the North celebrated this day, but the festivities died out after a while. Black Americans were dismayed that even though the international trade was supposed to end many slaveholders violated the law. January 1 celebrations would not make a reappearance until Lincoln issued the executive order ending slavery on January 1, 1863. The other two celebration days for African Americans fell on July 5 and August 1. The fifth was special because it coincided with July Fourth celebrations. August 1 held meaning for celebrants because the enslaved in the British West Indies gained their freedom on August 1. All of these celebrations centered around the participants' strivings for freedom, but they also had very somber elements because organizers took the time to remember those who remained in bondage.[84] The Cotton Makers Jubilee differs from these celebrations mainly because they were in the nineteenth century, but the messages are the same. The organizers and the participants were looking to stake their claim on the promises of this nation. For the Cotton Makers Jubilee organizers, the activities surrounding the event made a bold statement that they mattered just as much as the white participants in the Cotton Carnival. The jubilee reminds us that these supporters and organizers were not just Americans, they were Memphians, they were what made the South its own unique place. Finally, the jubilee reminds readers that "I Too Make Cotton."

6

BATTLE FOR A NARRATIVE

History seemed to be on the side of the jubilee organizers as they strove to promote a positive image of African Americans. From the *Brown v. Board of Education* decision to school desegregation in Little Rock, Arkansas, Americans became more intolerant of racial segregation. In Memphis, no dramatic court decision or violent street demonstration reflected this growing unpopularity. Instead, a group of concerned local business leaders emerged, inspired by the South's violent response to court-mandated desegregation, to facilitate Memphis's transition to a freer society.

Civic leaders approached desegregation in Memphis in an understated manner. Organizations like the Memphis Committee on Community Relations (MCCR) worked with local businesses to soften the impact of new legislation that allowed Black people into venues previously unavailable to them. Desegregation occurred at a steady pace in the city but ventured only so far. Despite the efforts of the MCCR and other similar organizations, Memphis persisted as a city divided in two; in government, Black representation remained negligible, and schools showed little movement toward desegregation. The National Association for the Advancement of Colored People (NAACP) fought such exclusion of African Americans from public service and schools, but their fight against segregation placed the NAACP at odds with the organizers of the jubilee. NAACP leaders urged an end to the event, labeling it a segregated relic of society. In response, Jubilee organizers pointed to the event's Black origins, characterizing the jubilee itself as a Black institution deserving of protection.[1]

The tension between groups that promoted integration and groups like the jubilee planning committee was not an unusual occurrence during the sixties. By 1961, the NAACP decided to issue a statement condemning the Nation of Islam as "anti-white."[2] The leaders of the group decided that this was necessary because African Americans increasingly supported the concept of Black nationalism, and this was concerning for a class of people who wanted to keep the community focused on desegregation.[3] The preachings of Black nationalism were particularly salient to young people as evidenced by the fact that while the national committee of the NAACP condemned the Nation of Islam, student chapters across the country extended several invitations to Malcolm X to speak to their members. The Honorable Elijah Muhammad and Malcolm X embodied the concept that promoted "the creation and maintenance" of Black institutions without oversight by white people.[4] They believed that it was through these institutions that Black people would find the liberation they sought. The obvious problem here is that the NAACP had spent the previous half century fighting to desegregate America, and here was a group encouraging the practices that served to marginalize Black people. While men like Malcolm X would claim that racial segregation (involuntary) and racial separation (voluntary) were two completely different things, his comments fell on deaf ears within pro-integration circles.[5]

This pull between integrationist and segregationist forces was not just a local phenomenon. Throughout the latter part of the twentieth century, vestiges of the Jim Crow past remained. While one group believed that these segregated institutions represented a way station to full integration, countervailing views believed that these segregated institutions, while valuable when people created them, were now a hindrance to full citizenship for the segregated group. In their study concerning the competing ideologies of Black nationalism and interracial integration, Jason Shelton and Michael Emerson hold that these two philosophies need not be mutually exclusive.[6] The jubilee was a Black nationalist event in that the organizers worked toward developing a sense of racial and regional identity, and they demonstrated political self-determination.[7]

Nationalism provided African Americans a framework to criticize inequality, but it also set the faction up for isolation and distrust from outside groups. The Cotton Makers Jubilee came to exist because the Cotton Carnival organizers excluded members of the Black community. Leaders like R. Q. Venson had to push their way into the festival activities so that Black Memphians would have a place of respect in the annual celebrations. Within the confines of the festival, Black people created their own narrative about the role of cotton in their lives. By the sixties, though, this nationalist movement in Memphis became plagued with the attitudes that normally accompany such associations. Members in this community became distrustful of the leaders of the group due the jubilee's association with the larger all-white carnival.[8]

The jubilee became a point of contention in the conversation over the methods of protest Black Memphians used to challenge white supremacy. Unlike the position the leaders of the jubilee took in the 1930s—a position more conciliatory to the white-led carnival—jubilee leaders of the 1960s found themselves grappling for relevance in a rapidly changing South. To protect their weakening status, jubilee leaders aggressively denounced attacks made against them. Many of them argued that the jubilee was in essence a protest against white oppression, a Black display of strength in the face of white racism.[9]

This opposition within the Black community in Memphis crystallized in 1961 when the Memphis chapter of the NAACP called for an end to the separate carnivals. The *Tri-State Defender* reported in May of 1961 that NAACP officials denounced the continuation of the jubilee. NAACP officials based their opposition on the civil rights organization's commitment to desegregation, believing the jubilee promoted continued segregation of public life. The organization issued a statement to the press in which it "strongly [urged] all Negro citizens not to participate [in the jubilee] in any way." The statement continued, "This action is being taken because of this organization's firm belief in Freedom, Justice and Equality, which by no means, [is] reflected in segregated events." The Ministers Alliance joined the NAACP in protest, and its leaders issued the following statement: "In view of the ministers' stand on racial segregation, we strongly condemn any participation of our people in the Cotton Maker's Jubilee celebration. We take this action on the basis of our belief that the segregation of people on the basis of race is inconsistent both with Christianity and democracy."[10]

Since March of 1961, the NAACP had been involved in protests throughout Memphis that challenged racial segregation. These series of protests culminated in the Freedom Movement's "march a week," which began in June of 1961. Throughout the spring of 1961, readers of the city's *Tri-State Defender* were reminded of the historic struggle Memphians waged toward a more free and desegregated society. In a speech honoring the work of civil rights legends Jesse H. Turner and A. Maceo Walker Sr., Rev. Kelly Miller Smith of Nashville stated that "soon Negroes will be integrated into the total life of all American [communities]."[11] Turner held the positions of vice president and cashier of Tri-State Bank, and A. Maceo Walker Sr., held the position of president of Universal Life Insurance Company, as well as president of the Tri-State Bank. Both, too, had recently risen to prominent roles in city government. Walker was appointed to the Memphis Traffic Advisory Committee, and Turner was the first African American to be elected to the Shelby County Democratic Committee.[12] Smith believed that the protest marches and modest concessions by white-controlled local governments in the South were but the beginning of the desegregation movement and that celebrations of such achievements would become unnecessary as Black people continued to rise to office at all levels of government.[13]

Aside from marching and celebration of African American breakthroughs, the NAACP became involved in significant discussions with the Memphis school board in response to the board's slow adoption of desegregation. In a "hot letter," NAACP President Jesse Turner chastised the school board for their failure to desegregate over five years after the 1954 *Brown* decision. Turner argued further, "We also wish to vigorously protest the policy concerning the designation of school holidays which permits school children to participate in segregated events sponsored by private groups, thus your policy of giving Negro children a school holiday so that they may participate in the Cotton Maker's Jubilee, a segregated affair, and white children a school holiday, so that they may participate in the Cotton Carnival, a similar segregated affair, we find highly offensive."[14]

President Frank Scott of the jubilee countered in 1961 that the jubilee did not support segregation. Quite the contrary, he believed that the jubilee was a "Negro" institution built and supported by "Negroes," and unlike the carnival, the jubilee welcomed all people, regardless of race, to participate. Echoing the sentiments of Malcolm X, Scott argued that there existed a "clear difference between All-Negro and segregated." From his perspective, to end the jubilee would be a destruction of heritage and was therefore a shortsighted resolution. Scott defended the jubilee by characterizing the attacks leveled against the organization as ignorant of the "aims and purposes of the Jubilee." Scott argued that work in the cotton industry remained a reality for people of color in the mid-South and encouraged the "Negro" population itself to "struggle for dignity of all mankind with King Cotton in a changing world." For Scott and other organizers, the jubilee was an effort to build a better future culturally, economically, and politically for Black people in the mid-South.[15]

Another organizer, Clifton Satterfield, examined the controversy in the jubilee's 1961 program. In response to those who asked, "Why celebrate cotton, a product of slave labor and the profit of plantation owners?" Satterfield argued that "cotton, as a product for human needs, should not be penalized for past experiences out-lived, and enslaved circumstances outlawed."[16] Satterfield believed that Black people were held to an economic obligation to cultivate the crop and be part of the "economic security of the South from which all of us benefit." He responded to those who complained about the segregated nature of the Cotton Fiesta (the original name for the jubilee) by drawing attention to the lack of carnival support the event received in its infancy. Nevertheless, the event grew slowly in participation and prominence in the eyes of regional and national observers. He further argued in favor of the benefits the jubilee offered to Black people as a "Negro Carnival," a space where the Black community was offered the opportunity to demonstrate their talent while also promoting cotton and the city of Memphis. At the carnival's beginning, no displays of people of colors' ingenuity, ambition, or enterprise were included. Satterfield reminded the public that in the 1930s, no vehicle existed for Black people to protest their white-controlled portrayal in the Cotton Carnival. He goes on to describe the few Black participants who were included at that carnival: "Negroes [who] participated in the Carnival . . . Wore dusters, pulled floats, picked banjoes, sang spirituals, and ate watermelons atop floats. They dressed like plantation slaves." Rather than wage a formal protest, R. Q. Venson and other Black community leaders organized to present an alternative image, another memory, of Black people's investment in cotton. Satterfield argued against the call to terminate the jubilee outright in the name of total integration, a proposal he described as analogous to "setting [your] house on fire on the theory that [you] will secure a house [you] do not yet have."[17]

Nat Williams furthered the argument made by Satterfield. He determined that the attacks on the jubilee required a decision from Black Memphians: to either "[hold] fast" to the tenets of Black culture that formed and nurtured Black racial identity, or to "cast aside" all fixtures and institutions "suggestive of the "Negro." To defend his stance, he turned to the Vensons' mission to reclaim Black identity:

> [T]he picture of the Negro as portrayed by the Carnival promoters was unsatisfactory, undignified, and embarrassing to the self-respecting Negro. R. Q. Venson noted that few, if any Negroes, relished the sight of "Negro" men pulling Carnival floats down Main Street parades . . . in the role of mules. He voiced the inner resentment of Negroes at seeing the world being given an image of "Negro" women as 'ole Black mammies, contentedly spinning cloth in downtown store windows' of "Negro" children being portrayed as 'pickaninnies,' . . . He knew the uneasiness in Negro breasts when they saw Negro [professionals] assembled at the riverfront to sing traditional Negro plantation songs as their Cotton Carnival 'majesties,' unrolled their regal splendor at the foot of Beale Street and Monroe Avenue.[18]

For Williams and his fellow jubilee organizers, Venson was a visionary who developed a "positive protest"; he created an event that presented a different image of Black people to both Memphis and the nation.[19] Jubilee organizers believed the city needed this alternate narrative. To promote a public image of the jubilee that extended beyond cotton, Williams pointed to the investments the jubilee made in the education of Black youth. The jubilee encouraged Black children to participate in competitions that awarded scholarships to Black students, including essay contests concerning the contention of cotton and its many issues. The jubilee's floats and parades, Williams argued, taught children about the lives of their ancestors, instilling a responsibility for further racial progress in the city. Organizers argued that this celebration was not the "Negro version of the Carnival," but rather "a purely Negro expression of pride of race, self-respect, and self-projection common to other groups all over America."[20]

In an editorial for the *Tri-State Defender* entitled "Sick, Sick, Sick!" Williams questioned the motives of civil rights protesters. He asked why no protests were called when the Elks Lodge held a segregated meeting on Beale Street. He noted that many schoolchildren participated in the Elks parade, marching past churches pastored by the same ministers who now protested the jubilee. He wanted to know why the jubilee offended these leaders, but the Elks Lodge did not. He argued that the Black people of Memphis were "sick with resentment over real and fancied wrongs, until the very word 'cotton' [gave] them a back-set."[21]

While Williams leveled a diagnosis of "'colorphobia' and 'interracial indigestion'" in Memphis, NAACP leaders responded in a rebuttal letter to the paper two weeks later.[22] They stated that Williams's connection to the segregationist past distorted his present views. The NAACP vowed to continue the fight against all segregationists, both Black and white, until they eradicated the practice outright. Jesse Turner agreed with Williams that the city was sick, but he argued that the cure was the 1954 Supreme Court decision that made segregation in public arenas unconstitutional. However, to Turner, the need of a select group of Black Memphians to hold fast to the ways of the past was unacceptable. For these Memphians, Williams's positive image of the jubilee offered a flexible alternative to a civil rights revolution boasting few apparent weapons in its arsenal—sit-ins and battles with the local police. For his part, Williams hoped that the jubilee would remain an alternative to these methods—an alternative that would allow African Americans an opportunity to stand up for their dignity without the threat of violence.[23]

During this heated back and forth, the integrationists and the jubilee supporters came together to discuss the future of the celebration in Memphis. The Ministers Alliance, a partner of the NAACP in sit-ins and protest marches, had a set of questions they wanted the jubilee organizers to address. They wanted to know if, quite simply, the jubilee had outlived its purpose. They also wanted to know if the jubilee was a segregated appendage of the Cotton Carnival, as well as whether the event was an anathema to the struggle for freedom that had consumed the organization for most of the year. Nat Williams as well as Dr. and Mrs. Venson represented the jubilee. They countered with their own set of questions. They asked the board whether or not the Congress of Racial Equality (CORE), the NAACP, the Southern Christian Leadership Conference (SCLC), and the Black Muslims were the only organizations with effective means of challenging segregation. They wanted the alliance members to clarify if they sought to disassociate with any event or activity that "smacked of the Negro's history in America . . . blues, spirituals, eating watermelon?" Jubilee organizers also wanted clarification on how exactly their celebration stereotyped "Negroes." They characterized the jubilee as a form of passive protest just as valuable as the NAACP's and Ministers Alliance's sit-ins and marches. The meeting ended on a positive note when Ethyl Venson explained that the jubilee was not a segregated arm of the carnival, but a separate organization, founded, funded, and operated by "Negroes," to which a representative of the Ministers Alliance responded that "this throws a different light on the whole thing."[24]

The NAACP would emerge as the unofficial spokesperson for Memphis's Black community as over seven thousand Memphians joined the organization. The NAACP was not the only group in the city working to end Jim Crow in public facilities. The MCCR, too, worked to desegregate Memphis, but the group intended to accomplish this goal in a more discreet fashion than did the NAACP. Comprising Black and white leaders, the MCCR worried that Black ministers were the only group championing the issue of desegregation. Initially, Black Memphians believed members of the MCCR intended to impede race progress due to their stated mission to maintain law and order in the city. However, the committee did have some foresight. The racial disturbances in other southern cities did not escape the members' attention, and they sought to take "positive steps . . . to forestall the probability of similar occurrences in Memphis."[25] The committee also believed it to be their duty to promote "planned, voluntary and constructive change" in Memphis.[26]

Through what its leaders called "quiet persuasion," the MCCR convinced local businesses to desegregate, thereby diminishing the publicity power of the NAACP. As the MCCR attacked racial segregation "quietly," Black students, rallied by the student arm of the NAACP, took control of their city's racial destiny. Students began to sit-in at public libraries and to boycott "whites only" establishments. In response to public protest, the city began desegregating its facilities, including city buses and the zoo. The MCCR's efforts and those of the student arm of the NAACP were so effective that by 1964, Dr.

Hollis Price, president of Lemoyne College, told reporters that he could one day envision complete desegregation in Memphis. He also encouraged Black patronage at desegregated restaurants because he worried the businesses would revert to segregationist practices in the absence of Black diners.[27] Unfortunately, the city's efforts only went so far. No amount of MCCR persuasion or public NAACP protest would move the city council or the mayor to begin to appoint Black Memphians to important city positions. Another failure of the city's desegregation can be seen in the all but nonexistent enrollment of Black students in historically white schools: a mere 287 Blacks were enrolled in these schools, which included a total of 54,407 students.[28] To further avoid desegregation, city officials closed public pools until further notice, and hotels began to admit Black people on the condition that an excess of Black guests not be admitted at once. The lack of desegregation in city hall led Jesse Turner to conclude that, while the work of the MCCR was important, there remained much to do. He described the city's desegregation efforts up to that point as "token" and "half-hearted."[29]

Still, Black Memphians probably felt like uninvited guests in their own city as important organizations such as the Memphis Chamber of Commerce or Future Memphis persisted in ignoring Black voices. Despite early desegregation accomplishments, the city continued to exhibit two very distinct populations, a serious challenge for the Memphis business community to overcome.[30] To understand why this was, one need only look at the city's political history, beginning in the 1870s, at the height of the yellow fever epidemic. As Gerald Capers argues in *The Biography of a River Town,* Memphis suffered a drain on human and economic resources due to the widespread deaths caused by the fever. The surviving population of Memphis was described as "provincial," a shift from the formerly cosmopolitan population that once dominated Memphis. The repopulation of the city saw the creation of a homogenous white Memphis. These Memphians shared the same religion, the same prejudices, the same commitment to the supremacy of the white race, and a firm dedication to state's rights.[31]

For most of the twentieth century, Memphis operated much like a plantation with Mayor—and later US Representative—E. H. Crump acting as plantation master. Under Crump, no one made a decision without his direct knowledge or approval. While this form of governance proved efficient, it also produced a "leadership vacuum." Crump made all decisions without the involvement of the larger community. He even excluded the city commission, the very purpose of which was to be involved in public policy creation and implementation. The result was an atrophied body of government. After the fall of the Crump machine in 1956, Memphis politicians found it necessary to teach themselves the intricacies of self-government that had fallen into abeyance. But they did not have much time to learn. The greatest turmoil since the Civil War loomed.[32]

Public scrutiny of the Cotton Makers Jubilee among the Black population of Memphis rose as the NAACP and MCCR worked to further desegregate the city. To these organizations, the goal of desegregation was the integration of Black people into mainstream society—a goal that the jubilee, a vestige of the segregated past, hampered. In the 1960s, while the jubilee fell subject to criticism, jubilee organizer and historian Nat D. Williams noted that people in the Black community's growing disfavor toward the jubilee, which they saw to be a waste of time, adding that suspicions and jealousies of Black Memphians had initially stalled the event.[33] Opposition was not new to the jubilee. From its earliest conception, African Americans questioned the carnival's efficacy, considering any celebration of cotton to be suspect. Ethyl and R. Q. Venson understood this wariness when they first conceived of a separate carnival—one where Black people controlled the message. The Vensons met with Black community leaders and managed to convince the majority of the need for Black participation in all community celebrations.[34] It is not clear if the members of the Black community changed their minds because they believed cotton was worthy of an honored place within the community, or if they were swayed by the economic benefit of their own celebration. What is certain is that the Vensons had an uneasy relationship with the Black community at large. Though a segment of Black Memphians were unhappy with the Cotton Carnival, they doubted the Vensons' solution would prove any better.

The debate over the efficacy of the jubilee continued throughout the 1960s. With the 1966 theme, "King Cotton in Orbit," organizers hoped to capitalize on the US satellite launch. The jubilee sought to link Americans' unpreparedness for the satellite launch to Americans' neglect of the African American protests that had endured over three centuries. The jubilee program pointed out that many Black and white Americans were "not in step with the new age which the satellites announced." In an essay by Williams, penned on behalf of the entire jubilee board, Black men and women are said to have left many of these people behind wondering where all this "Negro resentment" came from. If they paid attention, the organizer surmised, the racial revolution of the sixties was no surprise; activism was but another step in a long line of protest. Williams thought that through the jubilee, the "Negro" displayed the hopes and desires of his race to the world. Just as important, the jubilee served as a notice to all people who believed Black inclusion in the carnival to be inevitable. The jubilee was a wake-up call for the nation, stating that African Americans were no longer fodder for white entertainment, especially with regard to the tragedy of slavery. They were people who made contributions to the economic development of the South. Williams stated: "One objective, for instance, was to take 'Negro' women out of store windows on Main Street serving as reproductions of ante-bellum 'Black mammy' figures . . . to take Black men out of Cotton Carnival parades where they served as 'mules' to pull the floats on which white Cotton Carnival Royalty rode . . . to take 'Negro' children from the curbs where they were being fed cotton candy for the benefit of the pickaninny hunting . . . white news media. To select 'Negro' men and women to serve as kings and queens and princesses and nobility and thus gain a sense of dignity and self-respect."[35] Organizers occasionally wrapped the jubilee in the American flag. In the 1967 program, Clifton Satterfield described the jubilee not as a form of Black power, but as "the power of fellowship, citizenship and a relationship of goodwill toward all Americans as a government of the people, by the people and for the people." He also believed that the "Negro" should sing America's praises; "Negroes" should, for example, promote the American system of democracy. Satterfield offered a harsh rebuke to those who "burned draft cards and criticized the struggle in Vietnam, while our fellow Americans are dying there in this Nation's struggle in the defense of its commitment to freedom loving peoples everywhere." Satterfield exhorted readers of the 1967 program to deny their selfish motives and remember the sacrifices of American soldiers who fought to make "America safe for democracy."[36]

Unfortunately, the jubilee organizers faced an increasingly angry Memphis public throughout 1967 and into 1968. A small labor strike turned into a revolution that shook the foundations of the civil rights movement. On January 31, 1967, sanitation workers showed up to their jobsite in Memphis, but managers sent the Black workers home due to inclement weather. The rain ended, the white workers went out to complete the day's assignments, and the city paid them for a full day's work. When the Black workers discovered that the sanitation managers paid the white workers, they complained. City officials gave them "call-up" pay, but this did not satisfy Black workers. The disgruntled workers gathered at the American Federation of State, County, and Municipal Employees (AFSCME) union hall. The sanitation workers expressed their desire to be eligible for promotion regardless of race. They wanted to be able to address their on-the-job concerns to a responsible party, so such incidents would never occur again. They also wanted decent wages, overtime pay, and a dues' check-off included with each paycheck. City officials did not recognize Local 1733, an all-Black union, as an official bargaining agent, and the workers fought to change that as well. Mayor Henry Loeb's refusal to grant these last two requests led the workers to walk out.[37]

The sanitation strike became a lightning rod for increased frustration within the Black community. The demonstrations reflected Black dissatisfaction with the city's handling of police treatment, housing, jobs, wage equity, and justice within schools. The Black citizens of Memphis demanded more from their city government, and they became quite impatient. The workers' concerns found an audience with one of the most influential civil rights leaders this nation has ever produced: Martin Luther King Jr. He decided to take on the cause of the sanitation workers. King expressed compassion for the sanitation workers, and he welcomed a fight for economic justice which he believed to be a crucial tenet of the civil rights movement.[38]

King's organizers scheduled a march for the morning of March 28. On the day of the march, the atmosphere was tense in part due to the presence of young people in the crowd. Rather than picket with typical protest signs with phrases like "We Shall Overcome," marchers chose to write their own, cruder, chants: "Damn Loeb—Black Power is Here." The SCLC and union officials present at the site grew concerned about crowd control, and they began to wonder if Dr. King should cancel the rally altogether. But Dr. King arrived, and the march began. Not long into the march, activists heard the sound of breaking glass. Rally organizers, including King, decided to suspend the march. Police arrived wearing masks and holding tear-gas containers. While many of the protesters returned to Clayborn Temple when prompted to do so by Rev. James Lawson, some of the crowd's younger demonstrators decided to stay and fight. They threw bottles and picket signs at the approaching officers, who attacked the crowds with billy clubs and tear gas.[39]

After his curtailed sanitation march, King left Memphis but vowed to return to lead a successful nonviolent march. In the meantime, King created a Poor People's Campaign with a march on the nation's capital as its centerpiece. He now envisioned a movement that addressed the economic disparity that so many southerners of all races had suffered from for decades. Southern representatives pointed to the violence that occurred at the demonstration in Memphis as evidence that the city of Washington, DC, could expect the same type of mayhem if Congress allowed the march the following spring.[40] Neither the remarks of the congressmen nor the events in Memphis discouraged King. He returned to the city in early April 1968 to prove his mastery of the movement. Yet, he would never lead the march he returned to undertake. On April 4, 1968, King was gunned down by an assassin on the balcony of the Lorraine Motel.

After King's assassination, the mayor of Memphis felt obligated to negotiate with Local 1773. He later agreed to the union's desired concessions. The sanitation workers received their dues check-off, an increase of forty-five cents to their hourly wage, and the city council moved to recognize the right of the Local 1733 to negotiate on behalf of its members. Unfortunately, other groups had to fight the sanitation workers' battle repeatedly. Later in 1968, hospital workers attempted negotiations with the city only to go unrecognized. In the minds of many disaffected activists, it was as if the sanitation workers' strike had never happened and King's sacrifice on the altar of racial progress was in vain.[41]

While the jubilee organizers tried to remake the event's image to coincide with the movements of the sixties, groups like the NAACP hoped to do the very opposite. For the NAACP and other organizations closely linked to the civil rights movement, the jubilee continued to serve as a reminder of racial struggles that should have ended at the close of the Civil War. The very existence of the Cotton Makers Jubilee was predicated on racial exclusion from the white-led carnival. Cotton was the crop that had made slavery attractive in the South; it forged a dual caste system by which white southerners could treat Black Americans horrifically. Though the jubilee showcased the various talents of young people within the Black community, jubilee organizers never quite convinced African Americans that the event was any more than the Cotton Carnival in blackface.[42]

The debate between the promoters of the jubilee and members of the NAACP should be placed within the context of the larger debate among the African American historians of the mid-1960s. A noticeable tension between the civil rights activists grew. There were those who believed that the passage of the Civil Rights Act called for the thwarting of segregation wherever the practice was observed; conversely, there were those who argued for exceptions on the basis of the preservation of Black traditions. The jubilee seemed entrenched in promoting the separate society that so many fought against—but there was a school of thought committed to developing a distinct Black identity that thought of integration as a "sham." These Black activists saw protest as a method to "recapture identity" in order to liberate Black Americans. According to this perspective, freedom would be elusive to the Black race until the people could shun the American dream in favor of their own institutions founded on character and self-esteem—and their own dreams.[43] Of course, there was a paradox between these ideals and the ones exhibited by the organizers of the jubilee. Jubilee organizers believed that developing a sense of pride among Black people was a necessity, but they in no way rejected the American dream. They wanted to be included in the larger society, but they also wanted to maintain their own institutions. Furthermore, jubilee organizers did not see how the dissolution of the jubilee would move Black people any closer to their goals. The founder of the jubilee remarked that if "King Cotton" was to remain king, then "he must realize the fact that there are . . . injustices in his domain, and he must have the courage and the will to do something about them."[44] For Venson and Williams, the jubilee righted the wrongs of King Cotton by showcasing talent from within the Black community, giving Black men and women a place of honor.[45]

When one reads the various essays published in the souvenir programs during the 1960s, jubilee organizers' philosophical struggle with the events occurring throughout the South is evident. In 1965, Nat Williams discussed the jubilee's changing image. He examined how the negative images of Black Memphians persisted during the white-led carnival and how the changes that the jubilee inspired had left him enthusiastic. He perceived the jubilee as an "avenue of expression for the talents, personalities, and aspirations of an important segment of the population."[46] By the 1960s, jubilee organizers such as Williams focused on the event as a form of protest for the "colored" population of Memphis. The organizers touted their desire to promote the use of cotton as the paramount goal of the first jubilee in the 1930s. They became more comfortable discussing the resistance they received from the African American community during the jubilee's early years; Williams argued that the jubilee overcame the "impatience of the fifties and the sixties" and that Black men and women of "insight" actively supported the jubilee. To Williams, the jubilee's ability to develop and solidify an image for the Black American was the crowning achievement of the event. Instead of succumbing to popular arguments about the jubilee's lack of relevance in the wake of the civil rights movement, Williams held fast to the belief that the jubilee was a step in the right direction.[47]

The organizers of the jubilee believed that people should not expect social justice in an instant, as is evidenced by the theme for the 1970 jubilee: "Where Do We Go from Here?" In the program, Dr. Venson published an essay discussing the greatness of America. While he conceded American democracy's imperfections, he wrote that democracy was the supreme form of government in the world. The jubilee was a festival that spoke to the greatness of America; only in this country could a formerly enslaved group muster the resilience to organize and fund its own carnival. Venson also argued that "as awful and sinful the blight of slavery is on America, it was a blessing in disguise when [he] thinks of the chaos and discord among the African nations from which the American 'Negro' came." He concluded that "there are far too many Black and White ingrates in America, who through their behavior are giving aid and comfort to the enemies of America in their program to over [throw] our form of Government." It is clear from Venson's words that the jubilee founder was someone who wholeheartedly believed in the "American way." It is arguable that he believed the jubilee was an avenue into white society. By electing kings, queens, and a Spirit of Cotton, Venson and the other organizers displayed the genteel side of Black Memphis society. Racial uplift permeated Williams's ideas. Throughout the 1960s, Williams constantly reminded jubilee attendees of the distance they had progressed since the festival's beginnings in the 1930s. The image of Black people had improved tremendously, Williams argued, because of the work of the jubilee.[48]

Organizers also relied heavily on religion, and specifically on Jesus Christ, to disseminate their message to the public. In his 1970 essay, Clifton Satterfield echoed some of Venson's statements, but he engaged in the culture wars as well: "Thrill seekers indulging in the consumption of dope in all its damaging forms . . . the scanty and colorful attire in today's fashions, the sexy pattern of youth behavior, the immoral practices of human conducts and the 'God is Dead' theory of a Godless generation." Satterfield believed that the path to end what he perceived as chaos lay in the Bible. He did not believe that advances such as walking on the moon, executive orders, legislation, or courtrooms held the same promise for the future of this country as did reliance on the word of God. To Satterfield, the only way for the nation to move forward was to remember the love that Christ had for all his people. Satterfield urged Memphians to practice that love of and for one another. Frank Scott, president of the Cotton Makers Jubilee, Inc., in 1970, also expressed this sentiment. He stated that "blessings do not drop out of the clear sky unsolicited or unmerited; nor do favors fall into idle laps seated in the market places where loafers congregate. You receive as you become fit to receive . . . Let us return to God, submit to His will and be at one with our fellow man."[49]

Venson, Scott, and Satterfield had clearly wearied of the protests by the late 1960s, as had much of the nation. From the words of Scott and Venson, one ascertains that these men did not receive gratitude from those who continued to push for equality before the law. By this time, they suggested that the civil rights activists and war protestors were "ingrates," lazy, atheists, and un-American. The Black race would never fit into the larger society if its most vocal members constantly raised their voices in anger to vilify the country.

The problems that the organizers experienced in accepting the dynamic trajectory of the direct-action campaigns of the 1960s falls squarely within the framework of the larger debates during the decade about the future of African American rights. While Williams, Venson, Satterfield, and Scott clearly fought the NAACP over the validity of the jubilee, their ideas for liberal reform of the political and social system did not contradict the civil rights organization at all. However, the problem that they faced was twofold. First, these men were clearly part of the Black bourgeoisie; they were all highly educated professionals, and at least two, Venson and Satterfield, were veterans of war.[50] Second, what happened to the organizers of the jubilee had already happened to an older class of civil rights leaders by the end of the decade—the movement surpassed it. The demands of young activists outpaced the organizers' philosophy. The bourgeoisie sought to become a part of the larger American dream; they saw young protestors as an equal threat to Black culture as the images of mammies and pickaninnies had been in the early 1930s.[51]

While jubilee organizers spoke constantly of the mighty ways in which the jubilee led to the advancement of Black freedom, they also placed limits on that freedom. For example, they required that all candidates for king and queen have their applications judged in order to determine their fitness to represent the jubilee. This was arguably an attempt to impose middle-class morality on the election of jubilee royalty. Only those who presented themselves as the right kind of "Negro" could be rewarded with entrance into polite society. The new protesters not only challenged this antiquated process but also began to ask why Blacks should want to be a part of this society. They criticized and rejected the old elite's methods of fighting segregation. Many young protesters believed the older class of civil rights leaders, including jubilee leaders, were tools of the very system they rallied against.[52]

Venson's initial goal was to secure a dignified role for the African American in the carnival. According to the writings of jubilee officials themselves, that had not happened by the 1960s. As long as the event remained separate, Cotton Carnival organizers faced very little pressure to include a dignified Black presence in their affairs. Furthermore, if the Black struggle for freedom meant that Black people had to define their places in an equal and just society, segregated carnivals ran contrary to that goal. The *Brown* decision was about integration, and if the decision was hailed by Black leaders, then the goal should not have been for Black Memphians to remain separated from white society. Segregation meant anything but freedom and equality, and the jubilee was a constant reminder to some that Black status remained second-class.

The Cotton Carnival was not just about socialites coming out or business leaders displaying their standing in the community. The carnival was about history—a defense of a particular history. The jubilee was about history as well; it was a counternarrative to the version of history that Lost Cause supporters sustained. The jubilee organizers wanted to write a more accurate account of African Americans' past, in order to showcase the race's accomplishments in the present and to transmit their hopes for the community's future. In the early 1930s, the absence of a truer representation of the role of African Americans in slavery was a form of cultural violence. Material culture holds historical messages. One can imagine the response of Black men, women, and children when faced with dreadful Black stereotypes at the white-led Cotton Carnival. Venson and the other organizers of the Cotton Makers Jubilee faced a daunting task when they decided to create their own festival. They used the streets of Memphis, a historically white space, to challenge the powerful, mythologized memory of slavery, the Civil War, and Reconstruction as the century progressed.[53]

The jubilee and the carnival continued well into the 1980s. The two eventually merged and became Memphis in May. This festival includes a barbeque and music festival that Memphians look forward to year after year. Though the two festivals have merged, the issues that first caused the two events did not disappear. The merger came about in 1981 when then Cotton Carnival chair Ben Woodson presented his ideas to the Jubilee Executive Board about jubilee participation in the carnival events. Woodson used that year to restructure the carnival. He wanted the event to represent all members of the Memphis community. He proposed that the jubilee would become a "grand krewe" ("krewe" is another term for the society organizations that made up the carnival). Woodson wanted jubilee participants to be involved in all areas of the carnival festivities, from the barge landing to the coronation ball that named a new king and queen of cotton for the upcoming year. The jubilee krewe would have to pay $1,010 per group member in order to participate. This, of course, was a sticking point for jubilee members, as those who participated in the festivities were by no means wealthy. The idea that organizers would charge such a steep fee troubled more than a few board members. In addition to the fee to participate, additional fees were required to attend the Cotton Carnival Coronation Ball. Ethyl Venson received phone calls from Black Memphians who were concerned about the viability of the jubilee if it was "swallowed up" by the carnival. Yet, what seemed to appeal to Venson most was the economic benefit that the jubilee could receive from their participation in the carnival. She believed that the jubilee would directly benefit from the money coming into the city, and that the jubilee would be recognized for their efforts in putting on events. Venson seemed delighted to be involved with the carnival and stated, "I really don't know how it's going to come out . . . but the young whites in the carnival association seem to be very positive and anxious to [include] the Cotton Makers Jubilee in with the carnival on some things. I think they are sincere, but time will tell."

Whether due to the earnest efforts of the white representatives of the carnival or a desire to finally reach the goal of inclusion that R. Q. Venson had first sought to achieve, the jubilee and the carnival merged successfully in 1981. Leaders in the African American community such as D'Army Bailey, chairman of the Grand Krewe of the Nile, stated that "it's well past the time to bring the communities together and declare the Civil [War] at an end." Minerva Johnican thought that the merger was long overdue. She stated, "I hope it won't be for Cotton Carnival time only, but will be an extension of improving race relationships which are so badly needed and that it will translate into economic development for Blacks." Participants in the 1981 celebration were most pleased by the possibility of dismantling the social barriers that had divided the races for so long. Some business owners were pleased with the economic aspects of the interracial gathering, but many Black participants emphasized that better social relationships resulted from mingling with each other.[54]

By 1985, Ethyl Venson was ready to retire from her leadership role at the jubilee. Her retirement led many within (and without) the organization to reflection. They wondered whether the jubilee should retire with its founder. By 1981, the jubilee had reached its goal of inclusion, but just as in 1961 organizers defended the jubilee as a Black institution with its own traditions that were well worth preserving. These growing pains could be seen in the 1985 celebration where, rather than merge the jubilee's parade with the carnival's, leaders in the jubilee marched in a separate event. It was the fifty-year anniversary, and that alone provided a source of pride that jubilee participants vividly displayed. Venson again expressed her satisfaction with the way the two organizations worked together and said that she could see there being only "one celebration in . . . five or six years."[55]

Whatever success or sense of accomplishment Ethyl Venson achieved because of the merger did not last long. She did not see the jubilee thrive under the Carnival Memphis umbrella. Her nephew Clyde Venson agreed with this assessment and believed that the more the jubilee organizers tried to align their values with those of the larger carnival organization the more distance they created between the jubilee and the Black community. So, while the jubilee maintained some ties to the carnival, the jubilee board members decided to change the name to the Kemet Celebration, and they continued in the original tradition of R. Q. Venson, which was to highlight the accomplishments of Black Memphians.[56]

There were no more direct challenges to the jubilee after the 1961 controversy, but anger over segregation and its destructive impact continued to simmer within the Black community. Activists moved their fight from the jubilee to symbols that they believed more readily exhibited hostility toward the Black race. In the early seventies, one of those symbols was Nathan Bedford Forrest.

7

A SHRINE OF HEALING

The citizens of Memphis experienced a definite change in perspective after the assassination of Martin Luther King Jr. Community activists wanted to improve the standard of living for the poorest members of the community. The Memphis Chamber of Commerce operated the "Greater Memphis" campaign, which was designed to expand opportunities for economically depressed areas. After Dr. King's death, the Memphis Chamber of Commerce experienced an unprecedented amount of donations. The local government also developed a program in which the business community hired Black people who they believed were difficult to place in permanent positions. Business leaders offered so-called unemployables the minimum wage, and the municipal government reimbursed them through a federal grant. Another program offered by the city included "Food for Fitness." Black and white women operated this program at two local schools to provide students with healthy meals at breakfast and lunch. St. Jude's Hospital also began a program to help undernourished children by providing free examinations for the poor. When physicians detected malnutrition, the program coordinators put the family in touch with the local food banks. Skeptics commented that much of the activity taking place had to do with the fact that the city's image needed a face lift; they doubted that city leaders had any real desire to lift Black families out of poverty.[1]

A biracial group of leaders in the city decided that they needed to address the disparities between the two races so that white and Black citizens could become partners in a better future for the city. Business and local leaders formed Memphis Community Leadership Training, Inc., after the assassination of Dr. King to address the disparities in the Memphis community. Local businesses funded the commission, and its director sponsored biweekly gatherings of white and Black citizens concerned about the racial tone of the city. The goal of the organization was to encourage people to exchange their views on race. The meetings became very popular, and eventually the editors of the two local newspapers attended, as well as several local bank presidents. One bank president, after attending several of these gatherings, admitted that his concern for the plight of the Black community was minimal before he had gone to the meetings. However, since his attendance he believed that he was committed to the ideals of racial and economic justice. While business and community leaders participated in these meetings, there was one very visible absence. Neither Mayor Loeb, nor anyone on his staff, attended these meetings, and this demonstrated the lack of political leadership on the issue of desegregation.[2]

Elements within the Memphis community searched for ways in which the two races could live together in peace; however, this element was very small. One glance at the larger Memphis society, and one could see that the majority of white residents continued to favor a segregated community. One blatant example of their stubbornness to let go of the Jim Crow past was on the issue of school desegregation. In 1961, the federal government singled out Memphis because of the smooth transition that the school board had made toward a more integrated system. One of the reasons there was not as much violence as in other southern cities was because the Memphis School Board took bold steps to quell the chaos. The reason for the success of Memphis's school desegregation plan can be attributed to three factors. First, on the day Black students entered the schools the police commissioner charged more than 160 officers with keeping order at any cost. Second, the news media completely underplayed the event. It worked with the school board to not report on the event until after the students already entered the school. Finally, and most importantly, the fact that only eleven students enrolled in all-white schools throughout the city kept many of the violent tempers under control.[3]

As the decade progressed, more Black children enrolled in all-white schools, but their enrollment was at a pace the NAACP deemed unacceptable. The NAACP returned to court to ask the judiciary to force desegregation at a more rapid pace. While the courts never enforced the desegregation plans of the NAACP (because they believed them to be too drastic), they did favor more expansive plans than the school board implemented. In 1971, the US Supreme Court forced the issue in the *Swann v. Board of Education* decision. The justices ruled that busing was an acceptable method for school boards to use to achieve racial balance in schools. This ruling sent shockwaves through the Memphis community. The public school system began to experience a mass exodus of white students into private schools. Two such organizations committed to blocking desegregation were the Citizens Against Busing (CAB) and local Protestant churches. By the end of the seventies, the white student population in Memphis public schools dropped to 32 percent, which was down from 50 percent just ten years earlier.[4]

School desegregation is a practical example of how racial justice played out in the city of Memphis. While members of organizations like the Memphis Community Leadership Training, Inc., talked about community values or goals for the city to meet, average white and Black citizens confronted the reality of what racial desegregation meant. The fact was that no matter how many conversations about race occurred among the city's elite, rank-and-file white Memphians did not accept the social changes that organizations like the NAACP demanded. What also disturbed many Black observers was the complicity of the white church in the efforts of white Memphians to skirt the desegregation orders of the courts. These churches maintained that they wanted to give parents an opportunity to have their children educated in an environment that stressed a "Christian philosophy." However, the creation of these Christian-education institutions proved the underlying reason had more to do with white flight than anything else. The heads of these academies also claimed they opposed busing and not school desegregation. But as one critic pointed out, "The interest in God generated by busing is phenomenal. It's amazing how many people opposed to busing have their kids riding buses to private schools."[5]

Obviously, the movement for equality had its limits. King's assassination occurred, and the business community attempted to come together and affect real change for the citizens of Memphis. However, most white people resisted desegregation efforts. This left many Black Memphians feeling as if all the marching and even the death of King were in vain, as the city returned to its former racial attitudes. Despite all of the efforts of the reform-minded business organizations, by 1971, 75 percent of the Black population lived below the poverty line. Many of them could still only get "nigger jobs," which were the lowest-paying and dirtiest sort of employment. African Americans also still suffered from police brutality, despite a Police Community Relations Board, established by the city to address and curtail abuses by the police force. One of their main problems was that even though the city founded the board it did not fund them. The board relied on gifts from the community, and after King's death the board received plenty of donations, but by the early 1970s people no longer felt obligated to give.[6]

Activists began to turn in different directions to vent their frustrations at the stagnation of the civil rights movement. Some began to attack symbols that they believed promoted the racial views of the Old South and prevented the region from moving toward a more equitable existence. One such symbol, the Nathan Bedford Forrest statue, went unmolested and unchallenged for the majority of the twentieth century. However, in the post–civil rights environment in Memphis, the statue became a focal point for much of the anger and frustration surrounding race and desegregation. For example, in 1979 a Congress of Racial Equality (CORE) activist named Isaac Richmond led a one-man protest against the statue and what he believed it symbolized. He called the monument an "insult" to Black Memphians and demanded that it be torn down.[7]

Richmond made a name for himself within CORE as a man who challenged the established civil rights leaders. His defiance cost him his CORE membership after he staged a protest at a Jackson, Tennessee, store.[8] Upon his dismissal Richmond decided to form his own organization called the Commission on Religion and Racism, or CORR. Roy Innis, president of CORE, was not amused. He sued Richmond over the name because he stated that the name of Richmond's new organization sounded too similar to the organization Innis headed. He did not want people to confuse the two groups. Innis stated that CORE would "not tolerate any infringement on our 40-year-old name."[9] This is a battle that Richmond won. The court ruled that he could keep the name.

Richmond decided to take on the Forrest statue during a particularly tense time in Memphis. Several events that season turned people's attention to the matter of race. To begin with, there was a dramatic mayoral race in 1979. Otis Higgs, a Black man, ran against the white incumbent mayor,

Wyeth Chandler. During this very contentious campaign, Chandler went so far as to ask the city election office for a list of the white voters who did not participate in the last primary election. He wanted to contact each voter and encourage him or her to vote for him in the general election. Eventually Chandler backed off his request, but he irreparably damaged his campaign from the perspective of Black voters. Chandler claimed to relinquish his request for the list because many people called his campaign headquarters and chastised him for violating their privacy. He further defended his decision by claiming, "Our request was no different from Higgs busing people in to register. The people he bused in were not white. It cuts both ways, but nobody has said anything about that. It's interesting that the people brought to the Election Commission to register were all Black." The Higgs campaign seized on this request as further evidence that Chandler persisted in his insensitivity toward Black voters. Higgs's campaign also cited Chandler's meetings with the White Citizens' Council, where Chandler "put his hand over his heart and pledged allegiance to the Confederate flag."[10]

As an editorial in the *Commercial Appeal* summarized, Chandler played "racial hardball." The editor also stated that while Black people had made significant progress under Chandler's administration, most of them knew their success was not the mayor's doing. They knew that the federal courts ordered a lot of the improvements, and Chandler needed more than political favors to get their vote. Mary Todd, a Memphis woman, wrote the *Commercial Appeal* about Chandler's comments during the election. Chandler stated that Black people voted the way someone told them to vote. She reminded Chandler that a number of white candidates "received a tremendous amount of Black votes," so the reason Black people did not support him had nothing to do with his skin color. She felt that his "condescending" and "tacky" attitude toward the majority population of Memphis was reason enough for him to lose the election.[11]

If Wyeth Chandler's actions were not enough to stir up racial tensions, then the cross burning on the lawn of Otis Higgs definitely confirmed the racial animosity that existed in the city. At 3:30 a.m. on November 14, 1979, Higgs's wife woke him when she heard a window break in the living room. When the couple went to investigate, they saw a cross burning on the front lawn. Chandler expressed his shock and outrage the next morning at a press conference. He wanted the city council to offer a reward for any information about the incident. Many on the city council agreed, but just as many thought a reward was inappropriate. Councilman Robert James wanted to know what the guilty person or persons would be charged with if the police apprehended the culprit. When he found out that the charge was malicious mischief, he stated "I hate to see us offer rewards like that for malicious mischief when we have hardened criminals out killing people and raping them all the time." James believed that if they offered a reward in the Higgs case then the council should offer a reward in other cases as well. Although the council did not offer a reward, it did direct the police chief to "spare no effort to bring the perpetrators of this heinous deed" to justice.[12]

Higgs was not the only one threatened with violence. In another incident, someone attacked the home where the mother of Higgs's son lived. On the same night of the cross burning on Higgs's lawn, Mrs. Rosie Lee Williams and her husband, Archie, reported to police that they heard some kind of crash in the house. They found a makeshift cross burning on their den floor. Along with the cross was a note that stated, "If not Otis, then his son." The fact that Higgs had had a son out of wedlock when he was a teenager proved to be shocking news for most Memphians. For others, the fact that someone provoked an incident which caused the disclosure of this information on the eve of the election was no coincidence and not shocking at all.[13]

There was even more fuel to add to this racial fire. The *Commercial Appeal* began running a series of exposés on the growth of the Ku Klux Klan since the civil rights movement. In 1979, Irwin Suall, the chief of the Anti-Defamation League in New York City, stated that the Klan's numbers increased at about 20 percent a year. Suall showed that the Klan members of his day did not compare to the Klan at the end of the Civil War. The articulate and convincing manner with which the leaders of the Klan in the post–civil rights era spoke created a lot of interest in the organization. They appealed to white people with high incomes and higher degrees. The type of organization that developed was not one of a bunch of beer drinking "rednecks," but a group that could attract high school students and college graduates.[14]

William Thomas, the reporter for the *Commercial Appeal,* met and talked with various Klan leaders who attributed the resurgence of the organization to the events of the 1960s. James Venable, an imperial wizard in the Klan, told Thomas that "when the need arises so does the Klan." Apparently, the need arose because of the Civil Rights Act, so-called reverse discrimination, and what the Klan believed were the negative effects of desegregation. This Klan did not handle these new threats to white power in the conventional manner, because for the most part they shunned the idea of violence. In the words of David Duke, "this is a new Klan. . . . I feel violence is stupid. . . . Violence is the way to destroy the movement. I don't mind seeing people carry clubs on a march; they're not going to attack anybody. But I can't see our marchers carrying weapons that make us look like the Mafia." While Duke and other Klansmen insisted that they had no interest in committing violence against others, they also stated that they had no problem defending themselves against aggression. Mack Bowles, a plant mechanic in Memphis and a cyclops within the Klan, stated that their members committed themselves to achieving their goals politically. He believed that in the meantime the organization needed to teach white families how to defend themselves when the revolution came.[15]

In every interview with the Klansmen, one name popped up repeatedly: Nathan Bedford Forrest. All of the Klansmen claimed Forrest as their fearless leader, and they believed their present work continued his tradition of race pride and activism. The Klan made its presence known in the mid-South that fall because of a case of police brutality that led to the suspension of two white officers. Many civil rights organizations traveled to Tupelo, Mississippi, to express their outrage at what happened. The Klan also showed up to demonstrate that they supported the actions of the police.

In Tupelo, many African Americans stated clearly that the Klan did not have the power that it once had. Willie Patterson, a Black construction worker, even gathered his grandchildren on the lawn to watch the Klan parade as it passed. He stated, "I think the kids ought to see this because the Ku Klux Klan is on the way down. There will always be a few folks dressin' up in sheets and hoods, but it don't mean anything anymore. That day has done [sic] gone by." Another Black man, Clinton Sanderford, expressed the same sentiments. He had suffered a police beating at the hands of a Black Tupelo policeman while participating in a march that condemned the shooting death of an eighteen-year-old county jail inmate. The officers beat him with a rifle, and at the time of the interview he claimed to suffer from periodic numbness in his arm that prevented him from brushing his teeth. He believed that the white officers used the Black officer intentionally, because everyone knew that the white officers supported the Klan. Even though he suffered that beating, he still had the courage to state:

> White robes don't prove nothin' to black folks no more. . . . We showed that last year on Thanksgiving day. We were marching down the street when about 30 Klansmen came right through us. We could have picked 'em off easy if we'd wanted to. But we're trying to enlighten our people. We wanted them to see that putting on a white robe don't mean nothin' no more. We stopped and let 'em go right through the ranks. They rubbed right up against us, like they was one of us. And nothin' happened. Maybe they don't know it, but the Ku Klux Klan man don't scare nobody no more.

The author of the exposé believed that such sentiments "may be the most significant development of all."[16]

Editorial writer Peter B. de Selding believed that "the new sophisticated racism" had replaced the old-style Klan violence. This racism was different from that of the early twentieth century, which municipal and state legislators sanctioned. This racism did not put up any "colored only" signs. Instead, it claimed reverse discrimination when affirmative action programs appeared to be squeezing white people out of their traditional managerial jobs. This racism committed acts of police brutality in the name of law and order. This racism allowed Klansmen to wrap themselves up in the Constitution and go free when they committed acts of cold-blooded murder.[17] Even if these acts of violence did not stir up the activists, the bitter and racially tense mayoral campaign was enough. Wyeth Chandler, as far as anyone knows, was not a member of the Klan, yet he thought his request for a list of all-white voters was appropriate. The reason he believed that this was an acceptable tactic could lie on Union Avenue. The majority of white Memphians still shared the attitudes and perspectives that put Nathan B. Forrest on one of the city's main thoroughfares. The new Klan regenerated Forrest, and as long as a statue to the first imperial wizard of the Klan still enjoyed such a prominent place within the city of Memphis, the issue of race progress stalled.

Richmond's protest consisted of only himself and his petition, which he read at the foot of the statue. Despite this small demonstration, his request that the city tear down the Forrest statue sparked quite a reaction throughout the South. Locally, the descendants of Forrest, like Mrs. Lucille E. Landry, wrote to Mayor Chandler and told him that "it upsets [her] very much that any group of people would even think of removing the statue!" Another writer, Ralph Green, who was a member of the Sons of Confederate Veterans in Mississippi, wrote that it was "with combined sorrow and fury that [he] learned of the CORE request for Memphis to tear down the statue of General Forrest." Green believed that Richmond's efforts were just one more example of "the inability of some to accept other races as people with equal rights and [his] fury came from seeing one more attempt to obliterate history." Dean Allen Sr. from Texas wrote Mayor Chandler. He not only asked him to resist any effort to destroy the monument, but he also encouraged the mayor to turn his attention to the "communist rabble-rousing trash known as the Congress of Racial Equality." He thought the mayor would do the community a service if he would "investigate the subversive aspects of the CORE, NAACP, ad nauseum."[18]

Jack Balch sent a letter to the mayor that reflected the opinions of other writers. He also included a brief history lesson. He told the mayor that the complaint about Forrest being a slave trader was really unfair because "dealing in slaves prior to the war was a legitimate business." He also believed that the second charge against Forrest concerning the general being the head of the Klan was from miseducation, because when the events of Reconstruction are put into "proper historical perspective," one can easily see that the South desperately needed the Klan. There were "disreputable northern politicians and profiteers" who took advantage of southerners. There was no organized police force, so the former Confederates had to come together to be "keepers of the peace." Balch also stated that the only reason the former Confederates wore hoods was because the South was under martial law, and these keepers of the peace did not want to be arrested by federal officials. He made the point that this "idea blossomed even further when they realized that a great many of the former slaves were superstitious and that they would flee in terror at the site [*sic*] of these hooded riders." Finally, the Klan of 1865 was very different from the Invisible Empire people heard about in 1979 because Forrest broke this group up in the late 1860s by his own "Disbandment Order." Balch in his letter divorced racism from the history of Forrest and the Civil War. Where issues of race could not be avoided, he made the Klan appear innocuous.[19]

Calvin Queen of the Memphis KKK also wrote a noteworthy letter to the mayor. Mr. Queen expressed his outrage that "this CORE group [was] allowed to push its way down the throats of decent law-abiding citizens," but he had a special warning for the mayor as well. Queen asked the mayor to take special note of an article that he included with his letter. The article came from *The Klansman,* the official newsletter of the organization. The title read "Mayor Resigns Under Klan Pressure." The mayor of Selma, Alabama, had resigned, and the Klan took responsibility for his political downfall. The message was clear: Mayor Chandler should stop any attempt to remove the Forrest monument if he did not want the same thing to happen to him. Unfortunately for Richmond, except for this smattering of letters, Memphians paid little attention to his protest, and the controversy subsided.[20]

More than a decade later, the presence of the Forrest statue drew negative attention again. The University of Tennessee at Memphis (UT Memphis) decided to honor its exiting chancellor, Dr. Edward Boling, for all of his years of service to the college. The organizers planned to have his retirement ceremony at Forrest Park. This action enraged members of the Memphis chapter of the NAACP. Much of the animosity between the NAACP and the UT Memphis board of trustees traced back to the university's extremely low acceptance and retention rate of African Americans. The situation greatly concerned many within the city, which led to a series of articles in the *Commercial Appeal* in September 1987. The articles prompted the university to develop several programs that identified African Americans who showed special talent in the areas of math and science as early as junior high and encouraged them to consider UT Memphis as an option for higher education. The Tennessee Higher Education Commission (THEC) and Dr. James Hunt, the chancellor of UT Memphis at the time, believed that this outreach program was the first step toward making some needed change.

However, their efforts did not excite all observers. Shelby County commissioner Vasco Smith, an African American activist who had since retired from the commission, concluded that programs like this presumed that African American students did not meet minimum standards. He did not like that the university promoted the program as one in which the university helped students who could not finish medical school in the traditional four years. He thought that the assertion was "insulting and degrading and [he] thoroughly resented it."[21]

Despite Vasco Smith's concerns, the university reported that by April of 1988 they had met their recruitment goals. Evidence of this lay in the fact that the university offered twenty-three Black applicants a position at the school. This increased from the previous year, when the admissions office accepted only eight. Still, there was a lingering feeling within the African American community that the university could do more to increase enrollment. Mr. A. C. Wharton, a member of the panel to aid in the school's desegregation, commented that although the university made some improvements in their admissions practices, "all of this is for naught . . . if the perception exists in the community that you're not trying to reach out to Blacks."[22]

The issue that really made UT Memphis's efforts seem disingenuous to Black Memphians was its decision to adopt Forrest Park. While at the beginning of the century, Memphis honored and appreciated Forrest for his sacrifice, the social and political atmosphere of the city had changed by the 1980s. During the 1960s, activists revealed Forrest's past as a slave trader and as the first imperial wizard of the Ku Klux Klan. Further, during the 1970s, Isaac Richmond turned the city's attention to the alternate side of Forrest's history when he presented a petition to the county commission and the city council in favor of removing the statue. Nevertheless, UT Chancellor James Hunt explained that the motivation for the university to adopt the park grew out of concern for the "safety and security" of the student body and faculty. In a letter dated May 2, 1988, he outlined the goals of the board with regard to the park. According to Hunt, students, faculty, and administrators at UT Memphis already considered the park a part of their institution, and some even referred to the park as "Memphis Medical Center Park." He continued to explain that while the university maintained the property, the city still owned the land. The university would improve the physical character of the area, as evidenced by the fact that they had already invested a sizable amount on a fitness trail and other amenities for the park.[23] While improving the look of the park was undoubtedly an added benefit, some members of the board maintained that there were genuine safety concerns surrounding the park's operations. In a letter to Maxine Smith, UT President Edward Boling confirmed this sentiment. He told Smith, "The University of Tennessee is committed to the expansion of minority enrollment and employment on all of its campuses" and that Smith need not worry because "we [the board of trustees] do not wish to do anything to detract from achieving our objectives." Boling reiterated that the university's adoption of the park was solely for the "safety, security, cleanliness, and care of the park, not to promote the person for whom the park has been named."[24]

Another issue that aggravated this already tense set of circumstances was the university's plan to hold a very large public ceremony for Boling and to formalize the transfer of the park to the university. Maxine Smith implored Dr. Hunt to reconsider this ceremony. She asked him to think of the message this type of ceremony sent to the African American community. For Smith, the celebration signaled an approval of Forrest and everything he stood for—namely, the Confederacy and white supremacy. Smith made her feelings clear on the issue in a letter to Sam Cooper, a prominent Memphian and member of the UT Memphis board of trustees, who wrote to her earlier in the summer about the board's decision to adopt the park. In July of 1988 Smith stated: "Forrest Park is an affront to all Black citizens. The southern confederacy was established to maintain Black people in slavery and General Forrest is one of the most honored leaders of the confederacy [sic] . . . the University of Tennessee is a public institution that serves all . . . citizens, and for its chancellor to be honored before a symbol of the legacy of slavery is both insensitive and unconscionable." In this same letter Maxine Smith also invoked the language of the Holocaust. She asked Cooper, "How would you feel if a statue of Adolf Eichmann were erected in front of the Jewish Community Center?"[25] This exchange between Cooper and Smith is significant when one considers the timing. Smith mailed her letter to Cooper after the NAACP and UT Memphis had supposedly resolved the issues concerning the park. Judging from the language and tone of the letter the issue was anything but resolved for Smith and her camp.

The people who occupy the position that the statue should stay where it is consider Smith and her supporters myopic. They continue to believe that the people who want the statue removed neglect to examine the complete character of Forrest. They also believe that the attempt to remove the statue reflects a serious misunderstanding of his legacy. In 1988, when anti-Forrest representatives spoke about why they wanted the park renamed and the statue removed, they often dwelt on his slave-trading business, the massacre at Fort Pillow, and his "creation" of the KKK. Forrest supporters believed that because activists did not have the full facts, they blamed Forrest for occurrences out of his control. As with the previous controversy in the seventies, many of them agreed with novelists such as Shelby Foote, who believed that even though Forrest sold slaves, he never sold them to cruel masters.[26]

In his book *An Unerring Fire,* historian Richard Fuchs agreed with the assessment of some who believed that the troops had a deep antipathy toward the garrison in Fort Pillow; however, the similarities in their analysis ends there. The author asserts that Forrest was a man who was committed to the "utter . . . annihilation of his adversaries."[27] As an example, he recounted the story of an artillery officer involved in a confrontation with Forrest. The officer shot Forrest, and his comrades thought the injuries were fatal. Forrest vowed that "no man shall kill me and live," and he immediately jumped on a horse in pursuit of his assailant. Fuchs's argument was that Fort Pillow was not out of Forrest's control. The situation was just an inevitable occurrence given his previous actions when dealing with an enemy, especially when he felt the enemy had personally crossed him. In Fuchs's opinion, incidents like the one mentioned above reveal a propensity for violence on the part of Forrest, and this led the author to conclude that the incident at Fort Pillow was "an intentional design to annihilate the garrison for reasons unrelated to strategic or military necessity . . . [and that] the massacre was a natural and intended consequence of General Forrest and his troops' enmity toward this particular garrison."[28]

With regard to the Klan, Robert Corlew, a Tennessee historian, recognizes that the KKK started as a social club, but he documents a very rapid and vicious turn early on in the organization's history. He believes that by 1867 the intention of the group was to "frighten Blacks from the polls and Union Leagues across the South." Because the activities of the KKK greatly concerned the governor and state legislators, they held hearings in 1868 to hear testimony that revealed the beatings, robberies, and rapes that the KKK perpetrated on African Americans. Forrest allegedly disbanded the Klan in 1869, and Corlew points out that the reason behind the dissolution was that Forrest believed "the Klan in large measure had accomplished its objectives and he regretted that many acts of violence not committed by Klan members had been blamed upon the organization."[29]

Thinking back to the first chapters of this book, one wonders what Corlew could be referring to when he states that the acts of violence accredited to the Klan saddened Forrest. Clearly, whether one was in the mid-South, Alabama, or Mississippi, there were no boundaries when it came to Confederates regaining their dominance. It was this effort by white southerners to reassume positions of power that caused much of the tension in the twentieth century between African American civil rights activists and those who wanted to hold on to the ideals and principles of the Lost Cause.

Elizabeth Avery Meriwether's book sheds some light on the matter of whether Forrest knew and consented to the violence and intimidation in which the Klan participated. Meriwether's son (who wrote the foreword to her book) stated unequivocally that Forrest and his father met to discuss the tragedy of Reconstruction. They committed to physical and verbal punishment for any Black person who got out of line. Meriwether stated that the plan was "illegal, fantastic, but self-preservation [was] the first law of Nature."[30] For southerners, getting a handle on the freed population was a matter of survival. The freedmen threatened their political, social, and economic existence. Southerners needed someone to stand up for the challenge of reclaiming white dominance in the face of federal government opposition. The man who could handle the pressures and perform the unpleasant duties in order for white southerners to regain their footing in southern society was Nathan Bedford Forrest. Forrest and others in his social class were the type of men to make the white southern world right again.

To avoid the charge of promoting racism, Forrest supporters redefined southern history. The Confederate soldiers did not fight to maintain slavery; they fought against a tyrannical federal government that forced southern citizens to pay an unfair share of taxes. Confederate soldiers did not massacre Black soldiers at Fort Pillow; they were victims of their own inexperience. The KKK was not a terrorist organization; it was dedicated to the preservation of order. In the final analysis the argument attempts to take race out of historical events clearly saturated with the concept.[31]

The struggle between these two camps about their different visions of Forrest is the conflict that lies at the crux of this work. There is an ongoing struggle between these two narratives, and the winner will get to control the collective memory concerning the Confederacy and the South. This struggle was quite evident in 1988 during the conflict between the NAACP and UT Memphis. While the NAACP pushed for change, many others in the community pulled just as hard to maintain the status quo. The editorial page of the *Commercial Appeal* on May 15, 1988, offers some insight into how white Memphians felt about the idea of the removal of the statue. Edward Malone of Memphis, who was related to Forrest, stated, "I believe the NAACP is going too far in this instance." Mavis Bull, also of Memphis, claimed that the "NAACP [was] trying to rewrite history by demanding that the University of Tennessee . . . sever ties to Confederate General Nathan Bedford Forrest." In an anonymous letter to Maxine Smith, dated May 24, 1988, the writer warned, "I believe his spirit will be watching you and your kind and you will feel his presence. . . . If you have a conscience you'll think of this constantly." Once again, the fury of the white backlash outweighed substantive change on the issue. The university adopted the park and the ceremony occurred as planned.[32]

Close to ten years after this park controversy, an African American activist organization called Inward Journey attempted to change the community's perception of Forrest Park. The group's intentions differed from the NAACP's in that they did not wish to have the park removed and the statue torn down. They did wish to reclaim it and transform the park from one of shame to "a shrine of healing." The organizers of the rededication quickly pointed out that the purpose of their gathering was not to mount some kind of protest against Nathan Bedford Forrest, and to that end they immediately paid homage to his military brilliance. They pointed out, however, that Forrest was responsible for the massacre of Black troops at Fort Pillow and that he was a founder of the KKK. They considered this an organization that was responsible for the persecution of Blacks, Jews, and other oppressed groups throughout the twentieth century.[33]

For the most part, the speakers at the ceremony concentrated on African American history and the powerful people who made strides in improving the group's condition. Besides a brief history about Nathan Forrest, which lasted all of two minutes, there was very little said about him. That was because Forrest's history as a general in the Civil War is not particularly relevant to African Americans. Nevertheless, the activists said enough about Forrest to warrant some pretty powerful responses to the ceremony from the general's supporters throughout western Tennessee.

Letters from disgruntled Forrest supporters filled the *Commercial Appeal* editorial pages the following week. One writer wrote, "If Inward Journey, African American Council, hopes to succeed in teaching African American history to others, it should get a spokesman who is more knowledgeable of history than executive director Al Lewis appears to be." This writer was angry because Lewis painted such a dim picture of Forrest. Many letters echoed the sentiment that Forrest was not responsible for the creation of the Klan, nor was he responsible for the massacre at Fort Pillow. Leslie Birchfield argued that "while there was frightful carnage at Fort Pillow [there was] no massacre." Another writer from neighboring Ripley, Tennessee, concerning Inward Journey's decision to unofficially rename Forrest Park as Nat Turner Park, stated that "If I were a Black leader, I would not want to hold up Nat Turner as a role model" because "his followers killed unarmed white people, including women and children. Some were killed in their beds; some were killed with axes. He admitted at his trial that none of those people had mistreated him."[34]

For Inward Journey, it seems as if the statue was a prop to advance the cause of cultural nationalism. Remember that they wanted to reclaim the park, unlike Isaac Richmond and the NAACP, who wanted to have the statue removed and the park renamed. Over the course of the twentieth century, the meaning of the Forrest statue had changed, and people who opposed what the Confederate loyalist idealized became empowered through the growth of the civil rights movement. They began to amplify the counternarrative of Forrest and his activities before and after the war. This transition of meaning is not unusual though. Often times, the significance one group puts on a monument becomes a source of provocation for another, especially after time has passed and more people have reflected on the meanings of the memorial.[35]

Inward Journey's demonstration was about how African Americans could improve their lives. Just like the controversies before it, the Inward Journey demonstration did little to alter Nathan Bedford Forrest Park physically. The demonstration did add to the increased cacophony of voices that continued to ask why this park and statue remained in a modern southern city, and since it had been transferred back to the city, why should African Americans' tax dollars support this man, his park, and what he represents? The questions only got louder at the beginning of the twenty-first century.

EPILOGUE

On the evening of June 17, 2015, I was watching cable news when a "breaking news" alert crossed my screen. Rachel Maddow, the commentator, informed viewers that there had been a shooting in a Charleston, South Carolina, church. The name of the church was Emanuel African Methodist Episcopal. I was stunned as I continued to watch the coverage. An hour or so later, I switched to the local Charleston news stations, which reported that the shooter had killed nine worshippers during a Bible study meeting at the church. Among the dead was Clementa Pinckney, who was not only the senior pastor at Mother Emanuel but also a South Carolina state representative.[1] For days, a shocked nation watched as details of the mass shooting emerged. They learned that the shooter committed this act of violence out of racial hatred. Emanuel AME was not just some random choice by the assassin. Emanuel had been an integral part of the Black community since its inception. Denmark Vesey was a member of the church when he plotted his rebellion against slaveholders in 1822. It was that attempt that created the need for the Citadel, an armed fort constructed to keep members of the church as well as the larger Black community in line.[2]

Not even twenty-four hours after this horrific event in Charleston, a New York real estate giant turned reality television star descended onto the ground floor of his self-named skyscraper, riding a gold-plated escalator. He was welcomed by a few hundred supporters holding signs in praise of his new endeavor. He wanted to become president of the United States. The man, Donald J. Trump, took to the stage to make his case for why he should defeat Hillary Clinton in the 2016 election.[3] Using his well-known meandering way, then-candidate Trump criticized everything from Obamacare to the war in Iraq. The aspect I would like to focus on in his speech as it relates to the topic of this book is Trump's ability to tap into the feelings of loss many of his supporters felt in regard to America and its promises. He stated: "Our country is in serious trouble. We don't have victories anymore. We used to have victories, but we don't have them. When was the last time anybody saw us beating, let's say, China in a trade deal? They kill us. I beat China all the time. All the time."

Throughout his speech he continued this theme of loss, from United States trade negotiations with Japan to his evidence-free claim that the unemployment rate was really 18 to 20 percent and not the 5 percent reported by the Bureau of Labor Statistics in June 2015.[4] The doom and gloom expressed in Trump's speech was not just to denigrate the accomplishments of Democrats in general, and Barack Obama in particular, in order to get elected to the presidency. Trump keyed in on the Republican base voters' apprehensions about the rapidly changing and increasingly global interconnectedness of nations. He also fed into the voters' beliefs that the institutions that were supposed to be unbiased and fairly reporting on these issues were in fact corrupted. Further, he implied that they were corrupted in a way that harmed real (read white) Americans.[5]

Trump's ability to connect with white voters by highlighting the loss of American exceptionalism is particularly relevant to this study.[6] In a recent speech the journalist Nikole Hannah-Jones stated that in order for white Americans to hold on to the idea of American exceptionalism and the origin story of the "City on a Hill," Black people cannot have their narratives centered.[7] As Court Carney points out in *Reckoning with the Devil,* when Black voices are disappeared from the narratives of US history, white Americans can create the perception that there is consistency and agreement among all peoples concerning their (white) accounts.[8]

In her essay "The 'Colorblind' Trap: How a Civil Rights Ideal Got Hijacked," Hannah-Jones argues that right-wing activists since the time of Barry Goldwater have stressed that the Constitution is colorblind. Conservative activists, who occupy Lost Cause organizations, are expanding that notion of colorblindness to their pet project of redeeming the plantation South.[9] For insight into the more recent battles over Confederate memorabilia, Nicole Maurantonio offers valuable analysis. In her work *Confederate Exceptionalism,* Maurantonio attempts to understand how race and racism became divorced from the vision of the Confederacy held by modern-day adherents to the Lost Cause. She concludes that the only way this Confederate exceptionalism (a method of remembering and revisioning Civil War and Reconstruction history) can exist is if it is separated from any discussion of race or racism and housed in the realm of "neutrality and objectivity." Adherents to the Lost Cause frown upon conversations that include race because race interjects emotion, and as Maurantonio points out, emotionalism is a tool of the "raced body" or the enemy to all things Confederate.[10] With this information in mind, it is not difficult to understand why Lost Cause advocates excluded and continue to exclude the narratives of Black Americans. The mere presence of the African American is a dent in the fortress of American exceptionalism and by extension the exceptionalism of the Confederacy.

Reportedly, as Dylann Roof massacred parishioners of Emanuel AME Church, one of his victims confronted him and asked him why he was killing them. Roof responded: "I have to do this. You are raping our women and you are taking over the world."[11] Again, Roof was expressing a sense of loss. To cement these two events, the Charleston Massacre and the connection of Donald Trump to white nationalist voters, one only needs to look at the work of R. Derek Black (now Adrianne Black), who was the child of Don Black. The elder Black was the creator and founder of the website Stormfront, a white-nationalist media source.[12] Black offers an intimate portrait of the goals of white nationalism, which she does not differentiate from white supremacy. She asserts that the media mistakenly try to draw a line between the two ideologies when they are really interconnected. Black states that white supremacy is part of the fabric of America. Its principles hold that white people are at the top of the social, political, and economic pecking order. She states: "Everyone is affected by White supremacy, because it is woven into the fabric of our society, and its history has a strong legacy. It is what props up the 'garden variety' racism you find in any majority-White suburb, workplace, or institution, and it is what props up White nationalism."[13]

Black lists a myriad of guiding principles for white nationalism. Skin color is very important, and it is essential to white nationalists that the color of the white citizen not be diluted through interracial relationships. The white nationalist believes he is faced with extinction due to out-of-control immigration and the spread of hip hop culture. One important tenet of white nationalism that relates to the 2016 election is the belief that if only more white people could hear their message, the numbers of white nationalists would increase.[14] In that way Donald Trump was a perfect messenger. He often made (and still makes) outlandish comments on immigration and the assault on white culture. He provided a full-throated defense of Confederate statues and monuments and rejected any efforts to remove them.[15] Black writes that she was struck by the fact that many of the talking points she and her dad (and their good friend David Duke) developed were received quite favorably by white audiences at Trump rallies.[16] This same dynamic is at work with neo-Confederates.

The Dylann Roof shooting caused an unusual shift in the public zeitgeist concerning Confederate symbols and their place in the public sphere. For decades critics had challenged the prominent placement of the Confederate flag on the grounds of the South Carolina legislature. Pastor Clementa Pinckney had been one of those critics, and community members began to ask whether it was appropriate for Pinckney to lie in state at the capitol building in Columbia, South Carolina, under the shadow of that flag. After some debate, state officials decided to have a public viewing, but maintenance supervisors would cover a window in the room with a black cloth so that the flag would not be visible to mourners as they passed the casket. This response was amazing, given the intransigence of the members of the legislature to having the flag removed and their intolerance of disparaging it on state grounds in any way. A surprising ally appeared for those who believed that the death of these nine individuals provided an opportunity to finally rid the state of this albatross. Governor Nikki Haley threw her support behind critics of the flag and called for its removal.[17]

Born Nimarata Randhawa, the governor grew up in Bamberg, South Carolina, where her father's Sikh faith and her family's brown skin were stark indicators of their outsider status. In the aftermath of the church shooting, Haley recalled an incident that was burned into her memory. In her youth, she and her father stopped at a local farmer's stand. Her father was his usual jovial and polite self. He greeted the owner, picked out produce, and paid for it. This scene plays out a thousand times on roadsides throughout the state, but what made this particular incident distinct was that the owner took one look at the pair and decided to call the police. The officers arrived on the scene and stood over Haley and her father while they made their purchases.

The situation was still vivid for her, and she recounted that when she passes that same vendor's stand the pain of that day overwhelms her. The stand remains a symbol of the prejudice she and her father experienced that day.[18]

It was the pain of this symbol that motivated Haley to push for the removal of the Confederate flag from the state grounds. After attending all nine funerals, Haley's thoughts began to crystallize around symbols and how those symbols hurt. She held four separate meetings with stakeholders regarding the flag. The individuals participating in the meetings were lawmakers from both parties and civic leaders who had been active in state politics. She told everyone in attendance at the June 19 meeting that at 4:00 p.m. she would hold a press conference to call for the removal of the flag, and she invited them to come stand with her as she made this difficult announcement. She let activists who supported allowing the flag to remain on the capitol grounds know that she respected them but argued that the state needed to heal. She also assured lawmakers that she would not hold any grudges against those who decided not to support her at the press conference that afternoon.[19]

The NAACP had long targeted the state of South Carolina because the Confederate flag flew atop the capitol building. Though the flag had flown at the state house and senate chambers since the late thirties, lawmakers did not raise it over the statehouse building until 1962. At the time flag promoters said it was to commemorate the one-hundred-year anniversary of the Civil War, but observers also noted that the civil rights movement had momentum at this time. For these people, the flag was a signal that the state was not going to let go of its racial hierarchy easily. Since its appearance, citizens and numerous civil servants had called for the flag's removal. One servant, Republican governor David Beasley, developed a plan for its removal in the mid-1990s. He believed that the flag would be better served if it were moved to a museum. Once flag supporters became aware of this proposal, they campaigned fiercely to stop the proposal from becoming legislation. They even assisted Beasley's opponent in the primary of 1998. Beasley lost his re-election bid despite promising never to raise the flag issue again.[20] The NAACP excoriated the state in the press and even called for a boycott until officials removed the flag. The organization and the state then reached a type of "compromise." Those in charge decided that they would remove the flag from the flagpole on top of the capitol and place it on the grounds of the building. What this act did was remove the flag from the sky and put it in the faces of those people who traveled through the area. The flag was even more prominent than it had been before. Further, the legislature passed the Heritage Act, which holds that the legislature has to approve any changes or removal of any "monument, marker, memorial, school, or street erected or named in honor of the confederacy or the civil rights movement located on any municipal, county, or state property."[21]

The battle over the prominent placement of the flag continued, but it was not until nine people spilled their blood on the floor of one of the most historic churches in the nation that legislators voted to remove the flag. In the senate the vote was quick. Thirty-seven voted in favor of removal, and three were opposed, but the measure was held up in the house. Republican Mike Pitts from Laurens County tried to delay passage by adding at least twenty amendments to the bill. The members of the legislative body decided to allow him to speak on his additions. They also did not interrupt or challenge other members who supported the flag and wanted it to remain on the capitol grounds. The session took more than twelve hours. Another issue that slowed the process in the house was that Democratic legislators gave interviews in which they said they would not accept anything other than a clean bill. Flag supporters thought that this attitude represented an "in-your-face" position, which only served to harden their opposition to removing the flag. The debates continued into the night, and it was not until Representative Jenny Horne spoke that debate finally ended. Her passionate plea to remember those slain in Charleston and to comfort the state by bringing its citizens together propelled members to vote to remove the flag, without further delay and without amendments to water down the measure.[22] Haley signed the bill for removal on July 9, 2015, and at least ten thousand people gathered the next day as South Carolina state troopers lowered the flag for the final time on statehouse grounds.[23]

Shockwaves reverberated throughout the South. Not only did the flag come down in South Carolina, but citizens in other states like Mississippi and Louisiana also saw cherished Confederate memorabilia come down. Those officials did not have some of the same roadblocks that South Carolinians faced when legislators finally had the will to remove the flag. For instance, in 2000, the ongoing criticism and boycotts motivated legislators in South

Carolina to build a blockade of laws to protect the flag by passing legislation like the Heritage Act. No such obstacles existed in other places where the presence of the flag was just a fact of life. So, when the governor of Mississippi decided to remove Confederate symbols like the flag from the state house grounds, he only had to answer to a few constituents.[24]

Just as in other states, activists in Memphis began to make louder demands for the removal of Confederate statues in the city. What also motivated these activists was the fact that the city was having a fifty-year commemoration of the assassination of Martin Luther King Jr. in 2018 and concerned citizens believed the presence of these memorials to the Old South were inappropriate. Take 'em Down 901, led by Tami Sawyer, was one such group whose members were committed to bringing an end to the Forrest statue's presence on Union Avenue. One of the first meetings of the organization occurred on June 20, 2017, at Bruce Elementary school. Speakers took to the podium to talk about both the Forrest and Jefferson Davis statues and how the presence of those statues colored their experience in the city of Memphis. One participant stated that when he was a child and had played in Medical Plaza Park, he saw the Forrest statue and thought that the person the statue represented must have been "a great guy." This sentiment was reasonable. It was not like the statue has any context, which is what Bill Black, another speaker, pointed out. He stated that "these monuments, themselves, are an erasure of our past. These monuments do not teach. They humiliate. They denigrate. They lie."[25] While the meeting focused on both statues, the group recognized that there was a special connection with the Forrest statue due to his prominent presence in the Memphis community.

Throughout 2017, Take 'em Down 901 had its starts and stops. Like the Heritage Act in South Carolina, the Tennessee legislature passed the Tennessee Heritage Protection Act in 2016. This law held that "no monument on public property can be relocated, removed, altered, renamed, rededicated, or otherwise disturbed without a waiver."[26] The Tennessee Historical Commission (THC) is the state agency that approves waivers, and throughout the ideological battle in Memphis it was not forthcoming with an agreement to remove either statue from either park. The body also delayed votes on the measures in order to set guidelines for approval of waivers. The intransigence of the commission is what led activists like Hunter Demster to conclude that the city should sell "the parks to a nonprofit that could remove the statues and sell the parks back to the city."[27] This is where the people opposed to the presence of the statues landed.

This plan to sell the property to a nonprofit did not materialize overnight. In 2012, Councilman James Strickland read the Tennessee Heritage Act and immediately recognized the loophole in the legislation. Again, the act stated that no monument on public property could be moved without a waiver from the Tennessee Historical Commission. Strickland believed then that the city would be well within its rights to sell the land to a private developer and allow the owners to do whatever they wanted with the statues. By 2016, Strickland became the mayor of Memphis, and he still had his eye on the removal of those statues. At first, he wanted to take "the less politically alienating" route. He met with the THC in Athens, Tennessee, to request a waiver. Also in attendance at the meeting was City Attorney Bruce McMullen. McMullen described the atmosphere as "surreal." He noted that the team attended dinner at a local restaurant where they saw the spokesperson for the Sons of Confederate Veterans (SCV), Lee Millar, sitting with members of the commission. Not surprisingly, the THC denied the request for the waiver.[28]

Strickland continued on the path of least confrontation. He tried to have a mediation with the SCV on December 1, 2017, but the group rescheduled to meet on December 12 but ultimately put off that meeting as well until March of 2018. The city appealed the THC ruling, and the chancery court set a hearing for December 20, but the courts delayed that hearing and set a new one for January 2018. By this time, Strickland had had enough of these delaying tactics. He had already worked with McMullen to create a deal to sell the parks, and on December 15 he signed the agreement to sell the parks to Greenspace, a nonprofit, with the city council's approval. On December 20, 2017, the Memphis City Council sold Health Sciences Park and Memphis Park. These grounds contained monuments to Nathan Bedford Forrest and Jefferson Davis, respectively. Greenspace, headed by Shelby County Commissioner Van Turner, bought the parks at the bargain basement price of $2,000. Because Greenspace is a private entity, it had the legal right to remove the statues, and they were removed expeditiously. Once the city approved the sale, the police went into action. They cordoned off both parks as citizens began to assemble at both locations. The council meeting ended at 5:00 p.m., and Strickland Construction had their cranes in place by 6:00 p.m. Once the council approved the deal, McMullen took the ordinance upstairs to the mayor's office, where he signed the legislation. After he signed, he then alerted the police chief and state lawmakers as to what happened, and at 9:01 (a reference to the Memphis area code), the cranes removed the statues from their bases.[29]

This feels like a victory to me. People who understood the meaning of the statues to be a monument to white supremacy were able to break through the fierce resistance of those who wanted to hold on to what they perceived to be southern civilization immortalized in stone. Yay, team equality! But of course, nothing is that clear-cut. For instance, as F. Sheffield Hale points out in "Finding Meaning in Monuments," that while the removal of the statues appears to be a palate cleanser for advocates of equality, these removals have unintended consequences. Southern heritage (which Sheffield defines as "history without all the unpleasant parts") supporters see the disappearance of their relics, and they harden the historical inaccuracies and mythmaking that had led to the statues being erected in the first place. Contextualization is the watchword for Sheffield. He believes that the statues can serve public memory if they are discussed in a way that makes clear that the people who erected the objects did so to strengthen and/or preserve white supremacy.[30] In "Epistemological Crises Made Stone: Confederate Monuments and the End of Memory," Ryan Andrew Newson continues this line of thought on contextualization. He believes that removing the monuments is counterproductive to the goals of racial equality advocates as this action only serves to "assuage white guilt."[31] Assuaging that guilt leads the citizenry to historical forgetting and to an inability to see how the policies and attitudes that motivated officials to build the statues are still evident in society today. One way to address the eradication of these statues and avoid the issue of historical forgetting that Newson raises comes from historian Kirk Savage, who believes that even though the personage depicted in white-supremacist statuary should be removed, the columns that held the figures up should remain. In that way there is always a prompt in place to remind those who interact with the statue of the progress the citizenry has made.[32]

Hale, Savage, and Newson propose similar solutions to the vexing issue of Confederate memorials. They all believe that contextualization is the key to addressing the concerns of those who want the statues gone. Either through oral interpretation or the addition of plaques around the statues, historians can give a more accurate account of the history of the person or concept being honored with a statue, and they can also talk about the forces in society that led to the statue's creation in the first place.[33] My initial analysis of this situation was to argue that the contextualization concept would appease people on both sides of this controversy, but I realized that is a mistake. Though the statues would remain, which Confederate loyalists would see as a victory, the context of these statues is the issue that drives the southern heritage advocates and what divides them from the groups that want those statues gone.

On the one-year anniversary of the removal of his statue, the descendants of Forrest and the SCV launched a lawsuit against the city. The plaintiffs claimed that the incident caused them "embarrassment, humiliation, and mental anguish."[34] Just like the backlash that followed proposals for removal in the seventies and nineties, the pro-Confederacy group declared that removing the statues was an attempt to obliterate history. As journalist Paul Duggan concluded, people who support the display of Confederate symbols do not look at these items "as a reminder of racial oppression, but of courage, devotion to duty, devotion to family, honor, valor, and a lot of other qualities that we should aspire to in life."[35] As one letter to the editor points out, Forrest was a "great and terrible man," but people should focus on his contrition later in life when he supposedly rejected the racism that made him a fortune and called for the races to reconcile.[36] Another editorial comment suggests that the monuments and parks that honored Confederate leaders provide the community with "civic bearings." The author of this letter is basing his comments on the work of Thompson Mayes, who is deputy general counsel at the National Trust for Historic Preservation. Mayes contends that old places provide observers with a "sense of continuity, memory, and identity." He also believes that these statues allow individuals to feel like they are a part of a larger community, a community that aspires to something greater than the individual.[37] Mayes's assessment permits readers to move beyond the "heritage not hate" arguments that inevitably occupy neo-Confederates' positions about the importance of these statues.

Old South loyalists—persons who believe a collection of mythologized events and personalities of the antebellum era—have a lot tied up in these memorials. In his article "Living with Confederate Symbols," Franklin Forts points out that their mythmaking becomes foundational in the creation of white southern identity. This is important because when people base their identities on myth they only focus on the positive aspects of the past. Any negative characteristics or behaviors from the past are readily dismissed. As an example of this dynamic, Forts puts forth that a person from the nineteenth century could believe that slavery was wrong and that the Union needed to be preserved, but at the same time hold the belief that white people would always be superior. He argues that this position was the most common among white people during that era. Conversely, maybe someone has an ancestor who lived during the ante- and postbellum periods who showed great kindness to his or her neighbors and passionate love for a spouse. However, this same person could have been a vicious master who committed atrocious acts against their slaves. Two things can be true at once; however, for those citizens who build their identity on myths about this time period, any negative characteristics of their loved ones would be obscured by the myth of all-benevolent ancestors.[38]

The battle over the statue of Nathan Bedford Forrest may seem tangential to some observers. Many people believe that there are more important issues for African Americans to be concerned with, and fighting about this issue is a waste of energy. However, this perspective neglects the real essence of this fight. This argument about the prominence of place that Nathan Bedford Forrest enjoyed in Memphis is about more than the structure. Its placement and continued existence is about a people's history and experience, and who is going to define what that experience encompassed. For too many years, white southerners who controlled the memory of southern history have not been honest in their representation of African American life. During the Depression in Memphis, this took the form of the Cotton Carnival, where organizers muted the harshness of slave society in favor of plantation fantasies in which Black men and women were portrayed as enjoying positions of servitude. African American men and women like the Vensons took on these powerful memories and images and tried to reveal a more inclusive and accurate portrait of slave life. They also strove to represent the best parts of Memphis's Black community and the important role it had in the future development of the city. Unfortunately, neither the jubilee nor the civil rights movement completely overcame the negative stereotypes left over from slavery. But they did provide an impetus for Black Memphians to question and challenge the memories of white southerners of the Civil War and their heroes with great vigor.

The Forrest statue is about identity and who controls the public's memory of historical events. With the guidance of the United Daughters of the Confederacy, neo-Confederates have held a firm grip on the memory of the ante- and postbellum South for most of the twentieth century. They look on this statue as a representation of all the valiant men who fought for states' rights, and they long for a time when they assume that men like them had authority in local and national politics. More importantly, though, at the dawn of the twentieth century the statues erected by town councils and cities were not just sites of remembrance. As Adelia A. Dunovant pointed out in a 1901 address she delivered at a UDC general meeting in Wilmington, North Carolina: "It seems to me that our error lies in embalming, as it were, historic truths and putting them away in the tomb of the Confederacy—making them as devoid of energizing influence as an Egyptian mummy—instead of bringing them and keeping them ever before us in the vital, living present. Memory is not a passivity, but an ever active faculty—History should be made to serve its true purpose by bringing its lessons into the present and using them as a guide to the future."[39]

In her article on catechisms the UDC members taught children, Amy Heyse gives readers a framework by which they can understand the connections between these lessons on southern history and the way that information infiltrated American history throughout the twentieth century. Capturing the memories of the children was essential for organizations such as the UDC because through the children the history of their South would continue. Children not only participated in catechisms, but they also played an important role in public commemorations. Remember, as was discussed in the introduction, it was Kathleen Bradley, the great-granddaughter of Forrest himself, who pulled the cord to release the drapery surrounding the monument to him and his wife. For Bradley and the children watching, not only did history live through the unveiling, but they were active participants in keeping that history alive.[40]

While the statue is a good indication of where the citizens of Memphis stood on the issue of race, the statue is also the symbol of where these men and women wanted to take the city in subsequent years.[41] White Memphians were greatly invested in the myth as it defined who they were and by extension the way they viewed African Americans. Neo-Confederates argue that their memories and their reverence for the heroes of the old South have nothing to do with the slaves who made these men great. They contend that they are celebrating the honor and dignity that men like Lee, Davis, and Forrest embodied in their efforts to live out the true meaning of the Constitution.[42] Of course as observers review history this claim has little credibility. As Gerald Webster and Jonathan Leib point out in "What Would Robert E. Lee Do?" the popularity, and therefore visibility, of the Confederate flag skyrocketed after the *Brown v. Board of Education* decision of 1954. In the deep South, legislatures began raising the flag over all types of public spaces to show their defiance of what they believed to be federal government intrusion into their affairs.[43] Southern heritage advocates from the previous chapter would argue that these racists appropriated the flag and distorted its meaning, but did they really?

The celebrations surrounding the statues and the honorifics Lost Cause advocates bestow on the flag are about white history and white identity. In their public ceremonies African Americans are nowhere to be found. How can they participate when the only role for them to play is one of a servant? There are no dignified roles in the world of the Confederate loyalist for their Black neighbors, at least as Black citizens interpret the word "dignity." For Lost Cause advocates, there is no more a dignified role for Black people than that of the hapless devoted attendants who were willing to come to the aid of their masters.[44]

African Americans cannot participate in these celebrations because their presence exposes the contradictions in the myths about the Confederate cause. "Negro" Americans fought in the Civil War to work toward one goal: freedom for them and their families. There is no way to marry freedom for slaves and freedom for the Confederates because any truthful accounting of history shows that the two groups worked at cross purposes. Had the Confederates won the war, slavery would have continued. There is no easy way around that fact, so neo-Confederates ignore the harshness of slavery in order to rehabilitate the practice, and thus they can pretend that the Civil War was about anything else other than the abolition of slavery. In the world of happy slaves and chivalrous gentlemen, the valuable contributions of enslaved Black workers to the economy and social life of the South disappear. The reason for the erasure can be found in the Newson article. He makes the point that America has never reckoned with its racial past. He uses the example of the Wilmington, North Carolina, insurrection of 1898, when Black and Republican officeholders, who had been duly elected by the people of Wilmington, were forced to resign because a white-supremacist mob held them at gunpoint. The mob violence and forced resignations were undertaken because the Democratic Party had been successful in taking over key positions across the state in the 1898 election. The party did not secure any leading positions in Wilmington because of the "fusion" government that stood strong against the specter of "Negro" domination. For these people, the government could not stand, so they used violence to end these democratic institutions.[45] The key to this discussion is not just understanding the violent overthrow of the local government. What is also impactful is the fact that there were absolutely no repercussions for the outlaws, who rampaged through the city looking to "kill every damn nigger in sight." That there were no consequences for this brazen act led the white supremacists down a road of absolution, and further justified, in their minds, that their cause was righteous—just like their ancestors who felt justified in fighting the Civil War. The problem is that if there is no justice, there can be no healing. If there is no healing, victims are unable to move past hurtful events.[46] Extrapolating on Newson's thesis, healing is a nonstarter for communities where the injustices have been immortalized in bronze or fly proudly from a flagpole on government property.

Black Memphians, starting with the jubilee, decided to use public space to offer the public a counternarrative of the Black experience during slavery and afterwards. They also used the jubilee, as well as protests against the Forrest statue, to have a discussion about where the race is and how Americans have or have not lived up to the promises of the Constitution. In the end, what the struggles between these two groups show is that white southerners' efforts to erase African American participation from the pages of history have proven to be a fruitful endeavor up to a point. The changes and challenges of the twentieth century have caused a definite push by Black Memphians to counter the narrative put forth by the neo-Confederates. By developing and participating in the jubilee and protests surrounding the Forrest statue, they have made an important statement about their citizenship and proven that they were not invisible actors in history.

The statue and the carnival provide evidence that white southerners wanted to dominate public space. They served as a reminder of the good old days when people respected white privilege, and "colored" people had to swallow their discontent and obey the racial hierarchy. But that was then, what about now? Inward Journey tried to "reclaim" the meaning of the park, but I think the park continues to symbolize what white Memphians were trying to hold onto in 1905. The removal of the statue just increases the desire of Confederate loyalists to hold on to a time when white supremacy was an accepted fact, because the removal represents a weakening of the values that elevated their ancestors. For white Memphians, the statue is about dominance of the past and scrambling to be heard in the present and the future. White, racially conservative southerners have not been able to get over the trauma of the new social order in places like Memphis. From Elizabeth Avery Meriwether, claiming to being accosted on the streets after the war, to the mayoral race of 1979, when Wyeth Chandler made his plea for white solidarity in order to secure a win, some white southerners have seen their histories upended by "aggressive" Black men and women who, in their estimation, want to tear down everything that they hold dear. The statues and what they represent will remain in place as long as this very vocal minority continues to feel restricted in their ability to not only claim their history but stake out a place for themselves and their families in all areas of public life in the city.

Although not nearly as many people gathered that chilly December night when the Forrest monument was removed as had gathered on that warm day in May back in 1905 when it had been erected, the air was just as anxious. At long last, opponents of the statues won a victory in the battle for an image, an image that did not promote white supremacy and the values of a slave society, but one that adhered to the promises of America.

NOTES

INTRODUCTION

1. Coleman Hutchison, "In the Land Where We Were Dreaming," *South: A Scholarly Journal* 48, no. 1 (Fall 2015): 47. Throughout this book I will use the term *Old South* to refer to the myth of antebellum life and the Civil War promoted by the United Daughters of the Confederacy and other southern heritage organizations. It is a myth in which the slaves sang happily in the fields while the master and mistress of the house lounged around their homes, wore fine clothes, and sipped cocktails. In this narrative slave owners were benevolent. They were guardians of their slave family, offering advice, love, and of course discipline. The men, whether slave or free, practiced honor and chivalry. The society was organized based on gender and race. Everyone had their role to play, and they accepted their place, making southern society the height of civilization.

2. George W. Gordon, *At the Dedication Ceremonies of the Forrest Monument at Memphis Tennessee, May 16, 1905* (Memphis: Forrest Memorial Association, 1905), 12–16; *The Forrest Monument: Its History & Dedication* (Memphis: Forrest Monument Association, 1905), 16. Both texts are at the Memphis Room, Central Location, Memphis & Shelby County Libraries and Public Information Center.

3. From the inscription on the statue in Memphis.

4. Gordon, *At the Dedication Ceremonies of the Forrest Monument,* 64.

5. Gordon, *At the Dedication Ceremonies of the Forrest Monument,* 12–16; *The Forrest Monument,* 16.

6. "Journey to Forrest Statue Bold Step to Wholeness," *Commercial Appeal* (hereafter referred to as *CA*), June 20, 1999; Al Lewis, interview by author, July 8, 1999, Memphis, TN; *CA,* May 12, 1988.

7. Gordon, *At the Dedication Ceremonies of the Forrest Monument,* 3–4.

8. Johan Fornäs, *Signifying Europe* (Intellect, 2012), 43–45, 51.

9. Fornäs, *Signifying Europe,* 43–45, 51; John J. Winberry, "'Lest We Forget': The Confederate Monument and the Southern Townscape." *Southeastern Geographer* 55, no. 1 (Spring 2015): 19–31, 20, 29. Martha E. Kinney, "'If Vanquished I Am Still Victorious': Religious and Cultural

Symbolism in Virginia's Confederate Memorial Day Celebrations, 1866–1930," *Virginia Magazine of History and Biography* 106, no. 3 (1998): 239; For Kinney, the point of the celebration is about how the symbol makes participants feel and what types of memories the symbol evokes.

10. Joan Marie Johnson, "Drill into Us . . . the Rebel Tradition: The Contest over Southern Identity in Black and White Women's Clubs, South Carolina, 1898–1930," *Journal of Southern History* 66, no. 3 (2000): 530; Jennifer Gross, "The United Daughters of the Confederacy, Confederate Widows, and the Lost Cause," in *Women on Their Own: Interdisciplinary Perspectives on Being Single,* ed. Rudolph M. Bell, and Virginia Yans (Rutgers University Press, 2008), www.jstor.org/stable/j.ctt5hj2wd.Gross explains that the work of the UDC included the memorial projects to further the narrative of the rightness of the Lost Cause. She also focuses on the fact that these memorial ceremonies to Confederate soldiers provided an opportunity for the men who survived the conflict to continue to act as the guardians of their fallen brethren's family as well as of their memory.

11. Karen Cox, *Dixie's Daughters: The United Daughters of the Confederacy and the Preservation of Confederate Culture* (University Press of Florida, 2003), 48; Winberry, "Lest We Forget," 26.

12. F. Sheffield Hale, "Finding Meaning in Monuments: Atlanta History Center Enters Dialogue on Confederate Symbols," *History News* 71, no. 4 (Autumn 2016): 20.

13. Johnson, "Drill into Us," 535; Johnson makes the point that there was great crossover between the United Daughters of the Confederacy and white women's social clubs in the South. The membership rolls were often the same so that the agendas of both groups were identical. This point is also supported by Gross, "The United Daughters of the Confederacy," as she notes similar ties between the Ladies Memorial Association in Raleigh, North Carolina, and the local chapter of the United Daughters of the Confederacy. See also Cox, *Dixie's Daughters,* 29.

14. For a discussion on how southern identity has become synonymous with white identity, see Ashley B. Thompson and Melissa M. Sloan, "South Polls: Race as Region, Region as Race: How Black and White Southerners Understand Their Regional Identities," *Southern Cultures* 18, no. 4 (2012): 73, www.jstor.org/stable/26217396. For information on the types of narratives that southern white women bored into the southern landscape, see Johnson, "Drill into Us," 542, 543. For information on what the southern narrative entailed, see Cox, *Dixie's Daughters,* 11–13; David Blight, *Race and Reunion: The Civil War in American Memory* (Harvard University Press, 2001), 1, 2, 313; Orville Vernon Burton, "The South as 'Other,' the Southerner as 'Stranger,'" *Journal of Southern History* 79, no. 1 (2013): 13.

15. Thompson and Sloan. "South Polls," 73. The authors note that there are "very few" Black southerners who have been memorialized by any southern heritage preservation groups. This serves as another example of white southerners' attempts to erase Black southerners' role in the development of the region.

16. Johnson, "Drill into Us," 549. See also Judy Barsalou and Victoria Baxter, Report, US Institute of Peace, 2007, www.jstor.org/stable/resrep12524, 12. Barsalou and Baxter state plainly that outsiders are not welcome in the memorialization process because the creators of the memory material are interested in establishing a certain truth.

17. "Journey to Forrest Statue"; "The 9:01: Movement Against Confederate Monuments," *CA,* July 22, 2017, A3.

18. Barsalou and Baxter, Report, 17; Kirk Savage, *Standing Soldiers, Kneeling Slaves: Race, War, and Monument in Nineteenth-Century America* (Princeton University Press, 1991), 3–4, 6, 131, 152.

19. Brian D. Page, "'Stand by the Flag': Nationalism and African-American Celebrations of the Fourth of July in Memphis, 1866–1887," *Tennessee Historical Quarterly* 58, no. 4 (1999): 286–88; Peter C. Myers, "'A Good Work for Our Race To-Day': Interests, Virtues, and the Achievement of Justice in Frederick Douglass's Freedmen's Monument Speech," *American Political Science Review* 104, no. 2 (2010): 211. Myers analyzes Frederick Douglass's speech on the occasion of the eleventh anniversary of Lincoln's assassination (210). In his speech Douglass expresses his pleasure at seeing Black Americans at the civic ceremony as free people, as citizens, where they would have been excluded just a decade before (211). See also George Barr et al., "'What to the Slave Is the Fourth of July?' (1852)." In *The Speeches of Frederick Douglass: A Critical Edition,* ed. John R. McKivigan, Julie Husband, and Heather L. Kaufman, (Yale University Press, 2018), 68, 72.

20. Robert Emmett McLean, "Cotton Carnival and Cotton Makers Jubilee: Memphis Society in Black and White," master's thesis, George Mason University, 1994, 87–89; "The Memphis Cotton Makers Jubilee: A Historical Sketch," Container 1, Folder 4, 1940, Ethyl Q. Venson Collection, Memphis Room, Memphis & Shelby County Library (hereafter Venson Collection); Nat Williams, "Historical Resume," Container 1, Folder 8, 1949, Venson Collection; Amy Lynn Heyse, "The Rhetoric of Memory-Making: Lessons from the UDC's Catechisms for Children," *Rhetoric Society Quarterly* 38, no. 4 (2008): 415. The myth of the Old South is just one of four myths that Heyse points to as sustaining and living memorials to the Confederacy.

21. Clippings File: Cotton Carnival, Memphis Room, Memphis & Shelby County Library; Genevieve Fabre, "African American Commemorative Celebrations in the Nineteenth Century," in *History and Memory in African American Culture,* ed. Genevieve Fabre and Robert O'Meally (Oxford University Press, 1994), 72–73, 78, 88. African Americans in Memphis did not always protest negative images in a direct way. Through their celebrations, they also rejected the notion that they were anything but full citizens of this country.

22. David Blight, "W. E. B. Du Bois and the Struggle for American Historical Memory," in, *History and Memory in African American Culture,* ed. Fabre and O'Meally, 46; Johnson, "Drill into Us," 531.

23. Robert Glaze, "Saint and Sinner: Robert E. Lee, Nathan Bedford Forrest, and the Ambiguity of Southern Identity," *Tennessee Historical Quarterly* 69, no. 2 (Summer 2010): 167–68. Glaze makes the point that both of these men, though very different in character, represented a link to the religiosity, honor, and manhood of the antebellum South. Lee and Forrest took charge during the supposed chaos of Reconstruction to keep "the vulgar mob in its place and to ensure its deference to its betters" (167). Further, Glaze argues that for southerners Forrest was a symbol of "defiance of Yankee modernity and elitism" (168). See also J. C. M., "Just a Word About the Lost Cause," *Register of Kentucky State Historical Society* 1, no. 3 (September 1903): 91; Heyse, "The Rhetoric of Memory-Making," 409. The Daughters of the Confederacy were responsible for creating and compiling the information that constitutes the Lost Cause; see Burton, "The South as 'Other,'" 14.

24. Linda Shopes and Paula Hamilton, *Oral History and Public Memories* (Temple University Press, 2008), ebscohost.com, 4. Shopes concludes that the Singapore History Centre worked to exclude the voices of the poor and disenfranchised in its history and attempted to describe the nation by focusing on the accounts of the affluent. This is similar to how African Americans have had great difficulty being able to include their history and that of their ancestors in the narratives created by southern heritage organizations. Slavery complicates the narrative, and it is unwelcome.

25. Court Carney, "The Contested Image of Nathan Bedford Forrest," *Journal of Southern History* 67 (August 2001): 621–22, 624.

26. Court Carney, *Reckoning with the Devil: Nathan Bedford Forrest in Myth and Memory* (Louisiana State University Press, 2024), 12, 13, 29, 46.

27. Winberry, "Lest We Forget," 20.

28. Jody Stokes-Casey," Richard Lou's ReCovering Memphis: Conceptual Iconoclasm of the Nathan Bedford Forrest Monument," *Tennessee Historical Quarterly* 75, no. 4 (Winter 2016): 325; Tom Vincent, "'Evidence of Womans Loyalty, Perseverance, and Fidelity,': Confederate Soldiers' Monuments in North Carolina, 1865-1914" *North Carolina Historical Review* 83, no. 1 (January 2006): 63–64, 74, 81. Vincent argues that the women of the memorial associations recast these structures so that the spirit of mourning that the monuments represented would be replaced by the strength of Confederate values. The monuments were now handy guidebooks on how southerners should conduct themselves in American life.

29. "Negroes in the City," *Memphis Daily Eagle,* November 8, 1849; Beverly Greene Bond and Sarah Wilkerson Freeman, eds. *Tennessee Women: Their Lives and Times* (University of Georgia Press, 2015), 13–15.

30. For information on the atmosphere in the city of Memphis after the Civil War, see Elizabeth Avery Meriwether, *Recollections of 92 Years* (EPM Publications, 1994), 154; Marius Carriere, "An Irresponsible Press: Memphis Newspapers and the 1866 Riot," *Tennessee Historical Quarterly* 60, no. 1 (2001): 7–8.

31. W. E. B. Du Bois, "The Talented Tenth," in *The Negro Problem: A Series of Articles by Representative American Negroes Today* (James Pott and Co., 1903), 33–34; Booker T. Washington, "Booker T. Washington Delivers the 1895 Atlanta Exposition Speech," http://historymatters.gmu.edu/d/39/. The talented tenth refers to a philosophy developed by W. E. B. Du Bois that held that while industrial education may have its place, Black people and philanthropists needed to develop a select number of African Americans for leadership and political action to lift up African Americans as a whole.

32. "The Memphis Cotton Makers Jubilee: A Historical Sketch," Venson Collection; Williams, "Historical Resume," Venson Collection.

33. Fornäs, *Signifying Europe,* 54.

34. Winberry, "Lest We Forget," 20.

35. Modupe Labode and Kevin M. Levin, "Reconsideration of Memorials and Monuments," *History News* 71, no. 4 (Autumn 2016): 8.

36. Winberry, "Lest We Forget," 26–27.

37. "Foreword," Folder 3, 1939, Venson Collection. The executive committee of the Cotton Makers Jubilee was made up of Dr. J. J. Raines, treasurer; Clifton Satterfield, secretary; Dr. R. Q. Venson, chairman; Prof. Nat D. Williams, publicity director; Prof. H. B. King, comptroller; and Eddie Hayes, vice chairman.

38. Matthew 13:3–9 (New Living Translation).

1. DEFINING FREEDOM IN ANTEBELLUM AND POSTBELLUM MEMPHIS

1. H. M. Henry, The Slave Laws of Tennessee, *Tennessee Historical Magazine,* 2, no. 3 (September 1916): 180.

2. "Negroes in the City," *Memphis Daily Eagle,* November 8, 1849.

3. "Negroes in the City"; Bond and Freeman, eds. *Tennessee Women,* 13–15.

4. "Negroes in the City"; on the slave population in the city, see Marius Carriere, "Blacks in Pre–Civil War Memphis," in *Trial and Triumph: Essays in Tennessee's African American History,* ed. Carroll Van West (University of Tennessee Press, 2005), 26.

5. Here and throughout, I have consistently put quotations marks around this term and also 'colored' to indicate that, while both were commonly used terms in antebellum America and long after, they are pejorative. In a few instances when context indicated and when syntactic awkwardness might arise, I have left the quotation marks off.

6. William Lloyd Imes, "The Legal Status of Free Negroes and Slaves in Tennessee," *Journal of Negro History,* 4, no. 3 (July 1919): 262.

7. Emily West, *Family or Freedom: People of Color in the Antebellum South* (University Press of Kentucky, 2012), 23.

8. Gerald Capers Jr., *The Biography of a River Town,* 2nd ed. (Tulane University Press, 1966), 68. Capers supposed that the restrictions in the 1830s were due to the Nat Turner rebellion in Virginia. See "Duties of Town Watchman" from Memphis Board of Alderman minutes, March 18, 1839, at the Memphis & Shelby County Library, Central Location, Memphis Room; Carriere, "Blacks in Pre–Civil War Memphis," 33.

9. Carriere, "Blacks in Pre–Civil War Memphis," 33.

10. West, *Family or Freedom,* 29. West is just one of the historians who have written about the efforts to control the behavior of free people and the enslaved. In contrast to what happened in Memphis, West argues that there is no correlation between an increase in the population and the proliferation of these ordinances. In the cities and states she is referring to, there was no upsurge in the population of Black people. In Memphis, there was a noticeable rise in the Black population, and I submit that this fact was a strong motivation for Memphis council members to act. Another article that gives a compelling account of the changes in law, in this case in the state of Louisiana, is Amy Sumpter, "Segregation of Free People of Color and the Construction of Race in Antebellum New Orleans," *Southeastern Geographer* 48, no. 1 (May 2008): 31, 33.

11. "Regulation for Slaves," *Memphis Daily Appeal,* December 28, 1860. Memphis was not the only city where authorities enforced these kinds of laws; many of the statutes were in effect across Tennessee. See Imes, "The Legal Status of Free Negroes," 257–58. Imes also dis-

cusses the situation regarding "hiring out," which is when slaves purchased their time from their masters.

12. Kathleen Christine Berkeley, "'Like a Plague of Locusts': Immigration and Social Change in Memphis, Tennessee, 1850–1880" (PhD diss., University of California Los Angeles, 1980), 144.

13. Bobby Lovett, "The Negro's Civil War in Tennessee, 1861–1865," *Journal of Negro History* 61, no. 1 (January 1976): 36. Deborah Gray White, *Ar'n't I a Woman? Female Slaves in the Plantation South* (Norton, 1999), 129; Stephanie Camp, *Closer to Freedom: Enslaved Women and Everyday Resistance in the Plantation South* (University of North Carolina Press, 2004), 119; Antonette G. Van Zelm, "Too Much of the Yankees about Them, to Suit Me" Wartime Emancipation and Tennessee's Slaveholding Women," *Tennessee Historical Quarterly* 72, no. 4 (2013): 269–70.

14. Lester Lamon, *Blacks in Tennessee 1791–1970* (University of Tennessee Press, 1981), 29–30, 33; Lovett, "The Negro's Civil War in Tennessee," 38; Sherman's attitude was not unusual. Before 1963 and the Emancipation Proclamation, for instance, Lincoln himself framed the war in terms of keeping the Union together. While southerners understood and explicitly stated that they were at war to preserve their free labor, northerners focused on the reunification of the states. See Ira Berlin et al, *Slaves No More: Three Essays on Emancipation and the Civil War* (Cambridge University Press, 1992), 4–5.

15. Lamon, *Blacks in Tennessee*, 38; *Memphis Public Ledger*, March 7, 1867. The article reported on a Mississippi farmer who complained about not being able to find enough help for plantation work. One of the reasons for this shortage he highlights is that city merchants "[took] laborers from the farmers." Because of the opportunities for employment in the city, former slaves did not feel chained to the plantation. See United States Bureau of Refugees, Freedmen, and Abandoned Lands, Roll 24. These documents record the many labor disputes that came about as a result of these labor contracts. They also point out that freed people were not easily intimidated into accepting unfair wages as they took their disputes to the Bureau to seek resolution; for more on this resistance, see Noralee Frankel, *Freedom's Women: Black Women and Families in Civil War Era Mississippi* (Indiana University Press, 1999), 29; Hannah Rosen, *Terror in the Heart of Freedom: Citizenship, Sexual Violence, and the Meaning of Race in the Postemancipation South* (University of North Carolina Press, 2009), 32, 62, 66; Eric Foner, *Reconstruction: America's Unfinished Revolution, 1863–1877* (Harper Perennial, 2014), 129; and Nell Irvin Painter, *Southern History Across the Color Line* (University of North Carolina Press, 2002), 113.

16. Beverly Bond, "'Til Fair Aurora Rise': African American Women in Memphis Tennessee, 1840–1915" (PhD diss., University of Memphis, 1996), 140; C. Stuart McGehee, "E. O. Tade, Freedmen's Education, and the Failure of Reconstruction in Tennessee," *Tennessee Historical Quarterly* 43, no. 4 (1984): 376–89.

17. Berkeley, "Like a Plague of Locusts," 229, 231, 236. Missionary education heavily relied on instruction in piety and industriousness; see E. Franklin Frazier, *The Black Bourgeoisie* (Falcon's Wing Press, 1957), 70–71.

18. Berkeley, "Like a Plague of Locusts," 236–39; Bond, "'Til Fair Aurora Rise," 140.

19. Alrutheus Ambush Taylor, *The Negro in Tennessee, 1865–1880* (Reprint Company, 1975), 1–2.

20. *Nashville Daily Times,* January 18, 1865; Taylor, *The Negro in Tennessee,* 2.

21. House Journal, 34th Tenn. General Assembly, 1st Session, 1865; Senate Journal, 34th Tenn. General Assembly, 1st Sess., 1865, 42; Taylor, *The Negro in Tennessee,* 4–5, 7; *Harper's Weekly,* June 10, 1865. The tactic of diluting the African American vote during Reconstruction was not the sole province of the Tennessee state legislature. Across the South state governments enacted "Black Codes," which were designed to keep freed people as close to slave status as possible. See Stephen Middleton, ed., *Black Congressmen During Reconstruction: A Documentary Sourcebook* (Greenwood Press, 2002), xix; Christopher Waldrep, "The Politics of Language: The Ku Klux Klan in Reconstruction," in *Warm Ashes: Issues in Southern History at the Dawn of the 21st Century,* ed. Winfred B. Moore Jr. (University of South Carolina Press, 2003), 143; Minion K.C. Morrison, ed., *African Americans and Political Participation Reference Handbook* (ABC-CLIO, 2003), 45.

22. "The Beale Street Baptist Church, a story," African American Registry, effective August 19, 2022, https://aaregistry.org/story/the-beale-street-baptist-church-a-story/.

23. Meriwether, *Recollections of 92 Years,* 43, 46, 143.

24. Meriwether, *Recollections of 92 Years,* 154; Berkeley, "Like a Plague of Locusts," and Bond, "'Til Fair Aurora Rise." Readers can surmise for themselves if Meriwether's estimate of Black people in Reconstruction was accurate. What we learned from the early pages of this chapter is that Black men and women worked diligently to establish schools and churches to serve the newly freed population.

25. Editorial, *Memphis Daily Avalanche,* January 23, 1866; Carriere, "An Irresponsible Press, 4.

26. Editorial, *Memphis Daily Avalanche,* March 20, 1866.

27. Kevin Hardwick, "'Your Old Father Abe Lincoln Is Dead and Damned': Black Soldiers and the Memphis Race Riot of 1866," *Journal of Social History* 27 (Fall 1993): 110.

28. E. B. Washburne, *Memphis Riots and Massacres* (Arno Press & *New York Times,* 1969), 7; Bond, "'Til Fair Aurora Rise," chap. 3; Altina Waller, "Community Class and Race in the Memphis Riot," *Journal of Social History* 18 (Winter 1984): 233–46; James G. Ryan, "The Memphis Riot of 1866," *Journal Of Negro History* (July 1977): 243–57.

29. Washburne, *Memphis Riots and Massacres,* 7–8, 36; of that total, $110,000 was for damage done to private property. Sharon Wright, *Race, Power, and Political Emergence in Memphis* (Routledge, 2003), 14; "Value of $130,000 from 1866 to 2022," CPI Inflation Calculator, effective August 12, 2022, https://www.officialdata.org/us/inflation/1866?amount=130000.

30. Editorial, *Memphis Daily Avalanche,* May 5, 1866; Washburne, *Memphis Riots and Massacres,* 317; Waller, "Community, Class, and Race in the Memphis Riot," 237–38. Waller argues that the rioters targeted new migrants to the city. See also Ryan, "The Memphis Riots of 1866," 244. Ryan discusses at length the problems between the Black population and the Irish. He also notes the population increase between 1860 and 1865, as well as how the rioters focused attacks on those associated with the Union army.

31. "The Duties and Responsibilities of Enfranchised Colored People," *Memphis Daily Post,* February 27, 1867.

32. Brian D. Page, "'Stand by the Flag': Nationalism and African American Celebrations of the Fourth of July in Memphis, 1866–1887," in *Trial and Triumph,* ed. West, 189.

33. Middleton, ed., *Black Congressmen During Reconstruction,* xix; Waldrep, "The Politics of Language," in *Warm Ashes,* ed. Moore, 143; Morrison, ed., *African Americans and Political Participation Reference Handbook,* 45.

34. Paul Shackel, *Memory in Black and White: Race, Commemoration, and the Post-Bellum Landscape* (AltaMira Press, 2003), 28.

35. Blight, *Race and Reunion,* 48; Shackel, *Memory in Black and White,* 22. Shackel notes that the only time white veterans mentioned the presence of Black soldiers at reunion ceremonies was when one would "tune up a banjo and sing old plantation melodies."

36. Cox, *Dixie's Daughters,* 1–2, 22–23.

37. Annie Cody, "History of the Tennessee Division," *UDC Magazine* VII (November 1944): 11.

38. Cody, "History of the Tennessee Division," 11. See also Caroline Janney, *Burying the Dead but Not the Past: Ladies' Memorial Associations and the Lost Cause* (University of North Carolina Press, 2008), 2.

39. Cox, *Dixie's Daughters,* 105–6. For more on the sanitized version of slavery, see Janney, *Burying the Dead but Not the Past,* 172; and Reiko Hillyer, "Relics of Reconciliation: The Confederate Museum and Civil War Memory in the New South," *Public Historian* 33, no. 4 (November 2011): 37.

40. Blight, *Race and Reunion,* 311, 314, 316, 313, 319, 337; J. R. Oldfield, ed., *Civilization and Black Progress: Selected Writings of Alexander Crummell on the South* (University of Virginia Press, 1995), 204–5, 174–75; Crummell was a prominent leader in nineteenth-century politics. He advocated for Booker T. Washington's philosophy on industrial education, but he left room for men and women who showed promise in liberal arts. One issue that he championed was emigration of Black Americans back to Africa. He believed that hope for the "Negro" race lay in going to places like Liberia, where they would not continue to face their past as enslaved people.

41. Blight, *Race and Reunion,* 317.

42. Shackel, *Memory in Black and White,* 11, 13.

43. Cox, *Dixie's Daughters,* 60–61, 67.

44. Hillyer, "Relics of Reconciliation," 35–36, 40.

45. Cox, *Dixie's Daughters,* 94, 96, 101, 103–6.

46. Gary W. Gallagher and Alan T. Nolan, eds. *The Myth of the Lost Cause and Civil War History* (Indiana University Press, 2000), 27.

47. Blight, *Race and Reunion,* 309. There are a myriad of works that chronicle the legal setbacks suffered by African Americans at the close of Reconstruction and the remainder of the nineteenth century, among them Donald Neiman, *Promises to Keep: African Americans and the Constitutional Order, 1776 to the Present* (Oxford University Press, 1991).

2. THE CHALLENGES OF FREEDOM

1. Willard B. Gatewood, *Aristocrats of Color: The Black Elite, 1880–1920* (Indiana University Press, 1990), 302–3, 310–11; Deirdre Mullane, ed., *Crossing the Danger Water: Three Hundred Years of African American Writing* (Doubleday, 1993), 376, 384.

2. Kenneth Goings and Gerald Smith, "'Unhidden' Transcripts: Memphis and African American Agency, 1862–1920" in *The New African American Urban History*, ed. Kenneth Goings and Raymond Mohl (Sage Publications, 1996); Waller, "Community, Class, and Race in the Memphis Riot," 233.

3. Kenneth Goings and Gerald Smith, "Duty of the Hour: African American Communities in Memphis, 1862–1923," in *The New African American Urban History*, ed. Goings and Mohl, 230–39. My analysis relies on Goings and Smith, who identify three separate groups in Memphis during the late nineteenth century: the talented tenth, accommodationists, and finally the migrants. They argue that each group had its own approach to dealing with the daily abuse put forth by white southerners who refused to accept Black Memphians as equal participants in southern society. See also Frazier, *The Black Bourgeoisie*, 71.

4. Mia Bay, *To Tell the Truth Freely: The Life of Ida B. Wells* (Hill and Wang, 2009), 98–99; Linda McMcMurry, *To Keep the Waters Troubled: The Life of Ida B. Wells* (Oxford University Press, 1998), 143; Brian D. Page, "In the Hands of the Lord," in *An Unseen Light: Black Struggles for Freedom in Memphis, Tennessee*, ed. Aram Goudsouzian, Charles W. McKinney Jr. (University Press of Kentucky, 2018), 14.

5. Bay, *To Tell the Truth Freely*, 87–88; McMurry, *To Keep the Waters Troubled*, 135, 138; Alfreda M. Duster, ed., *Crusade for Justice: The Autobiography of Ida B. Wells* (University of Chicago Press, 1970), 47–52. In these three texts, Wells describes the lynching of three of her dear friends who owned a grocery store. Wells mentioned the men's good character and clean appearance more than once, indicating that she, and others in her social circle, believed that the reason mobs lynched Black men was because of something they did or because they did not fit neatly into mainstream society.

6. Philip S. Foner and Robert James Branham, *Lift Every Voice: African American Oratory, 1787–1900* (University of Alabama Press, 1998), 747.

7. Paula Giddings, *When and Where I Enter: The Impact of Black Women on Race and Sex in America* (William Morrow, 1984), 17–18.

8. Ida B. Wells, "Lynching, Our National Crime," Address at the National Negro Conference, June 1, 1909.

9. Giddings, *When and Where I Enter*, 29, 31, 97.

10. Darlene Clark Hine, Elsa Barkley Brown, and Rosalyn Terborg-Penn, eds., *Black Women in America* (Indiana University Press, 1993), 572–73.

11. Bond, "'Til Fair Aurora Rise," 155–56, 160; Page, "In the Hands of the Lord," 14.

12. Roberta Church and Ronald Walter, *Nineteenth Century Memphis Families of Color, 1850–1900* (Murdock Printing Co., 1987), 43; Selma S. Lewis and Marjean G. Kremer, *The Angel of Beale Street: The Biography of Julia Ann Hooks* (St. Luke's Press, 1986), 201, 205–8.

13. Church and Walter, *Nineteenth Century Memphis Families of Color,* 43–44; Julia A. Hooks, "Duty of the Hour," *Afro-American Encyclopedia* (Nashville, 1896), 334; Gatewood, *Aristocrats of Color.* Gatewood states, "They [Black aristocrats] assumed that proper conduct, manners, and other evidence of good breeding were indicative of one's character" (343). These aristocrats also believed that it was the character of Black men and women that led to the sexual and physical abuse Black people suffered daily.

14. Hooks, "Duty of the Hour," 335–37.

15. Robert R. Church/Church Family Papers, Container 1, Folder 9, Mississippi Valley Collection, McWherter Library, University of Memphis; Goings and Smith, "Duty of the Hour."

16. Lewis and Kremer, *The Angel of Beale Street,* 234–36.

17. Selma S. Lewis and Marjean G. Kremer, *The Angel of Beale Street,* 234–36; Kenneth Goings and Gerald Smith, "Duty of the Hour: African American Communities in Memphis, 1862–1923," in *Trials and Triumph: Essays in Tennessee History* (University of Tennessee Press, 2002), 234.

18. Thomas O. Fuller, *Twenty Years in Public Life, 1890–1910* (National Baptist Publishing Board, 1910), 9, 11–12.

19. Fuller, *Twenty Years in Public Life,* 18.

20. Fuller, *Twenty Years in Public Life,* 26–27, 29–30.

21. Fuller, *Twenty Years in Public Life,* 28, 30–31, 37–38, 44, 45.

22. Fuller, *Twenty Years in Public Life,* 52.

23. Fuller, *Twenty Years in Public Life,* 109, 111–12.

24. Fuller, *Twenty Years in Public Service,* 273–74.

25. David Tucker, *Black Pastors and Leaders* (Memphis State University Press, 1975), 115–16, 172, 273–74; Jacqueline Jones, *American Work: Four Centuries of Black and White Labor* (Norton, 1998), 284.

26. Kenneth W. Goings and Ray Mohl, "Toward a New African American Urban History," *Journal of Urban History* 21 (March 1995): 285–86; Joel M. Roitman, "Race Relations in Memphis, Tennessee, 1880–1905" (master's thesis, Memphis State University, 1964), 129; Robin D. G. Kelley, *Race Rebels: Culture, Politics, and the Black Working Class* (Free Press, 1996), 56.

27. Walter E. Campbell, "Tracking Jim Crow: Streetcar Segregation in the Urban South," paper presented at the Modes of Inquiry for American City History Conference, Chicago, October 1990; Howard Rabinowitz, *The First New South, 1865–1920* (Harlan Davidson, 1992), 2–6; Rayford Logan, *The Negro in American Life and Thought* (Dial Press, 1954), 9. De jure segregation refers to segregation by law.

28. Kelley, *Race Rebels,* 55–66; Goings and Smith, "Duty of the Hour," 59; Lamon, *Blacks in Tennessee,* 20; editorial, *CA,* February 8, 1903. Page, "In the Hands of the Lord," 14; Bertram Wilbur Doyle, *The Etiquette of Race Relations in the South* (Schocken, 1971), 113.

29. "Jim Crow Cars," *CA,* April 7, 1903; "Jim Crow Cars," *CA,* March 27, 1903; "Jim Crow Laws," *CA,* January 1, 1903. Streetcar company officials promised that they were diligently working to enforce the law; however, in the meantime they thought they could appease the public by placing a copy of the Hancock law in every car and training conductors on how to

uphold the provisions of the law. Despite their efforts to comply, local politicians sued the MSRC for nonenforcement and obtained a $200 fine against the company.

30. Jennifer Roback, "The Political Economy of Segregation: The Case of Segregated Streetcars," *Journal of Economic History* 46 (December 1986): 915; T. H. Tutwiler, General Manager, *Payroll & Statistical Report of Operation of the Memphis Street Railway Company,* July 1905.

31. August Meier and Elliott Rudwick, "The Boycott Movement Against Jim Crow Streetcars in the South, 1900–1906," *Journal of American History* 55 (March 1969): 760–62, 766; *CA,* January 24, 1903; Goings and Smith, "Duty of the Hour," 239.

32. Fuller, *Twenty Years in Public Life,* 261.

33. *Mary Smith (c) & W. C. Smith (c) v. Memphis Street Railway Company,* Circuit Court of Shelby County, Tennessee, Division #3, #17778, T.D., filed October 1, 1908, 4–5, 10–15; On page 7 of the transcript, Mrs. Smith testified that she had previously sued MSRC in 1905 because of injury she received on the cars.

34. *Mary Smith (c) & W.C. Smith (c) v. Memphis Street Railway Company,* 2, 5, 16.

35. *Mary Smith (c) & W.C. Smith (c) v. Memphis Street Railway Company,* 6, 17, 42–47, 70.

36. Doyle, *The Etiquette of Race Relations in the South,* 109; *CA,* 23 May 1910.

37. "Four Negroes Shot During Riot on Car," *CA,* October 22, 1916.

38. Fuller, *Twenty Years in Public Life,* 45; Booker T. Washington, "Atlanta Exposition Address," in *Let Nobody Turn Us Around: Voices of Resistance, and Renewal, an African American Anthology,* ed. Manning Marable and Leith Mullings (Rowman & Littlefield, 1999), 185; W. E. B. Du Bois, excerpts from "Conservation of Races," in *Let Nobody Turn Us Around,* ed. Marable and Mullings, 224. Du Bois maintained that the freedman felt the "weight of his ignorance . . . [and the] red stain of bastardy." He holds that the "Negro" was not only ignorant of "letters" but also of business.

39. I am making these assertions based on Fuller's statements about Black people who took official positions in government after the Civil War without being properly trained. As I stated earlier, he sympathized with white men who became enraged at the reality that they were shut out from government while their former uneducated slaves were active participants. Also Fuller became the president of the Howe Institute, and the goal of this organization was "to make the Negro fit for the world." See earlier discussion in this chapter. See also Fuller, *Twenty Years in Public Life,* 207–8, 273; Booker T. Washington, "Atlanta Exposition Speech," 184. Readers can also find similar views among prominent Black women, such as Mary Church Terrell. See Beverly W. Jones, "Mary Church Terrell and the National Association of Colored Women, 1896 to 1901," *Journal of Negro History* 67, no. 1 (Spring, 1982): 24–25, 27; Mary Church Terrell, "Lynching from a Negro's Point of View," *North American Review* 178, no. 571 (1904): 853–68; Giddings, *When and Where I Enter,* 95, 97.

40. Goings and Smith, "Duty of the Hour," 137, 140; Gregory Mixon, "Good Negro—Bad Negro: The Dynamics of Race and Class in Atlanta During the Era of the 1906 Riot," *Georgia Historical Quarterly* 81, no. 3 (1997): 594.

41. Ida B. Wells, "Southern Horrors," in Trudier Harris, *Selected Works of Ida B. Wells-Barnett* (Oxford University Press, 1991), 40, 59; Ida B. Wells, "Lynch Law in all Its Phases," in

Lift Every Voice, ed. Foner and Branham, 753. W. J. Cash offers yet another perspective, however. W. J. Cash, *The Mind of the South* (Alfred Knopf, 1941), 113.

3. BUILDING THE LEGACY OF NATHAN BEDFORD FORREST

1. Mrs. Hugh Hicks, "Nathan Beford Forrest," *UDC Magazine* (November 1944): 12–13.

2. "Confederate Clans," *Richmond Dispatch,* May 29, 1890; Untitled, *Richmond Dispatch,* May 28, 1890.

3. "Confederate Clans"; Untitled, *Richmond Dispatch.*

4. "Unveiled," *Richmond Dispatch,* May 30, 1890.

5. "Unveiled."

6. Janney, *Burying the Dead but Not the Past,* 7, 110–14.

7. Glaze, "Saint and Sinner," 164, 166, 170.

8. Adam H. Domby, *The False Cause: Fraud, Fabrication, and White Supremacy in Confederate Memory* (University of Virginia Press, 2020), 4, 6.

9. "Decoration Day," *Richmond Dispatch,* May 31, 1890.

10. Douglas Massey, "Confederate Revisionist History," in *Antidemocracy in America: Truth, Power, and the Republic at Risk,* ed. Eric Klinenberg, Caitlin Zaloom, and Sharon Marcus (Columbia University Press, 2019), 195; "Decoration Day."

11. "Decoration Day."

12. "Decoration Day."

13. "The Heathen Rage," *Richmond Dispatch,* May 23, 1890.

14. "Sickles at Boston," *Richmond Dispatch,* May 31, 1890; "The Heathen Rage."

15. Barsalou and Baxter, Report, 4.

16. Beverly Bond and Janann Sherman, *Memphis in Black and White* (Arcadia, 2003), 74–75; Wanda Rushing, *Memphis and the Paradox of Place: Globalization in the American South* (University of North Carolina Press, 2009), 36–37. Rushing points out that at the turn of the century Memphis leaders emphasized the city's New South potential by building the first bridge across the Mississippi River south of the city of St. Louis.

17. Hillyer, "Relics of Reconciliation," 36.

18. Charles Reagan Wilson, *Baptized in Blood: The Religion of the Lost Cause, 1865–1920* (University of Georgia Press, 1980), 80, 82. For more information on the building of the New South at the turn of the century, see Lawrence H. Larsen, *The Urban South: A History* (University Press of Kentucky, 1990), 60–95; Harold D. Woodman, "How New Was the New South?" *Agricultural History* 58, no. 4 (October 1984): 530–31; James Cobb, "Beyond Planters and Industrialists: A New Perspective on the New South," *Journal of Southern History* 54, no. 1 (1988): 53–54.

19. Gallagher and Nolan, eds., *The Myth of the Lost Cause and Civil War History,* 112–13.

20. Rushing, *Memphis and the Paradox of Place,* 42; Wilson, *Baptized in Blood,* 29; Domby, *The False Cause,* 9.

21. Ryan Andrew Newson, "Epistemological Crises Made Stone: Confederate Monuments and the End of Memory," *Journal of the Society of Christian Ethics* 37, no. 2 (Fall/Winter 2017):

137–39. Newson makes the point that these statues appeared in southern communities just as white violence against Black citizens increased.

22. Glaze, "Saint and Sinner," 170, 175. See also John Scales, *The Battles and Campaigns of Confederate General Nathan Bedford Forrest, 1861–1865* (Savas Beatie), 2016. The introduction to Scales's book begins with a quotation the author attributes to Sherman. Sherman wants every soldier focusing on killing or capturing Forrest because the Union forces would never see peace in Tennessee until they stopped Forrest's campaigns. See also Jack Hurst, "Tennessee Turning Point: Nathan B. Forrest Took Matters into His Own Hands at Ft. Donelson—and a Legend Was Born," *America's Civil War* 21, no. 6 (January 2009): 29, 35; John Rosenberger, "Nathan Bedford Forrest: Lessons from a Master of the Science and Art of Warfighting," *Cavalry & Armor Journal* 7, no. 4 (October 2016): 31, 32.

23. Andrew Ward, *River Run Red: The Fort Pillow Massacre in the American Civil War* (Viking Press, 2005), 142–43. Lovett, "The Negro's Civil War in Tennessee," 44. Lovett explains that Forrest also claimed that he thought of the captured troops as property, and he would not damage property; he would only "preserve and protect" these valuable interests. For information on the Paducah battle, see Ronald K. Huch, "Fort Pillow Massacre: The Aftermath of Paducah (1908–1984)," *Journal of the Illinois State Historical Society* 66, no. 1 (Spring 1973): 62–70.

24. Ward, *River Run Red,* 165, 178, 187, 189; Paul Ashdown and Edward Caudill, *The Myth of Nathan Bedford Forrest* (Rowman & Littlefield, 2005), 32. On refusal of the federal troops to surrender, see Kenneth Bancroft Moore, "Fort Pillow, Forrest, and the United States Colored Troops in 1864," *Tennessee Historical Quarterly* 54, no. 2 (Summer 1995): 113.

25. Ward, *River Run Red,* 192–93, 207–8. Eric William Sheppard was a contemporary Forrest biographer, and he is quoted by Ward as stating that the attack on Fort Pillow was "all for the best [because] inside its walls were the two breeds of men they hated most in life—the Tennessee Tories and the nigger dressed up as a soldier—the nigger fit for nothing but slavery—the nigger that had set white men all over America for four years at each other's throats." See also Ashdown and Caudill, *The Myth of Nathan Bedford Forrest,* 32, 37. Robert Browning, *Forrest: The Confederacy's Relentless Warrior* (Potomac Books, 2004), 56–7; Lovett, "The Negro's Civil War in Tennessee," 44. Lovett explains that out of the 262 Black soldiers at Fort Pillow, Forrest and his men killed 238.

26. John Cimprich, *Fort Pillow: A Civil War Massacre, and Public Memory* (Louisiana State University Press, 2005), 97–98, 101–2; For information about how many Black troops died at Fort Pillow, see John Cimprich and Robert C. Mainfort Jr., "The Fort Pillow Massacre: A Statistical Note," *Journal of American History* 76, no. 3 (December 1989): 837; Scales, *The Battles and Campaigns of Confederate General Nathan Bedford Forrest,* 263. While Scales acknowledges that Forrest's soldiers gunned down Union soldiers "out of hand" even as they tried to surrender, he dismisses the carnage at Fort Pillow by comparing it with other wars in which combatants committed atrocities.

27. Cimprich, *Fort Pillow,* 255–57, 258; Scales, *The Battles and Campaigns of Confederate General Nathan Bedford Forrest,* 444.

28. Claude G. Bowers, *The Tragic Era: The Revolution after Lincoln* (Riverside Press, 1929),

306; For information on the Reconstruction period in Tennessee and the actions of Brownlow that enraged ex-Confederates, see R. L. M'Donnold and R. L. McDonnold, "The Reconstruction Period in Tennessee," *American Historical Magazine* 1, no. 4 (October 1896): 314, 316–18.

29. Bowers, *The Tragic Era,* 307; H. Grady McWhiney and Francis B. Simkins, "The Ghostly Legend of the Ku Klux Klan," *Negro History Bulletin* 14, no. 5 (February 1951): 109. The authors lay out two personality types for the freed man back in the mythology of whites during the Reconstruction era. There was the "good darky" and the "bad 'Negro.'" The good darky was a person who acted subservient to his former masters and was always ready to entertain them with a song. He was also slow and superstitious. The "bad 'Negro'" was, in the minds of ex-Confederates, someone to be watched because he could not be trusted as his primary purpose in life was to "deflower" the white women of the South.

30. Winfield Jones, *Story of the Ku Klux Klan* (American Newspaper Syndicate, 1921), 15–16; M'Donnold and McDonnold, "The Reconstruction Period in Tennessee," 318. The entire article is a treatise on the supposed incompetence of northern and freedmen leadership; H. Grady McWhiney and Francis B. Simkins, "The Ghostly Legend of the Ku Klux Klan,"110.

31. Jones, *Story of the Ku Klux Klan,* 23–24. For more information on this supposed tyranny of the Republican Congress and "Negro" rule, see David Lowe, *Ku Klux Klan: The Invisible Empire* (Norton), 1967.

32. Allen W. Trelease, *White Terror: The Ku Klux Klan Conspiracy and Southern Reconstruction* (Louisiana State University Press, 1999), 10. Eric Foner supports Trelease's conclusions about the origins and purpose of the Klan. See Eric Foner, *Reconstruction: America's Unfinished Revolution 1863–1877* (Harper Perennial, 2014), 425–26; Richard Tucker, *"The Dragon and the Cross": The Rise and Fall of the Ku Klux Klan In Middle America* (Archon Books, 1991), 19; Elaine Frantz Parsons, "Midnight Rangers: Costume and Performance in the Reconstruction-Era Ku Klux Klan," *Journal of American History* 92, no. 3 (December 2005): 811. Parsons discusses how the founders of the Klan (James R. Crowe, Frank McCord, Calvin Jones) emphasized that in the early days of the organization the members liked to roam the streets to sing to their sweethearts while several of them played musical instruments.

33. M'Donnold and McDonnold, "The Reconstruction Period in Tennessee," 318; Robert Browning, *Forrest: The Confederacy's Relentless Warrior* (Potomac Books, 2004), 98.

34. Bowers, *The Tragic Era,* 310; Robert Selph Henry, *"First with the Most: Forrest"* (Bobbs-Merrill, 1944), 444, 446. On Forrest's Congressional testimony, see Ashdown and Caudill, *The Myth of Nathan Bedford Forrest,* 61–62. The congressional committee investigated the violent rampage of the Klan throughout the South. In the hearings Forrest was less than forthcoming about his role in the organization or its intentions; see M'Donnold and McDonnold, "The Reconstruction Period in Tennessee," 321. The authors state that "it was noticed that in localities where Klans existed there was a decided improvement in the behavior of the "Negroes" and of certain classes of whites who had been making themselves obnoxious."

35. Executive Document No. 1, Report of the Secretary of War, 40th Congress-House of Representatives, Chapter X, 193 (hereafter Executive Document No. 1); Cox, *Dixie's Daughters,* 37.

36. Executive Document No. 1, Chapter X, 193, 195–96.

37. Executive Document No. 1, Chapter X, 193, 195–96; M'Donnold and McDonnold, "The Reconstruction Period in Tennessee," 321; McWhiney and Simkins, "The Ghostly Legend of the Ku Klux Klan," 111.

38. Henry, *"First with the Most,"* 446; Ashdown and Caudill, *The Myth of Nathan Bedford Forrest,* 63; Trelease, *White Terror,* 180.

39. Ashdown and Caudill, *The Myth of Nathan Bedford Forrest,* 54, 63; Jack Hurst, *Nathan Bedford Forrest: A Biography* (Vintage, 1994), 379.

40. *The Forrest Monument,* 23–24; Gordon, *At the Dedication Ceremonies of the Forrest Monument,* 2–5. Although she is not mentioned in the Forrest dedication papers compiled by George Gordon, *UDC Magazine* honored Mrs. Thomas Jefferson Latham. In the November 1944 issue, the magazine publishers honored Mrs. Latham for her position as chair of the General Forrest Monument Association. See Janney, *Burying the Dead but Not the Past,* 15–38, 69–105. See also Domby, *The False Cause,* 15, where he states that white women were invested in lifting the profile of fallen soldiers and Confederate veterans. Winberry, "Lest We Forget," 24.

41. *The Forrest Monument,* 66, 68.

42. Gordon, *At the Dedication Ceremonies of the Forrest Monument,* 9–10, 52, 70; Hurst, *Nathan Bedford Forrest,* 8, 48, 52. Hurst argues that there was no discernable method to determine whether or not Forrest had anything to do with saving "Able" in a direct way. But he does believe that Forrest was among many in the crowd who gave an impassioned speech about the rule of law and its importance over mob rule. Hurst asserts that Forrest's actions in this incident raised his esteem among Memphians.

43. *The Forrest Monument,* 60; Domby, *The False Cause,* 9; Massey, "Confederate Revisionist History," 196. Massey argues that northerners became exhausted by trying to counteract the efforts of southern politicians to re-establish the antebellum racial hierarchy. The concept that became more important to northerners was reunion of the nation.

44. *The Forrest Monument,* 61–62.

45. *The Forrest Monument,* 72.

46. Blight, *Race and Reunion,* 2–3.

47. *The Forrest Monument,* 63.

48. Carney, "The Contested Image of Nathan Bedford Forrest," 602.

49. *The Forrest Monument,* 66, 68.

50. *The Forrest Monument,* 15.

51. *The Forrest Monument,* 15

52. Jody Stokes-Casey, "Richard Lou's Recovering Memphis: Conceptual Iconoclasm of the Nathan Bedford Forrest Monument," *Tennessee Historical Quarterly* 75, no. 4 (Winter 2016): 322. On the following page is a photograph of people roller skating through the park. This is an indication of how Lost Cause enthusiasts immersed Confederate symbols into the everyday life of Memphians.

53. *The Forrest Monument,* 78.

54. Winberry, "Lest We Forget," 20. Winberry argues that the meaning of a statue depends on the perspective of those who view the statue. See *The Forrest Monument: Its History & Dedication,* 15.

55. Glaze, "Saint and Sinner," 166–67, 169, 176–77, 180.

56. Shackel, *Memory in Black and White,* 11; Massey, "Confederate Revisionist History," 192.

57. Shackel, *Memory in Black and White,* 11; Winberry, "Lest We Forget," 20.

58. Cox, *Dixie's Daughters,* 60–61; Winberry, "Lest We Forget," 28.

59. Historiography on this time period is voluminous but contains gaps. See James Cobb, *The Most Southern Place on Earth: The Mississippi Delta and the Roots of Regional Identity* (Oxford University Press, 1992), 98–124. Cobb's discussion of the economic situation of African Americans relies heavily on white dominance, and very little on the powers that African Americans could utilize, such as moving or quitting, to improve their financial circumstances. See also Neil R. McMillen, *Dark Journey: Black Mississippians in the Age of Jim Crow* (University of Illinois Press), 1989, 4–5. While McMillen acknowledges that by the 1900s segregation was "irregular" (especially on the streetcars), he tends to focus on the laws that limited African American freedom and not necessarily their responses to those laws. See also Lamon, *Blacks in Tennessee,* 60–61; C. Vann Woodward, *The Strange Career of Jim Crow* (Oxford University Press, 1966), 82. Woodward dismisses African American agency during this time of great assaults on their freedom by stating that "the resistance of the "Negro" himself had long ceased to be an important deterrent to white aggression."

4. THE GREATEST PARTY IN THE SOUTH

1. Bond and Sherman, *Memphis in Black and White,* 106.

2. Roger Biles, "The Persistence of the Past: Memphis in the Great Depression," *Journal of Southern History* 52, no. 2 (May 1986): 185, 188.

3. Biles, "The Persistence of the Past," 185.

4. Larsen, *The Urban South,* 74, 82–85. The use of the term *progressive* in this paragraph only reflects Grady's desire to move the South beyond its agrarian past. See also Cash, *The Mind of the South,* x.

5. "Industrialism versus Agrarianism for the South," *The University Debater's Annual,* 1931–1928, 246.

6. Oliver Carson, "The Southern Worker Organizes," *The Nation,* September 26, 1934, 354; "Industrialism versus Agrarianism for the South," 246.

7. R. W. Henninger, "What the South Offers Industry," *Factory and Industrial Management* (April 1929): 716.

8. Henninger, "What the South Offers Industry," 715.

9. "Industrialism versus Agrarianism for the South," 246, 249, 248.

10. This is a bizarre argument. While agrarian proponents recognized the abusive nature of industry, they were uncomfortable with southern workers organizing to better their situation. They felt that unionization led to more federal government control.

11. "Industrialism versus Agrarianism for the South," 251, 241, 243, 235.

12. "Industrialism versus Agrarianism for the South," 251, 241, 243, 235.

13. Roger Biles, "The Persistence of the Past," 208; Jennifer Ritterhouse, *Discovering the South: One Man's Travels Through a Changing America in the 1930s* (University of North Carolina Press, 2017), 3, 6. For information on Walter White, see Edgar A. Toppin, "Walter White and the Atlanta NAACP's Fight for Equal Schools, 1916," *History of Education Quarterly* 7, no. 1 (Spring 1967): 15.

14.Biles, "The Persistence of the Past," 208.

15. Ritterhouse, *Discovering the South,* 3. See also Nell Irvin Painter, *Southern History Across the Color Line* (University of North Carolina Press, 2002), 112, 117–18. Painter points out that when white southerners used the term *social equality* they were really referring to miscegenation.

16. Michael Perman, *Pursuit of Unity: A Political History of the American South* (University of North Carolina Press, 2009), 231–33; Dewey W. Grantham, *The South in Modern America: A Region at Odds* (University of Arkansas Press, 2001), 120, 122.

17. Perman, *Pursuit of Unity,* 237, 239; Grantham, *The South in Modern America,* 125. Grantham points out that "the massive Democratic gains outside the South had drastically reduced the dependence of the national party on southern voters and . . . threatened the traditional power of southern leaders in Washington."

18. John Brueggemann, "Racial Considerations and Social Policy in the 1930s," *Social Science History* 26, no. 1 (Spring 2002): 144.

19. Jason Morgan Ward, "'The 'Negroes,' the New Deal, and . . . Karl Marx': Southern Anti-Statism in Depression and War," in *Nation Within a Nation: The American South and the Federal Government,* ed. Glenn Feldman (University of Florida, 2014), 102.

20. James Bealle, "Dixie Needs No Cotton Picker," *The Forum* (April 1937): 228.

21. Bealle, "Dixie Needs No Cotton Picker," 225.

22. Bond and Sherman, *Memphis in Black and White,* 110.

23. Biles, "The Persistence of the Past," 184.

24. Twelve Southerners, *I'll Take My Stand* (Harper & Brothers, 1930), ix–xx. In the introduction the authors lay out their principles. They conclude that industrialization is brutal, and every society should work to get rid of its evil influences.

25. Alva W. Taylor, "The Plight of the Southern Tenant," *Christian Century* 3 (April 1935): 428.

26. Taylor, "The Plight of the Southern Tenant," 428; The ten cotton states were North Carolina, South Carolina, Georgia, Alabama, Tennessee, Mississippi, Louisiana, Arkansas, Oklahoma, and Texas. See Peter Molyneaux, "The Second Civil War," *The Forum* (August 1934): 100.

27. Taylor, "The Plight of the Southern Tenant," 428; Molyneaux, "The Second Civil War," 100. Molyneaux suggests that even if there were no Depression the southern states would have to confront an economic transformation.

28. Ritterhouse, *Discovering the South,* 131.

29. Rodger Lyle Brown, *Ghost Dancing on the Cracker Circuit* (University Press of Mississippi, 1997), 192.

30. H. L. Mencken, "Uprising in the Confederacy," *American Mercury,* March 22, 1931, 379–81.

31. Brown, *Ghost Dancing on the Cracker Circuit,* 192; Mencken, "Uprising in the Confederacy," 379–81.

32. "Gaiety Prevails as King Cotton Takes Up Reign in Memphis," *CA,* May 12, 1932.

33. A. Irving Hallowell and Ralph Linton, "Nativistic Movements," *American Anthropologist* 45, no. 2 (1943): 231–32.

34. Hallowell and Linton, "Nativistic Movements," 233. The other subcategories are rational perpetuative (in which organizers attempt to create a sense of community within their chosen group), and magical nativistic (in which participants see their movement as messianic).

35. A. Arthur Halle, "History of the Memphis Cotton Carnival Association," unpublished essay, January 16, 1952, 3–4, 8, Memphis Room, Memphis & Shelby County Public Libraries, Memphis Room.

36. Halle, "History of the Memphis Cotton Carnival Association," 5–6.

37. Halle, "History of the Memphis Cotton Carnival Association," 1, 6.

38. Halle, "History of the Memphis Cotton Carnival Association," 1–2.

39. Halle, "History of the Memphis Cotton Carnival Association," 2–3.

40. Eda Clark Fain Jr., "'Cut Loose the Corset Strings of Dull Times': Attending Carnival in Memphis, Tennessee, through Newsprint Coverage, 1872–1901" (PhD diss., University of Memphis, 1999), 37, 307–8

41. Halle, "History of the Memphis Cotton Carnival Association," 3–4, 8.

42. Fain, "Cut Loose the Corset Strings," 37, 307–8; Halle, "History of the Memphis Cotton Carnival Association," 3–4, 8.

43. Bond and Sherman, *Memphis in Black and White,* 109.

44. Horace Gilmore, "Why I Like the South," *Publisher's Weekly,* February 8, 1930, 708–9; Bond and Sherman, *Memphis in Black and White,* 108; *CA,* May 12, 1932.

45. Halle, "History of the Memphis Cotton Carnival Association," 6.

46. "Memphis to Greet King Cotton at Noon," *CA,* March 2, 1931, 2; "King Cotton's Loyal Subjects Take City," *CA,* March 3, 1931.

47. Halle, "History of the Memphis Cotton Carnival Association," 10, 16; William McCaskill, "The National Cotton Show," 1935, 67; William McCaskill, "Memphis Cotton Carnival Association: Its Work and Plans," 1935, 77, 79; William McCaskill, "King Cotton in Memphis," 1936, 68, in A. Arthur Halle Collection, Memphis Room, Memphis & Shelby County Library.

48. "The Maid Gets Her Briefing," 1947, 169, 181, 199, 207, in A. Arthur Halle Collection.

49. McLean, "Cotton Carnival and Cotton Makers Jubilee," 87–89.

50. Larry Griffin, Ranae Evenson, and Ashley Thompson, "Southerners All?" *Southern Cultures* 11, no. 1 (Spring 2005): 7. This article analyzes the origin of the concept of "southern." The authors make the point that to refer to the South or to southern culture meant that the user meant white South or white southern culture.

51. "Feminine Beauty and Lore of 'Negro' Race Popular Themes in Carnival," *CA,* March 6, 1931.

52. Micki McElya, *Clinging to Mammy: The Faithful Slave in Twentieth-Century America* (Harvard University Press, 2007), 4.

53. Sen. Pat Harrison, "The Wages of Dixie," *Collier's,* January 1938, 46; "Memphis Makes War on CIO," *Christian Century,* October 13, 1937, 1273; R. C. Kennedy, W. Wilson, and H. Fuller, "The

Cotton Kingdom: 1931," *New Republic,* December 16, 1931, 133; Horace Mann Bond, "A 'Negro' Looks at His South," *Harper's,* June 1931, 38.

54. Mary Caputi, "National Identity in Contemporary Theory," *Political Psychology* 17, no. 4 (1996): 687, 689.

55. Kenneth W. Goings, *Mammy and Uncle Mose: Black Collectibles and American Stereotyping* (Indiana University Press, 1994), 20.

56. Nat D. Williams, "A Matter of Tactics," Folder 22A, 1969, Venson Collection; Nat D. Williams, "Battle for an Image," Folder 22, 1969, Venson Collection.

5. DEFINING BLACKNESS AND FEMININITY THROUGH THE COTTON MAKERS JUBILEE

1. M. G. Conover and L. Parrott, "Relief and the Color Line," *The Survey,* May 15, 1932, 204; Lauren Rebecca Sklaroff, *Black Culture and the New Deal: The Quest for Civil Rights in the Roosevelt Era* (University of North Carolina Press), 17.

2. R. Q. Venson, "The Memphis Cotton Makers Jubilee," Container 1, Folder 5, 1941, Venson Collection. This type of attitude was common across the South among the Black elite. See, for example, Karen Ferguson, *Black Politics in New Deal Atlanta* (University of North Carolina Press. 2002), 18.

3. "Negro Workers and the NRA," *Christian Century,* September 20, 1933, 1165; Patricia Sullivan, *Days of Hope: Race and Democracy in the New Deal Era* (University of North Carolina Press, 1996), 20–21, 44.

4. Jesse O. Thomas, "The Negro Industrialist: The Effect of Changing Economic Conditions upon the Living Standards of Negroes," *Proceedings of the National Conference of Social Work* (1928), 458, 461–62; "Negro Workers and the NRA," 1165; Michael Keith Honey, *Black Workers Remember: An Oral History of Segregation, Unionism, and the Freedom Struggle* (University of California Press, 1999), 43; Sullivan, *Days of Hope,* 44.

5. Toure F. Reed, *Not Alms but Opportunity: The Urban League and the Politics of Racial Uplift, 1910–1950* (University of North Carolina Press, 2008), 107; Ferguson, *Black Politics in New Deal Atlanta,* 167.

6. Douglas Smith, *The New Deal in the Urban South* (Louisiana State University Press, 1988), 232–35; Oliver Carlson, "The Southern Worker Organizes," *Labor and Industry,* September 1934, 354; Calvin White, *The Rise to Respectability: Race, Religion, and the Church of God in Christ* (University of Arkansas Press, 2012), 18.

7. Conover and Parrott, "Relief and the Color Line," 204. See also Honey, *Black Workers Remember,* 43. Memphis laborers, in their interviews with Honey for his book, repeatedly confirm the wage disparity between white and Black workers.

8. Conover and Parrott, "Relief and the Color Line," 204. See also Sklaroff, *Black Culture and the New Deal,* 17, 20.

9. Conover and Parrott, "Relief and the Color Line," 204. Conover was not alone in thinking this way. See Sullivan, *Days of Hope,* 20; Ferguson, *Black Politics in New Deal Atlanta,* 75.

10. Esther Morris Douty, "FERA and the Rural Negro," *The Survey,* July 1934, 215; John

Braeman and David Brody, eds., *The New Deal: The National Level* (Ohio State University Press, 1975), 124, 188–89, 222; Harry Hopkins, "Unemployment Relief and the Public Works Administration," *Proceedings of the Academy of Political Science* 15, no. 4 (January 1934): 81–83.

11. Douty, "FERA and the Rural Negro," 215–16.

12. Douty, "FERA and the Rural Negro," 215–16. For more information on landlords forcing their tenants off the land, see Biles, "The Persistence of the Past," 199.

13. Ferguson, *Black Politics in New Deal,* 73; Sullivan, *Days of Hope,* 43.

14. Douty, "FERA and the Rural Negro," 216.

15. Lisa Snowden-McCray et al., "110 Years: When We Fight, We Win," *Crisis* 126, no. 3 (Summer 2019): 25. See also Fern Gillespie, "Women Leaders Are Backbone of NAACP," *Crisis* 116, no. 3 (Summer 2009): 52; Gilbert Jonas, *Freedom's Sword: The NAACP and the Struggle Against Racism in America, 1909–1969* (Routledge, 2005), 2, 8; Manfred Berg, *The Ticket to Freedom: The NAACP and the Struggle for Black Political Integration* (University Press of Florida, 2005), 1, 12.

16. Smith, *The New Deal in the Urban South,* 256–57.

17. Mrs. Ethyl Venson, interview by Sanders Duke Williams, 3, Mississippi Valley Collection, McWherter Library, University of Memphis.

18. Venson, interview by Williams, 3.

19. Venson, interview by Williams, 8. By 1940, the jubilee directors thanked both the Black and white community for their participation. In a historical sketch printed in that year's program, the organizers thanked Groom Leftwich, who had been the president of the 1936 carnival. Mr. Leftwich helped the jubilee by getting floats for the effort as well as recognition of the jubilee from the Cotton Carnival organization. The program also mentioned a man named Henry Hazlip who provided the money for the cash prizes. See "The Memphis Cotton Makers Jubilee: A Historical Sketch," Container 1, Folder 4, 1940, Venson Collection.

20. Venson, interview by Williams, 8. For more information concerning the life and impact of Joseph Edison (J. E.) Walker on Memphis, see George Sewell and Margaret L. Dwight, *Mississippi Black History Makers* (University Press of Mississippi, 1984), 170–76. For additional information on Robert R. Church, see W. M. Brewer, "Robert R. Church," *Journal of Negro History* 38, no. 2 (1953): 249–51.

21. "Foreword," Folder 3, 1939, Venson Collection. The executive committee was made up of Dr. J. J. Raines, treasurer; Clifton Satterfield, secretary; Dr. R. Q. Venson, chairman; Prof. Nat D. Williams, publicity director; Prof. H. B. King, comptroller; and Eddie Hayes, vice chairman.

22. James Cobb, "Community and Identity: Redefining Southern Culture," *Georgia Review* 50, no. 1 (Spring 1996): 9; Sullivan, *Days of Hope,* 12.

23. "The Cotton Makers Jubilee: A Historical Sketch," Container 1, Folder 3, 1939, Venson Collection.

24. R. Q. Venson, "The Why What and How of the Memphis Cotton Makers' Jubilee," Container 1, Folder 8, 1949, Venson Collection.

25. "The Memphis Cotton Makers Jubilee," Container 1, Folder 5, 1941, Venson Collection.

26. "The Memphis Cotton Makers Jubilee," 1941.

27. Nat Williams, "The Jubilect," Container 1, Folder 5, 1941, Venson Collection.

28. Johnson Early Saulsberry, "How His Majesty and Her Royal Highness Is Selected," Container 1, Folder 15, 1958, Venson Collection.

29. Saulsberry, "How His Majesty and Her Royal Highness"; Johnson Saulsberry, "Their Majesties," Container 1, Folder 16, 1959, Venson Collection.

30. "The Cotton Makers Jubilee: A Historical Sketch," Container 1, Folder 3, 1939, Venson Collection.

31. "The Cotton Makers Jubilee Initiation and Aims," Container 1, Folder 1, 1937, Venson Collection.

32. "The Cotton Makers Jubilee: A Historical Sketch," Container 1, Folder 4, 1940, Venson Collection.

33. Kevin Gaines, "Assimilationist Minstrelsy as Racial Uplift Ideology: James D. Corrother's Literary Quest for Black Leadership," *American Quarterly* 45 (September 1993): 342, 344. Racial uplift was an African American middle-class plan of attack developed to combat the increasingly visceral racism Blacks faced in popular culture. Middle-class and elite Blacks believed that if they highlighted class differences within the race, they could demonstrate to white Americans that they were better and deserved appropriate treatment. It was a two-phase approach to end racism. Once elevated, the Black middle class could improve their status and that of others by uplifting the less-privileged classes of African Americans.

34. "Atlanta Exposition Address," in *Let Nobody Turn Us Around,* 184.

35. "Atlanta Exposition Address," in *Let Nobody Turn Us Around,* 185. See Gilbert Jonas, *Freedom's Sword: The NAACP and the Struggle Against Racism in America, 1909–1969* (Routledge, 2005), 9; Corey Seaton, "'W. E. B. Du Bois & Booker T. Washington: Approaches to Developing Citizenship Post-Reconstruction in the America,'" *Kola* 26, no. 1 (Spring 2014): 52–53.

36. Frazier, *The Black Bourgeoisie,* 72, 75, 77.

37. "Atlanta Exposition Address," in *Let Nobody Turn Us Around,* 187. W. E. B Du Bois, and Eugene F. Provenzo, *Illustrated Souls of Black Folk* (Routledge, 2015), 62; Frazier, *The Black Bourgeoisie,* 76.

38. "Atlanta Exposition Address," in *Let Nobody Turn Us Around,* 188.

39. Kevin Gaines, *Uplifting the Race: Black Leadership, Politics, and Culture in the Twentieth Century* (University of North Carolina Press, 1996), 40. See also Theodore Lewis, "Booker T. Washington's Audacious Vocationalist Philosophy." *Oxford Review of Education* 40, no. 2 (April 2014): 193–94.

40. R. Q. Venson, "The Memphis Cotton Makers Jubilee," Container 1, Folder 5, 1941, Venson Collection.

41. Venson, "The Memphis Cotton Makers Jubilee."

42. Venson, "The Memphis Cotton Makers Jubilee.

43. Venson, "The Memphis Cotton Makers Jubilee."

44. Ethyl Venson, "Digest of the Memphis Cotton Makers Jubilee," Container 1, Folder 9, 1951, Venson Collection.

45. Washington, "The Fruits of Industrial Training," in *Let Nobody Turn Us Around,* 194.

46. Nat Williams, "History of Jubilee," Container 1, Folder 7, 1948, Venson Collection.

47. Clifton Satterfield, untitled essay, Container 1, Folder 8, 1949, Venson Collection.

48. Williams, "Historical Resume."

49. Venson, interview by Williams, 7.

50. Venson, interview by Williams, 12.

51. Venson, interview by Williams, 12.

52. Venson, interview by Williams, 13.

53. Venson, interview by Williams, 13; "The Cotton Makers Jubilee Initiation and Aims."

54. George W. Lee, "Cabin in the Cotton," Container 1, Folder 8, 1948, Venson Collection. For more information on Black southerners claiming a piece of southern culture and their regional identity, see Cobb, "Community and Identity," 12.

55. Lee, "Cabin in the Cotton."

56. Lee, "Cabin in the Cotton."

57. Lee, "Cabin in the Cotton."

58. "ZoZo Club," Container 1, Folder 15, 1958, Venson Collection.

59. Cobb, "Community and Identity: Redefining Southern Culture," 18.

60. Erma Clanton, "Melrose High School ZoZo Club," Container 1, Folder 14, 1957, Venson Collection; Ethyl Venson, "Juvenile Activities," Container 1, Folder 8, 1949, Venson Collection.

61. Venson, "Juvenile Activities."

62. Lee, "Cabin in the Cotton"; Venson, "Juvenile Activities."

63. Venson, "Juvenile Activities"; Clanton, "Melrose High School ZoZo Club"; Venson, "Digest of the Memphis Cotton Makers Jubilee"; Ethyl Venson, "The Juvenile Royalty," Container 1, Folder 23, 1970, Venson Collection.

64. Ethyl Venson, "A Statement on 'Spirit of Cotton' Program," Container 1, Folder 10, 1952, Venson Collection.

65. Nat Williams, "The Jubilect," Container 1, Folder 8, 1949, Venson Collection; Nat Williams, "The Jubilee's Jubilect," Container 1, Folder 10, 1952, Venson Collection; Venson, "A Statement on 'Spirit of Cotton' Program." The Spirit of Cotton presented a direct contrast to the images of the fat and happy Black women who performed the role of mammies during the Cotton Carnival; see Jeanine Weekes Schroer, "The Terrifying Tale of the Philosophical Mammy," *Black Scholar* 43, no. 4 (Winter 2013): 101–7. Black women would have to struggle against the many negative stereotypes ascribed to their sexuality, femininity, and role in their families. See Melissa Harris-Perry, *Sister Citizen: Shame, Stereotypes, and Black Women in America* (Yale University Press, 2011), 5, 59. Harris-Perry offers an uncompromising critique of how white and Black Americans have internalized and accepted many of these images of Black women as hypersexual while at the same time these same women did what they could to defend themselves against these assaults. See also McElya, *Clinging to Mammy,* 11; K. Sue Jewell, *From Mammy to Miss America and Beyond: Cultural Images and the Shaping of US Social Policy,* Vol. Taylor & Francis e-Library ed. (Routledge, 2002), chap. 3.

66. Venson, "A Statement on 'Spirit of Cotton' Program."

67. Venson, "A Statement on 'Spirit of Cotton' Program"; Painter, *Southern History Across the Color Line,* 118, 128.

68. Jewell, *From Mammy to Miss America and Beyond,* chap. 3; Speculations about the lascivious nature of Black women reach far back to the first contact Europeans had with Africans. See Winthrop Jordan, *White over Black: American Attitudes Toward the Negro, 1550–1812* (University of North Carolina Press, 1968), 30–31. For a deeper understanding of the stereotypes that haunted Black women from slavery through the twenty-first century, see White, *Ar'n't I a Woman?,* 27–62, 176; Giddings, *When and Where I Enter,* 31, 43, 95.

69. Press release, Folder 10, 1952, Venson Collection.

70. M. N. Conley, "The Spirit of Cotton," Folder 9, 1951, Venson Collection.

71. Press release; Conley, "The Spirit of Cotton" (1951).

72. "The Spirit of Cotton," Container 1, Folder 7, 1948, Venson Collection,

73. "The Spirit of Cotton" (1948).

74. "The Spirit of Cotton," Container 1, Folder 7, 1949, Venson Collection.

75. "Presidents' Evaluations of 'Spirit of Cotton Makers Jubilee,'" Container 1, Folder 13, 1956, Venson Collection.

76. "Presidents' Evaluations of 'Spirit of Cotton Makers Jubilee.'"

77. Anna Julia Cooper quoted in Mullane, *Crossing the Danger Water,* 409.

78. Jewell, *From Mammy to Miss America and Beyond,* 8–9; Patricia Morton, *Disfigured Images: The Historical Assault on Afro-American Women* (Praeger Publishers, 1991), 31.

79. Deborah Gray White, *Too Heavy a Load: Black Women in Defense of Themselves, 1894–1994* (Norton, 1999), 89.

80. R. A. Lawson, *Jim Crow's Counterculture: The Blues and Black Southerners, 1890–1945* (Louisiana State University Press, 2010), 18–19, 29; White, *Too Heavy a Load,* 128–30.

81. Morton, *Disfigured Images,* 32, 36.

82. Jewell, *From Mammy to Miss America and Beyond,* 10, 17, 36–37, 39, 42; Morton, *Disfigured Images,* 32, 36.

83. "The Spirit of Cotton" (1952).

84. William B. Gravely, "The Dialectic of Double-Consciousness in Black American Freedom Celebrations, 1808–1863," *Journal of Negro History* 67, no. 4 (Winter 1982): 302–4, 306.

6. BATTLE FOR A NARRATIVE

1. *Tri-State Defender* (Memphis), May 6, 1961; Frank Scott, "The 1961 Jubilee & King Cotton in a Changing World," Container 1, Folder 17, 1961, Venson Collection. This debate is covered at length later in this chapter.

2. Garrett Felber, *Those Who Know Don't Say: The Nation of Islam, the Black Freedom Movement, and the Carceral State* (University of North Carolina Press, 2020), 7. Felber makes an important point that Americans' opinions concerning Black nationalism and Black Muslims were based on a documentary, *The Hate That Hate Produced,* featuring narration by Mike Wallace and interviews by Louis Lomax and produced in 1959 by CBS. Felber argues that Wallace

and Lomax treated the organization as the equivalent of the Ku Klux Klan. He further concludes that the coverage of the Nation of Islam by media outlets did not focus on their desire for self-determination, but instead the coverage led to the popularization of terms like "black supremacy" and "reverse racism" (35–36).

3. Felber, *Those Who Know Don't Say,* 38.

4. Jeffrey O. G. Ogbar, *Black Power: Radical Politics and African American Identity* (Johns Hopkins University Press, 2019), 3.

5. Felber, *Those Who Know Don't Say,* 3, 112–13.

6. Jason E. Shelton and Michael Emerson, "Extending the Debate over Nationalism Versus Integration: How Cultural Commitments and Assimilation Trajectories Influence Beliefs About Black Power," *Journal of African American Studies* 13, no. 4 (December 2009): 332.

7. Darren Davis and Ronald Brown, "The Antipathy of Black Nationalism: Behavioral and Attitudinal Implications of an African American Ideology," *American Journal of Political Science* 46, no. 2 (April 2002): 239–40.

8. Davis and Brown, "The Antipathy of Black Nationalism," 240; Scott, "The 1961 Jubilee & King Cotton." Assessing the role of the jubilee in the struggle for equality is a bit tricky. On the one hand, the jubilee represented Black self-determination, and the organizer's ideals aligned with the nationalist community. On the other hand, many of the goals of the jubilee organizers for fair and equitable treatment in Memphis society did not differ much from those of the pro-desegregation organizations.

9. Felber, *Those Who Know Don't Say,* 38; Ogbar, *Black Power,* 125.

10. Editorial, *Tri-State Defender* (Memphis), May 6, 1961.

11. Editorial, *Tri-State Defender* (Memphis), May 6, 1961.

12. Walker, "Turner Testimonial Speaker Says Negroes Soon Will Be 'Fully Integrated,'" *Tri-State Defender,* May 20, 1961.

13. "NAACP Plans Gigantic 'Town March,'" *Tri-State Defender* (Memphis), June 10, 1961; "NAACP Urges No 'Cool Off" for Freedom Riders," *Tri-State Defender* (Memphis), June 3, 1961; "Negroes Make Impressive Protest March," *Tri-State Defender* (Memphis), June 17, 1961; "NAACP Plans a 'March a Week' Protest of Bias," *Tri-State Defender* (Memphis), June 24, 1961; "Another Freedom March for Thursday Night," *Tri-State Defender* (Memphis), July 1, 1961; "In The Proper Manner," *Tri-State Defender* (Memphis), May 6, 1961; Walker, "Turner Testimonial Speaker Says."

14. "Hot Letter Sent: Asks Revision of Policies," *Tri-State Defender,* March 11–17, 1961.

15. Scott, "The 1961 Jubilee & King Cotton in a Changing World."

16. Clifton Satterfield, "Retrospection," Folder 17, 1961, Venson Collection; Clifton Satterfield, "A Chartered Course in Pursuit of Destiny," Container 1, Folder 17, 1961, Venson Collection.

17. Satterfield, "Retrospection"; Satterfield, "A Chartered Course." See also Laurie B. Green, *Battling the Plantation Mentality: Memphis and the Black Freedom Struggle* (University of North Carolina Press), 4, 7. Green argues that one way in which Black people fought the dominance of white society was to "assert views of themselves that countered racist thought." The Cotton Makers Jubilee was definitely a step in that direction.

18. Nat Williams, "The Cotton Makers' Jubilee: 'A Step Forwards or Backwards,'" Container 1, Folder 18, 1962, Venson Collection.

19. Williams, "The Cotton Makers' Jubilee."

20. Williams, "The Cotton Makers' Jubilee." See also Ogbar, *Black Power,* 136. Outreach to the youth of the community was very important as Black nationalism became a seductive philosophy in a post–civil rights America (146).

21. Nat Williams, editorial, *Tri-State Defender* (Memphis), May 20, 1961.

22. Editorial, *Tri-State Defender* (Memphis), June 3, 1961.

23. Editorial, *Tri-State Defender* (Memphis), May 27, 1961; Nat Williams, "A Matter of Tactics," Container 1, Folder 22, 1969, Venson Collection. See also Ogbar, *Black Power,* 149–50.

24. "Merits, Future of Cotton Makers Jubilee Aired by Ministerial Group," *Tri-State Defender,* June 24, 1961.

25. Benjamin Muse, "Memphis," in John Willard Brister Library Monograph Series 2, Container 9, Folder 67, 1964, The 1968 Sanitation Workers Strike, Memphis Multimedia Archival Project, 18–20. Muse reprinted the MCCR mission statement.

26. Muse, "Memphis."

27. Muse, "Memphis," 7–8, 11.

28. Anne Trotter, "The Memphis Business Community and Integration," 286–87; Muse, "Memphis," 25.

29. Trotter, "The Memphis Business Community and Integration," 286–87; Muse, "Memphis," 25.

30. Trotter, "The Memphis Business Community and Integration," 289. Future Memphis was an organization that sought out the future leaders of the city and trained them to be part of the business community and of the government as well.

31. Gerald M. Capers, *The Biography of a River Town* (University of North Carolina Press, 1939), 207; Lovett, *The Civil Rights Movement in Tennessee,* 108. See also Trotter, "The Memphis Business Community," 284.

32. Trotter, "The Memphis Business Community and Integration," 288.

33. Williams, "The Cotton Makers' Jubilee."

34. Venson, interview by Williams, 7; In the 1966 program Nat Williams also discussed the difficulties the Vensons faced when they attempted to organize the Black community. See Nat Williams, "Marching Through, with, for, and on . . .," Container 1, Folder 21, 1966, Venson Collection.

35. Williams, "Marching Through, with, for, and on. . . ."

36. Satterfield, "We Sing America with a Big 'A,'" Container 1, Folder 22, 1967, Venson Collection. For more on the relationship between civil rights and the Vietnam War, see Gregg L. Michel, "Surveilling the Memphis Movement: Police Spying in Memphis, 1968–1976," *Journal of Southern History* 87, no. 4 (November 2021): 676, 687, 702. The police and the press worked hand in hand to promote the fear of these groups (anti-war and/or pro–civil rights) and to discourage any Memphian from participating in any of their activities. Satterfield's comments speak directly to the rejection of what he considered to be anti-democratic radicals.

37. Michael Honey, *Going Down Jericho Road: The Memphis Strike, Martin Luther King's*

Last Campaign (Norton, 2007), 223–24; J. Edwin Stanfield, "In Memphis: More Than a Garbage Strike," 1–2, 25, in John Willard Brister Library Monograph Series 2, Container 9, Folder 67, 1964, The 1968 Sanitation Workers Strike, Memphis Multimedia Archival Project, March 22, 1968.

38. Honey, *Going Down Jericho Road,* 223–24.

39. Stanfield, "In Memphis," 3–4, 6; Lawson headed the Ministers Alliance and had directed the marches over the previous several weeks. See Sharon D. Wright, *Race, Power, and Political Emergence in Memphis* (Garland Publishing, 2000), 68–70; Honey, *Going Down Jericho Road;* Taylor Branch, *The King Years: Historic Moments in the Civil Rights Movement* (Simon & Schuster, 1988), 173–74.

40. Honey, *Going Down Jericho Road,* 298; Lovett, *The Civil Rights Movement in Tennessee,* 217, 219. For King's assessment of poverty and the disfranchised in the United States, see Martin Luther King Jr., "The Other America," Stanford University, April 14, 1967; for the organizing principles behind the Poor People's Campaign, see Martin Luther King Jr, Statement, Southern Christian Leadership Conference, December 4, 1967.

41. Pat Watters and J. Edwin Stanfield, "In Memphis: One Year Later," Southern Regional Council in Cooperation with the Tennessee Council on Human Relations, April 4, 1969, 9–10, in Maxine Smith unpublished collection, Memphis & Shelby County Archives.

42. Williams, "A Matter of Tactics."

43. Joanna Schneider Zangrando and Robert L. Zangrando, "Black Protest: A Rejection of the American Dream," *Journal of Black Studies* 1 (December 1970): 142, 150; Davis and Brown, "The Antipathy of Black Nationalism," 239, 241, 247. In this article Brown and Davis define Black Nationalism as the antithesis to Black reformist movements, such as those represented by the National Association for the Advancement of Colored People. See also J. Herman Blake, "Black Nationalism," *Annals of the American Academy of Political and Social Science* 382 (March 1969): 16–17. Herman argues that Black Nationalism is the result of the "duality of experience," further cultural nationalism grew out Black Americans' desire to create a sense of race pride and solidarity. See also August Meier and John H. Bracey, "The NAACP As a Reform Movement, 1909–1965: To Reach the Conscience of America," *Journal of Southern History* 59 (February 1993): 3.

44. R. Q. Venson, "King Cotton Moves Forward," Container 1, Folder 20, 1965, Venson Collection.

45. Venson, "King Cotton Moves Forward"; Nat Williams, "The Jubilee's Changing Image," Container 1, Folder 20, 1965, Venson Collection.

46. Williams, "The Jubilee's Changing Image."

47. Williams, "The Jubilee's Changing Image."

48. R. Q. Venson, "Where Do We Go from Here?," Container 1, Folder 23, 1970, Venson Collection. For Williams's assessment of African Americans' role in the Cotton Carnival as opposed to their role in the Cotton Makers Jubilee, see "Traditions or Not," Container 1, Folder 17, 1961, Venson Collection; "The Jubilee's Changing Image"; "Marching Through, with, for, and on . . .," Venson Collection; "Battle for an Image," Container 1, Folder 22, 1967, Venson Collection; "A Matter of Tactics."

49. Frank Scott, "Where Do We Go from Here?," Container 1, Folder 23, 1970, Venson Collection.

50. Williams, "The Jubilee's Changing Image"; Venson, "Where Do We Go from Here."

51. Cornel West, "The Paradox of the Afro-American Rebellion," *Social Text,* no. 9/10 (1984): 44.

52. West, "The Paradox of the Afro-American Rebellion," 44, 47.

53. Marianne Hirsch and Valerie Smith, "Feminism and Cultural Memory: An Introduction," *Signs: Journal of Women and Society* 28, no. 1 (Autumn 2002): 12; Michael Twitty, "The Persistence of Memory," *Journal of Negro History* 85 (Summer 2000): 179.

54. "Black Groups Join Cotton Carnival"; "Cotton Carnival Brings Communities Together," Clippings File: Cotton Makers Jubilee, Memphis & Shelby County Libraries.

55. "Dilemma Takes Root on Path Carved by Jubilee Tradition," Clippings File: Cotton Makers Jubilee, Memphis & Shelby County Libraries.

56. "Carnival Re-Invents Its Image: Big Party Continues but Bows to Changing Times," *CA,* June 4, 2006; Pamela Perkins, "Ball and Parade on Slate for 65th Jubilee," *CA,* May 3, 2001, B3.

7. A SHRINE OF HEALING

1. Watters and Stanfield, "In Memphis: One Year Later," 20–21, 24–25.

2. Watters and Stanfield, "In Memphis: One Year Later," 20–21, 26.

3. Roger Biles, "A Bittersweet Victory: Public School Desegregation in Memphis," *Journal of Negro Education* 55 (Autumn 1986): 471, 475.

4. Biles, "A Bittersweet Victory," 475–76.

5. Biles, "A Bittersweet Victory," 481; "After Five Years of Memphis Busing Desegregation Debate Rolls On," *Press-Scimitar* (Memphis), January 24, 1978.

6. Thomas A. Johnson, "3 Years After King Assassination, Many Memphis Blacks Are Discouraged," *New York Times,* April 4, 1971.

7. Clippings File: Isaac Richmond, Memphis Room, Memphis & Shelby County Library.

8. Marlene Davis, "Splinter Group from National CORE Faces Court Fight Over Its Name," *Press-Scimitar* (Memphis), May 18, 1983, Clippings File: Isaac Richmond. The article reports that Richmond threatened the owner of a Super-Save store with an economic boycott unless the owner bought ad space in Richmond's newspaper, the *Afro-American Voice.* The owner refused and reported this activity to the CORE national office; Richmond was reprimanded with suspension from the organization.

9. Davis, "Splinter Group from National CORE Faces Court Fight over Its Name."

10. "Chandler Campaign Drops Bid for List of Non-Voting Whites," *CA,* October 18, 1979.

11. "Chandler Campaign Drops Bid for List of Non-Voting Whites."

12. "Cross Burning Draws City Council's Anger," *CA,* November 14, 1979.

13. "Busy Polls Predicted for Mayoral Contest," *CA,* November 15, 1979.

14. "The Klan: Latest Warning Rattle May Bring Deadly Sting," *CA,* October 21, 1979.

15. Quotation from James Venable, "He Summons KKK Ghosts to Assemble," *CA,* Oc-

tober 22, 1979; quotation from David Duke, "Wizard Pushes New Image in Media Talks," *CA*, October 23, 1979; quotation from Mack Bowles *CA*, October 23, 1979; "This Klan Chieftain Still Believes Guns, Knives Relay Right Image," *CA*, October 25, 1979.

16. "This Klan Chieftain Still Believes Guns, Knives Relay Right Image"; "Some Police Sympathies Lay with Klan," *CA*, October 26, 1979.

17. Peter de Selding, *Commercial Appeal* series on the Klan, *CA*, October 21–27, 1979. Furthermore, on Saturday November 3, 1979, in Greensboro, North Carolina, demonstrators participated in an anti–Ku Klux Klan rally. Klan members showed up and opened fire on the crowd, killing four people and wounding ten more. Eventually, a jury found the perpetrators not guilty, and they never faced punishment for their actions.

18. Letter, Ralph Green to Mayor Wyeth Chandler, November 23, 1979; letter, Dean Allen Sr. to Mayor Wyeth Chandler, November 27, 1979; letter, Lucille Landry to Mayor Wyeth Chandler, November 5, 1979; Memphis Room, Central Location, Memphis & Shelby County Libraries. This is an unprocessed collection.

19. Letter, Jack R. Balch to Mayor Wyeth Chandler, December 26, 1979, Memphis Room, Central Location, Memphis & Shelby County Libraries.

20. Letter, Calvin Queen to Mayor Wyeth Chandler, November 5, 1979, Memphis Room, Central Location, Memphis & Shelby County Libraries.

21. Clippings File: Forrest Statue, Memphis Room, Memphis & Shelby County Library.

22. Clippings File: Forrest Statue.

23. Clippings File: Forrest Statue.

24. Letter, Edward Boling to Maxine Smith, May 17, 1988, Container 7, Folder 41, Maxine Smith Collection, Memphis & Shelby County Archives. Maxine Smith was president of the local chapter of the NAACP. She was a force in local politics, and she proved to be controversial in the city of Memphis as she pushed for civil rights for African Americans.

25. Letter, Maxine Smith to Sam Cooper, July 28, 1988, Maxine Smith Collection, Container 7, Folder 41.

26. Letter, Ralph Green to Mayor Wyeth Chandler, November 23, 1979; letter, Dean Allen Sr. to Mayor Wyeth Chandler, November 27 1979; letter, Lucille Landry to Mayor Wyeth Chandler, November 5, 1979; letter, Jack R. Balch to Mayor Wyeth Chandler, December 26, 1979; Letters to the Editor, May 24, 1988, Box 7, Folder 41, Maxine Smith Collection.

27. Richard Fuchs, *An Unerring Fire: The Massacre at Fort Pillow* (Stackpole, 2002), 32.

28. Fuchs, *An Unerring Fire*, 23–24. See also Litwack, *Been in the Storm So Long*, 90–93. Litwack points out that African Americans were outraged by the occurrences at Fort Pillow. However, Nathan Bedford Forrest just referred to Fort Pillow as "that place on the Mississippi River, 'dyed with the blood of the slaughtered' where his troops had conclusively demonstrated 'to the northern people that Negro soldiers can not cope with Southerners'" (91). Forrest acknowledges with this quote that there was massive bloodshed at Fort Pillow as well as a desire by his men to prove a point about African Americans in the military.

29. Robert Corlew, *Tennessee: A Short History*, 2nd ed. (University of Tennessee Press, 1981), 337–39. It is still not clear from the historical record how or even if Forrest disbanded

the group. This may just be a myth passed down from one generation of Confederates to the next and has just been accepted as fact by neo-Confederates.

30. Lee Meriwether, "My Mother," in Meriwether, *Recollections of 92 Years.* The one-page essay appears at the very beginning of the book.

31. Editorial, *CA,* June 27, 1999.

32. Letters to the Editor, *CA,* May 15, 1988; anonymous to Maxine Smith, May 24, 1988, Box 7, Folder 41, Maxine Smith Collection.

33. "Journey to Forrest Statue Bold Step to Wholeness," *CA,* June 20, 1999.

34. Editorial page, *CA,* June 27, 1999.

35. Barsalou and Baxter, Report.

EPILOGUE

1. *The Rachel Maddow Show,* hosted by Rachel Maddow, June 17, 2015.

2. Blain Roberts, "Uncovering the Confederacy of the Mind: Or, How I Became a Belle of the Ball in Denmark Vesey's Church," *Southern Cultures* 19, no. 3 (2013): 7, 9.

3. Adam Gabbatt, "Golden Escalator Ride: The Surreal Day Trump Kicked Off His Bid for President," *The Guardian,* June 19, 2019.

4. *Time,* June 16, 2015; US Bureau of Labor Statistics, "Unemployment Rate Falls from May to June 2015," July 7, 2015, bls.gov/opub/ted/2015/unemployment-rate-falls-from-may-to-june-2015.htm.

5. Hilde Restad, "Donald Trump's Calls to 'Make America Great Again' Show That American Exceptionalism Is Still a Powerful Idea," LSE (blog), *American Politics and Policy,* 2016. For more information and a comprehensive definition of American exceptionalism as it plays out on the world stage, see Hilde Eliassen Restad, "Old Paradigms in History Die Hard in Political Science: US Foreign Policy and American Exceptionalism," *American Political Thought* 1, no. 1 (2012): 54–55; Richard Gamble, "The Vanity of American Exceptionalism," *Reason,* September 19, 2013, https://reason.com/2013/09/19/the-vanity-of-american-exceptionalism/; Charles Murray, *Coming Apart: The State of White America, 1960–2010* (Crown Forum, 2012), 382, 401.

6. Restad, "Donald Trump's Calls"; Eli Saslow, *Rising Out of Hatred: The Awakening of a Former White Nationalist* (New York: Doubleday, 2018), 251.

7. Nikole Hannah-Jones, Public Address, Knight Center Charlotte, North Carolina, 11 July 2024.

8. Carney, *Reckoning with the Devil,* 154.

9. Nikole Hannah-Jones, "The 'Colorblindness' Trap: How a Civil Rights Ideal Got Hijacked," *New York Times* March 13, 2024.

10. Nicole Maurantonio, *Confederate Exceptionalism: Civil War Myth and Memory in the Twenty-First Century* (University Press of Kansas, 2019), 2, 8. Also, readers should think back to the chapter concerning the dedication ceremonies of Lee and Forrest. These ceremonies stressed American values like independence and honor. They focused on these men as heroes who embodied the principals of individualism.

11. Tonya Maxwell, "Witness in Dylann Roof Trial: 'I was just waiting my turn,'" *Citizen Times,* December 7, 2016, accessible at www.citizen-times.com.

12. Matt Lavietes, "Ex-KKK Leader's Child Comes Out as Transgender in New Memoir," NBC News, May 24, 2024, accessible at www.nbcnews.com/.

13. R. Derek Black, *The Klansman's Son: My Journey from White Nationalism to Antiracism: A Memoir* (New York: Abrams Books, 2024), chap. 1.

14. Black, *The Klansman's Son,* chap. 1.

15. Herb Jackson, "As Donald Trump Defends Confederate Statues, Cory Booker Wants Them Removed from Capitol," *Home News Tribune,* August 18, 2017, A3; Eric Foner, "Confederate History and 'Our' History: Commentary," *New York Times,* August 2, 2017, A25.

16. Black, *The Klansman's Son,* chap. 14.

17. "South Carolina Pays Respects to Slain Pinckney," *Post and Courier* (Charleston), June 23, 2015.

18. Jennifer Berry Hawes, "'On My Watch': Grieving Governor Forever Changed by Church Massacre," *Post and Courier* (Charleston), July 19, 2015, 1.

19. Hawes, "On My Watch," 1.

20. For information on the raising of the flag, see James Clyburn, *Blessed Experiences: Genuinely Southern, Proudly Black* (University of South Carolina Press, 2014), 147. Clyburn's book has a chapter entitled "The Confederate Battle Flag," 147–60. See also "Confederate Flag Timeline," *Charleston Post and Courier* (Charleston), July 11, 2015; Gerald R. Webster and Jonathan I. Leib, "What Would Robert E. Lee Do? Race, Religion, and the Debate over the Confederate Battle Flag in the American South," in *Faith and Race in American Political Life,* ed. Robin Dale Jacobson and Nancy D. Wadsworth (University of Virginia Press, 2012), 105. Authors in the latter book provide more information on the many iterations and complications that led to the starry cross.

21. Clyburn, *Blessed Experiences,* 147; Robert Behre, "Heritage Act Isn't Likely to Go the Way of the Confederate Flag," *Post and Courier* (Charleston), July 19, 2015, 3; Charles Joyner and Evan A. Kutzler, "Furling That Banner: The Rise and Fall of the Confederate Flag in South Carolina, 1961–2000," In *Citizen-Scholar: Essays in Honor of Walter Edgar,* ed. Robert H. Brinkmeyer (University of South Carolina Press, 2016), 22.

22. Cynthia Kropf, "Pitched Battle: How Democrats Lost, and Then Regained, the Needed Votes to Lower the Confederate Flag," *Post and Courier* (Charleston), July 10, 2015; Cynthia Roldan and Deanna Pan, "Haley Signs Bill That Removes Confederate Flag," *Post and Courier* (Charleston), July 10, 2015, 6; Behre," Heritage Act Isn't Likely to Go," 3.

23. "Confederate Flag Timeline."

24. Bryan Armen Graham, "Mississippi Lawmakers Vote to Remove Confederate Emblem from State Flag," *The Guardian,* June 28, 2020; Luke Ramseth, "Mississippi State Flag with Confederate Battle Symbol Will Be Replaced with Magnolia Design," *Clarion Ledger* (Mississippi), November 4, 2020.

25. "The 9:01: Movement Against Confederate Monuments," *CA,* July 22, 2017, A3.

26. Joel Ebert, "Tennessee House Votes for Heritage Protection Law," *The Tennessean,* February 18, 2016.

27. Ryan Poe, "Activists: We Can't Wait for a Waiver—Group Says City's Confederate Statues Need to Go by MLK50," *CA*, August 17, 2017, A3; Ryan Poe, "Forrest Statue Removal Hearing Delayed—Tennessee Historical Commission May Not Vote Until February 2018," *CA*, September 29, 2017, A12.

28. Ryan Poe, "How the Confederate Statues Came Down," *CA*, December 29, 2017, A8.

29. Poe, "How the Confederate Statues Came Down."

30. F. Sheffield Hale, "Finding Meaning in Monuments: Atlanta History Center Enters Dialogue on Confederate Symbols," *History News* 71, no. 4 (Autumn 2016): 21–23.

31. Newson, "Epistemological Crises Made Stone," 135.

32. For Savage's suggestion, see Labode and Levin, "Reconsideration of Memorials and Monuments," 7–11. See also Newson, "Epistemological Crises Made Stone," 137.

33. Newson, "Epistemological Crises Made Stone," 137–38; Hale, "Finding Meaning in Monuments," 21–23, 20.

34. Micaela A. Watts, "Nathan Bedford Forrest Descendants Sue Memphis, Demand Return of Equestrian Statue," *CA*, December 18, 2018.

35. Paul Duggan, "Mississippi Flag Voters Defend 'Heritage': 'I Don't Know if the Civil War Will Ever Be Over for Us,'" *Pittsburgh Post-Gazette*, April 19, 2001, A13.

36. Philip Altizer, letters to the editor, "Time to Forgive, Honor the Penitent Forrest," *CA*, January 21, 2018.

37. Thompson Mayes, "Why Old Places Matter," *History News* 71, no. 3 (2016): 20; Jim Williams, letter to the editor, "Preserving Good, Bad, Ugly Past," *CA*, November 7, 2017.

38. Franklin Forts, "Living with Confederate Symbols," *Southern Cultures* 8, no. 1 (2002): 66, 68.

39. Heyse, "The Rhetoric of Memory-Making," 408.

40. Heyse, "The Rhetoric of Memory-Making," 409. These statues embody the collective memories built by the shared myths of southerners. Heyes defines collective memories as those that are constructed by citizens and municipalities across the South that speak to where the community has been, the current status of the region, as well as how the citizenry sees itself in the future (411). According to Heyse, a group of people are able to build these memories because they share an imagined past, which Heyes refers to as myth (414).

41. Carney, *Reckoning with the Devil*, 66, 73.

42. Heyse, "The Rhetoric of Memory-Making," 416.

43. Webster and Leib, "What Would Robert E. Lee Do?" 106.

44. Heyse, "The Rhetoric of Memory-Making," 415.

45. Newson, "Epistemological Crises Made Stone," 139.

46. Newson, "Epistemological Crises Made Stone," 141.

BIBLIOGRAPHY

MANUSCRIPTS AND SPECIAL COLLECTIONS

McWherter Library, University of Memphis, Memphis, Tennessee.

40th Congress, House of Representatives Executive Document No. 1, Report of the Secretary of War, Chapter X, 193, 1868.

JW Brister Library Monograph Series 2, Memphis Multimedia Archival Project, The 1968 Sanitation Workers Strike.

Robert R. Church, Jr./Church Family Papers.

House Journal. 34th Tennessee General Assembly, 1st Session, 1865.

Senate Journal. 34th Tenn. General Assembly, 1st Sess., 1865.

Memphis & Shelby County Library, Memphis Room, Memphis, Tennessee.

Cotton Carnival Collection.

A. Arthur Halle Papers.

Memphis Board of Alderman minutes, March 18, 1839.

Shelby County Register's records. Book 16, p. 468.

Maxine Smith Collection.

Smith, Mary (c) & W.C. Smith (c) v. Memphis Street Railway Company. Circuit Court of Shelby County, Tennessee, Division #3, #17778, T.D., Filed October 1, 1908.

Ethyl Q. Venson Papers.

United States Bureau of Labor Statistics. "Unemployment rate falls from May to June 2015." July 7, 2015. Accessed at bls.gov.

United States Bureau of Refugees, Freedmen, and Abandoned Lands. Microfilm, Roll 24.

PUBLISHED PRIMARY SOURCES

Conover, M. G., and L. Parrott. "Relief and the Color Line." *The Survey,* May 15, 1932, 204.

The Forrest Monument: Its History & Dedication. Memphis: Forrest Monument Association, 1905.

Gordon, George. *At the Dedication Ceremonies of the Forrest Monument at Memphis.* Memphis: Forrest Memorial Association, 1905.

"Industrialism versus Agrarianism for the South." *The University Debater's Annual,* 1931–1928. Located on the second floor of the McWherter Library at the University of Memphis.

Robuck, J. E. *My Own Personal Experience and Observation as a Soldier in the Confederate Army During the Civil War, 1861–1865, Also During the Period of Reconstruction.* Memphis, TN: Burke's Bookstore, 1978.

Tutwiler, T. H. *Payroll & Statistical Report of Operation of the Memphis Street Railway Twyman's Memphis Directory & General Business Advertiser,* for 1850. Memphis Tennessee, 1849 *Company,* July 1905.

Wells, Ida B. "Lynching, Our National Crime," 1909.

NEWSPAPERS

Associated Press (2005)
Commercial Appeal (1903, 1910, 1916, 1931, 1932, 1979, 1987, 1988, 2001, 2005, 2006)
Memphis Daily Avalanche (1866)
Memphis Daily Eagle (1849, 1860)
Memphis Daily Post (1866, 1867)
Memphis Public Ledger (1867)
Nashville Daily Times (1865)
New York Times (1969, 1971, 2017)
The Tennessean
Tri-State Defender (1961)

INTERVIEWS

Al Lewis, cofounder of Inward Journey, interview by author, July 8, 1999, tape recording in the author's possession.

Lee Millar, president of the General Nathan Bedford Forrest Society, interview by the author, July 1, 1999, in the author's possession, Memphis, Tennessee

Mrs. Ethyl Venson, interview by Sanders Duke Williams, November 30, 1984, McWherter Library, University of Memphis, Memphis Tennessee.

SECONDARY SOURCES

African American Registry. "The Beale Street Baptist Church, a story." aaregistry.org/story/the-beale-street-baptist-church-a-story/.

BIBLIOGRAPHY

Altizer, Philip. Letter to the Editor, "Time to Forgive, Honor the Penitent Forrest." *CA*, January 21, 2018.

Ashdown, Paul, and Edward Caudill. *The Myth of Nathan Bedford Forrest*. Rowman & Littlefield Publishers, 2005.

Barker, Carol. "'Love Me Like I Like to Be': The Sexual Politics of Hurston's *Their Eyes Were Watching God*, the Classic Blues, and the Black Women's Club Movement." *African American Review* 32, no. 2 (Summer 1998): 199–213, www.jstor.org/stable/20064090.

Barr, George, et al. "'What to the Slave Is the Fourth of July?'" (1852). In *The Speeches of Frederick Douglass: A Critical Edition*, edited by John R. McKivigan, Julie Husband, and Heather L. Kaufman, 55–92. Yale University Press, 2018, doi.org/10.2307/j.ctv6hp3kt.9.

Barsalou, Judy, and Victoria Baxter. Report. US Institute of Peace, 2007, www.jstor.org/stable/resrep12524.

Bay, Mia. *To Tell the Truth Freely: The Life of Ida B. Wells*. Hill and Wang, 2009.

Bealle, James. "Dixie Needs No Cotton Picker." *The Forum*, April 1937, 224–28.

Beltramini, Enrico. "SCLC Operation Breadbasket: From Economic Civil Rights to Black Economic Power." *Fire!!!* 2, no. 2 (2013): 5–47, doi.org/10.5323/fire.2.2.0005.

Berg, Manfred. *The Ticket to Freedom: The NAACP and the Struggle for Black Political Integration*. University of Florida Press, 2005. Accessed at ebscohost.com/.

Berkeley, Kathleen. "'Like a Plague of Locusts': Immigration and Social Change in Memphis, Tennessee 1850–1880." PhD diss., University of California Los Angeles, 1980.

Berlin, Ira, et al. *Slaves No More: Three Essays on Emancipation and the Civil War*. Cambridge University Press, 1992.

Biles, Roger. "'A Bittersweet Victory': Public School Desegregation in Memphis." *Journal of Negro Education* 55, no. 4 (Autumn 1986): 470–83.

———. "Cotton Fields or Skyscrapers? The Case of Memphis, Tennessee." *The Historian* 50, no. 2 (1988): 210–33, www.jstor.org/stable/24447046.

———. "The Persistence of the Past: Memphis in the Great Depression." *Journal of Southern History* 52 (May 1986): 183–212.

Black, R. Derek. *The Klansman's Son: My Journey from White Nationalism to Antiracism, a Memoir*. Abrams Books, 2024.

Blackett, Richard J. M. "Resistance to Slavery in Middle Tennessee: Fugitive Slaves, the Underground Railroad, and the Politics of Slavery in the Decade before the Civil War." *Tennessee Historical Quarterly* 76, no. 4 (2017): 300–41, /www.jstor.org/stable/26540299.

Blake, J. Herman. "Black Nationalism." *Annals of the American Academy of Political and Social Science* 382 (March 1969): 15–25.

Blight, David. *Race and Reunion: The Civil War in American Memory.* Harvard University Press, 2001.

Bond, Beverly Greene. "'Til Fair Aurora Rise': African American Women in Memphis Tennessee, 1840–1915." PhD diss., University of Memphis, 1996.

Bond, Beverly G., and Janann Sherman. *Memphis in Black and White.* Arcadia Publishing, 2003.

Bond, Beverly Greene, and Sarah Wilkerson Freeman, eds. *Tennessee Women: Their Lives and Times.* University of Georgia Press, 2015, www.jstor.org/stable/j.ctt17575nc.

Bond, Horace Mann. "A Negro Looks at His South." *Harper's,* June 1931, 98–108.

Bowers, Claude G. *The Tragic Era: The Revolution After Lincoln.* Cambridge, MA: Riverside Press, 1929.

Braeman, John, and David Brody, eds. *The New Deal: The National Level.* Ohio State Press, 1975.

Branch, Taylor. *The King Years: Historic Moments in the Civil Rights Movement.* Simon & Schuster, 1988.

Breaux, Richard M. "'To the Uplift and Protection of Young Womanhood': African-American Women at Iowa's Private Colleges and the University of Iowa, 1878–1928." *History of Education Quarterly* 50, no. 2 (May 2010): 159–81, www.jstor.org/stable/40648057.

Brewer, W. M. "Robert R. Church." *Journal of Negro History* 38, no. 2 (1953): 249–51, www.jstor.org/stable/2715551.

Brown, David. "A Vagabond's Tale: Poor Whites, Herrenvolk Democracy, and the Value of Whiteness in the Late Antebellum South." *Journal of Southern History* 79, no. 4 (November 2013): 799–840.

Brown, Roger Lyle. *Ghost Dancing on the Cracker Circuit.* University of Mississippi Press, 1997.

Brown, Thomas. "Confederate Monuments." In *The New Encyclopedia of Southern Culture: Volume 4: Myth, Manners, and Memory,* 43–48. Edited by Charles Reagan Wilson. University of North Carolina Press, 2006, www.jstor.org/stable/10.5149/9781469616704_wilson.13.

Browning, Robert M. *Forrest: The Confederacy's Relentless Warrior.* Potomac Books, 2004.

Brueggemann, John. "Racial Considerations and Social Policy in the 1930s." *Social Science History* 26, no. 1 (2002): 139–77, doi:10.2307/40267773.

Burton, Orville Vernon. "The South as 'Other,' the Southerner as 'Stranger.'" *Journal of Southern History* 79, no. 1 (2013): 7–50, www.jstor.org/stable/23795402.

Byrne, Frank L. "Libby Prison: A Study in Emotions." *Journal of Southern History* 24, no. 4 (1958): 430–44, doi.org/10.2307/2954671.

Camp, Stephanie. *Closer to Freedom: Enslaved Women and Everyday Resistance in the Plantation South.* University of North Carolina Press, 2004.

Campbell, Walter E. "Tracking Jim Crow: Streetcar Segregation in the Urban South." Paper presented at the Modes of Inquiry for American City History Conference, Chicago, October 1990.

Capers, Gerald, Jr. *The Biography of a River Town*, 2nd edition. Tulane University Press, 1966.

Caputi, Mary. "National Identity in Contemporary Theory." *Political Psychology* 17, no. 4 (1996): 683–94, doi:10.2307/3792133.

Carby, Hazel V. "'On the Threshold of Woman's Era': Lynching, Empire, and Sexuality in Black Feminist Theory." *Critical Inquiry* 12, no. 1 (1985): 262–77, www.jstor.org/stable/1343470.

Carmichael, Peter S. "'Truth Is Mighty & Will Eventually Prevail': Political Correctness, Neo-Confederates, and Robert E. Lee." *Southern Cultures* 17, no. 3 (2011): 6–27, www.jstor.org/stable/26214302.

Carney, Court. "The Contested Image of Nathan Bedford Forrest." *Journal of Southern History* 67, no. 3 (August 2001): 601–30, doi.org/10.2307/3070019.

———. *Reckoning with the Devil: Nathan Bedford Forrest in Myth and Memory*. Louisiana State University Press, 2024.

Carriere, Marius. "An Irresponsible Press: Memphis Newspapers and the 1866 Riot." *Tennessee Historical Quarterly* 60, no. 1 (2001): 2–15, www.jstor.org/stable/42628498.

Carson, Oliver. "The Southern Worker Organizes." *The Nation*, September 26, 1934, 353–55.

Church, Roberta, and Ronald Walter. *Nineteenth Century Memphis Families of Color, 1850–1900*. Murdock Printing Co., 1987.

Cimprich, John. *Fort Pillow, A Civil War Massacre, and Public Memory*. Louisiana State University Press, 2005.

Cimprich, John, and Robert C. Mainfort. "The Fort Pillow Massacre: A Statistical Note." *Journal of American History* 76, no.3 (1989): 830–837, www.jstor.org/stable/2936423.

Clyburn, James. *Blessed Experiences: Genuinely Southern, Proudly Black*. University of South Carolina Press, 2014, doi.org/10.2307/j.ctv6wgcjm.23.

Cobb, James C. "Beyond Planters and Industrialists: A New Perspective on the New South." *Journal of Southern History* 54, no. 1 (1988): 45–68, doi:10.2307/2208520.

———. "Community and Identity: Redefining Southern Culture." *Georgia Review* 50, no. 1 (Spring 1996): 9–24.

———. *The Most Southern Place on Earth: The Mississippi Delta and the Roots of Regional Identity*. Oxford University Press, 1992.

Cody, Annie. "History of the Tennessee Division." *UDC Magazine*, November 1944.

Conway, James. "Beyond 1968: The 1969 Black Monday Protest in Memphis." In *An Unseen Light: Black Struggles for Freedom in Memphis, Tennessee*, 306–29. Edited by Aram Goudsouzian and Charles W. McKinney. University Press of Kentucky, 2018, doi.org/10.2307/j.ctt2111h1m.16.

Cox, Karen. *Dixie's Daughters: The United Daughters of the Confederacy and the Preservation of Confederate Culture.* University Press of Florida, 2003.

Cromwell, John W. "The Aftermath of Nat Turner's Insurrection." *Journal of Negro History* 5, no. 2 (1920): 208–34, doi.org/10.2307/2713592.

Crow, Jeffrey J. "Thomas Settle Jr., Reconstruction and the Memory of the Civil War." *Journal of Southern History* 62, no. 4 (November 1996): 689–726.

Davis, Darren, and Ronald E. Brown. "The Antipathy of Black Nationalism: Behavioral and Attitudinal Implications of an African American Ideology." *American Journal of Political Science* 46 (April 2002): 239–52.

Domby, Adam H. *The False Cause: Fraud, Fabrication, and White Supremacy in Confederate Memory.* University of Virginia Press, 2020, doi.org/10.2307/j.ctvvsqcqb.

Douglass, Frederick. *The Oxford Frederick Douglass Reader.* Edited by William L. Andrews. New York: Oxford University Press, 1996.

Douty, Esther. "FERA and the Rural Negro." *The Survey,* July 1934, 215.

Drabble, John. "From White Supremacy to White Power: The FBI, COINTELPRO-WHITE HATE, and the Nazification of the Ku Klux Klan in the 1970s." *American Studies* 48, no. 3 (2007): 49–74, www.jstor.org/stable/40644149.

Du Bois, W. E. B. "The Talented Tenth," in *The Negro Problem: A Series of Articles by Representative American Negroes Today,* 33–34. James Pott and Co., 1903.

Du Bois, W. E. B., and Eugene F. Provenzo. *Illustrated Souls of Black Folk.* Vol. An annotated, illustrated, documentary ed. Routledge, 2015. Accessed at ebscohost .com.

Duggan, Paul. "Mississippi Flag Voters Defend 'Heritage': 'I Don't Know If the Civil War Will Ever Be Over for Us.'" *Pittsburgh Post-Gazette,* April 19, 2001, A13.

Duster, Alfreda M., ed., *Crusade for Justice: The Autobiography of Ida B. Wells.* University of Chicago Press, 1970.

Ebert, Joel. "Tennessee House Votes for Heritage Protection Law." *The Tennessean.* February 18, 2016.

Equal Justice Initiative. "Confederate Iconography in the 20th Century." *Segregation in America.* Equal Justice Initiative, 2018, www.jstor.org/stable/resrep30692.9.

Fabre, Genevieve, and Robert O'Meally. *History and Memory in African American Culture.* Oxford University Press, 1994.

Fain, Eda Clark, Jr. "'Cut Loose the Corset Strings of Dull Times': Attending Carnival 'n Memphis, Tennessee, Through Newsprint Coverage, 1872–1901." PhD diss., University of Memphis, 1999.

Felber, Garrett. *Those Who Know Don't Say: The Nation of Islam, the Black Freedom Movement, and the Carceral State.* University of North Carolina Press, 2020.

Feldman, Glenn, ed. *Nation within a Nation: The American South and the Federal Government.* University Press of Florida, 2014.

Fellman, Michael. "Struggling with Robert E. Lee." *Southern Cultures* 8, no. 3 (2002): 6–17, http://www.jstor.org/stable/44376492.

Ferguson, Karen. *Black Politics in New Deal Atlanta.* University of North Carolina Press, 2002.

Fishwick, Marshall W. "Virginians on Olympus. II. Robert E. Lee: Savior of the Lost Cause." *Virginia Magazine of History and Biography* 58, no. 2 (1950): 163–80, www.jstor.org/stable/4245690.

Fleming, Cynthia. "'We Shall Overcome': New Direction of the Civil Rights Movement." *Tennessee Historical Quarterly* 54, no. 3 (Fall 1995): 230–45.

Foner, Eric. "Confederate History and 'Our' History: Commentary." *New York Times,* August 2, 2017, A25.

———. *Reconstruction: America's Unfinished Revolution 1863–1877.* Harper Perennial, 2014.

Foner, Philip S., and Robert James Branham. *Lift Every Voice: African American Oratory, 1787–1900.* University of Alabama Press, 1998.

Fornäs, Johan. *Signifying Europe.* Intellect, 2012.

Forts, Franklin. "Living with Confederate Symbols." *Southern Cultures* 8, no. 1 (2002): 60–75, www.jstor.org/stable/26236961.

Frankel, Nora Lee. *Freedom's Women: Black Women and Families in Civil War Era Mississippi.* Indiana University Press, 1999.

Frazier, E. Franklin. *The Black Bourgeoisie.* The Falcon's Wing Press, 1957.

Fuchs, Richard. *An Unerring Fire: The Massacre at Fort Pillow.* Stackpole, 2002.

Fuller, Thomas O. *Twenty Years in Public Life, 1890–1910.* Nashville: National Baptist Publishing Board, 1910.

Gabbatt, Adam. "Golden Escalator Ride: The Surreal Day Trump Kicked Off His Bid for President." *The Guardian.* June 19, 2019.

Gaines, Kevin. "Assimilationist Minstrelsy as Racial Uplift Ideology: James D. Corrother's Literary Quest for Black Leadership." *American Quarterly* 45 (September 1993): 341–69.

———. *Uplifting the Race: Black Leadership, Politics, and Culture in the Twentieth century.* University of North Carolina Press, 1996.

Gallagher, Gary W., and Alan T. Nolan, eds. *The Myth of the Lost Cause and Civil War History.* Indiana University Press, 2000.

Gamble, Richard. "The Vanity of American Exceptionalism." *Reason,* September 19, 2013, www.reason.com/2013/09/19/the-vanity-of-american-exceptionalism/.

Gatewood, Willard B. *Aristocrats of Color: The Black Elite, 1880–1920.* Indiana University Press, 1990.

Gayarré, Charles. "The Southern Question." *North American Review* 125, no. 259 (1877): 472–98, www.jstor.org/stable/25110134. S

Giddings, Paula. *When and Where I Enter: The Impact of Black Women on Race and Sex in America.* William Morrow, 1984.

Gillespie, Fern. "Women Leaders Are Backbone of NAACP." *Crisis* 116, no. 3 (Summer 2009): 52–55. Accessed at ebscohost.com.

Gilmore, Horace. "Why I Like the South." *Publisher's Weekly,* February 8, 1930, 708–9.

Glaze, Robert. "Saint and Sinner: Robert E. Lee, Nathan Bedford Forrest, and the Ambiguity of Southern Identity." *Tennessee Historical Quarterly* 69, no. 2 (Summer 2010): 164–85, www.jstor.org/stable/42628173.

Goings, Kenneth W. *Mammy and Uncle Mose: Black Collectibles and American Stereotyping.* Indiana University Press, 1994.

Goings, Kenneth W., and Gerald L. Smith. "'Duty of the Hour': African-American Communities in Memphis, Tennessee, 1862–1923." *Tennessee Historical Quarterly* 55, no. 2 (1996): 130–43, www.jstor.org/stable/42627273.

Goings, Kenneth W., and Ray Mohl. *The New African American Urban History.* Sage Publishing, 1996.

———. "Toward a New African American Urban History." *Journal of Urban History* 21 (March 1995).

Goudsouzian, Aram. "'If the March Cannot Be Here, Then Where?' Memphis and the Meredith March." In *An Unseen Light: Black Struggles for Freedom in Memphis, Tennessee,* 254–78. Edited by Aram Goudsouzian and Charles W. McKinney. University Press of Kentucky, 2018, doi.org/10.2307/j.ctt2111h1m.14.

Graham, Bryan Armen. "Mississippi Lawmakers Vote to Remove Confederate Emblem from State Flag." *The Guardian,* June 28, 2020.

Grantham, Dewey W. *The South in Modern America: A Region at Odds.* University of Arkansas Press, 2001.

Gravely, William B. "The Dialectic of Double-Consciousness in Black American Freedom Celebrations, 1808–1863." *Journal of Negro History* 67, no. 4 (Winter 1982): 302–17.

Green, Laurie B. *Battling the Plantation Mentality: Memphis and the Black Freedom Struggle.* University of North Carolina Press, 2007.

Griffin, Larry J., Ranae J. Evenson, and Ashley B. Thompson. "Southerners All?" *Southern Cultures* 11, no. 1 (2005): 6–25, www.jstor.org/stable/26390937.

Gross, Jennifer L. "The United Daughters of the Confederacy, Confederate Widows, and the Lost Cause: 'We Must Not Forget or Neglect the Widows,'" 180–200. In *Women on Their Own: Interdisciplinary Perspectives on Being Single,* edited by Rudolph M. Bell and Virginia Yans. Rutgers University Press, 2008, www.jstor.org/stable/j.ctt5hj2wd.11.

Hale, F. Sheffield. "Finding Meaning in Monuments: Atlanta History Center Enters

Dialogue on Confederate Symbols." *History News* 71, no. 4 (Autumn 2016): 20–24, www.jstor.org/stable/44605957.

Hall, Simon. "The NAACP, Black Power, and the African American Freedom Struggle, 1966–1969." *The Historian* 69, no. 1 (2007): 49–82, http://www.jstor.org/stable/24453911

Hallowell, Irving A., and Ralph Linton. "Nativistic Movements." *American Anthropologist* 45, no. 2 (1943): 230–40, www.jstor.org/stable/663272.

Hannah-Jones, Nikole. "The 'Colorblindness' Trap: How a Civil Rights Ideal Got Hijacked." *New York Times,* March 13, 2024.

———. Public Address, Knight Center Charlotte, North Carolina, July 11, 2024.

Hardwick, Kevin R. "'Your Old Father Abe Lincoln Is Dead and Damned': Black Soldiers and the Memphis Race Riot of 1866." *Journal of Social History* 27, no. 1 (Autumn, 1993): 109–28, doi:10.1353/jsh/27.1.109.

Harrison, Pat. "The Wages of Dixie." *Collier's,* January 1938, 46.

Harris-Perry, Melissa. *Sister Citizen: Shame, Stereotypes, and Black Women in America.* Yale University Press, 2011.

Hawkins, J. Russell. *The Bible Told Them So: How Southern Evangelicals Fought to Preserve White Supremacy.* Oxford University Press, 2021.

HeDren, Katarina, Jyoti Mistry, and Antje Schuhmann. "'Women, Use the Gaze to Change Reality.'" In *Gaze Regimes: Film and Feminisms in Africa,* 182–87. Edited by Mistry Jyoti and Schuhmann Antje. Wits University Press, 2015, www.jstor.org/stable/10.18772/22015068561.20.

Henneman, J. B. "Historical Studies in the South since the War." *Sewanee Review* 1, no. 3 (1893): 320–39, www.jstor.org/stable/27527761.

Henninger, R. W. "What the South Offers Industry." *Factory and Industrial Management,* April 1929, 714–17.

Henry, H. M. "The Slave Laws of Tennessee." *Tennessee Historical Magazine* 2, no. 3 (1916): 175–203, www.jstor.org/stable/42637977.

Henry, Robert Selph. *"First with the Most": Forrest.* Bobbs-Merrill, 1944.

Heyse, Amy Lynn. "The Rhetoric of Memory-Making: Lessons from the UDC's Catechisms for Children." *Rhetoric Society Quarterly* 38, no. 4 (2008): 408–32, www.jstor.org/stable/40232600.

Hicks, Hugh. "Nathan Bedford Forrest." *UDC Magazine,* November 1944.

Hillyer, Reiko. "Relics of Reconciliation: The Confederate Museum and Civil War Memory in the New South." *Public Historian* 33, no. 4 (November 2011): 35–62.

Hine, Darlene Clark. "Rape and the Inner Lives of Black Women in the Middle West." *Signs* 14, no. 4 (1989): 912–20, www.jstor.org/stable/3174692.

Hine, Darlene Clark, Elsa Barkley Brown, and Rosalyn Terborg-Penn, eds. *Black Women in America: An Historical Encyclopedia.* Jones and Bartlett Learning, 1993.

Hirsch, Marianne, and Valerie Smith. "Feminism and Cultural Memory: An Introduction," *Signs: Journal of Women and Society* 28, no. 1 (Autumn 2002).

Honey, Michael K. "Black Workers Matter: The Continuing Search for Racial and Economic Equality in Memphis." In *An Unseen Light: Black Struggles for Freedom in Memphis, Tennessee,* 366–92. Edited by Aram Goudsouzian and Charles W. McKinney. University Press of Kentucky, 2018, doi.org/10.2307/j.ctt2111h1m.19.

———. *Black Workers Remember: An Oral History of Segregation, Unionism, and the Freedom Struggle.* University of California Press, 1999.

———. *Going Down Jericho Road: The Memphis Strike, Martin Luther King's Last Campaign.* Norton, 2007.

Hooks, Julia A. "Duty of the Hour." *Afro-American Encyclopedia.* Nashville, 1896.

Hopkins, Harry. "Unemployment Relief and the Public Works Administration." *Proceedings of the Academy of Political Science* 15 (January 1934): 81–85.

Hoppe Sherry L., and Bruce W. Speck. *Maxine Smith's Unwilling Pupils: Lessons Learned in Memphis's Civil Rights Classroom.* University of Tennessee Press, 2007.

Huch, Ronald K. "Fort Pillow Massacre: The Aftermath of Paducah (1908–1984)." *Journal of the Illinois State Historical Society* 66, no. 1 (Spring, 1973): 62–70, www.jstor.org/stable/40191288.

Huebner, Timothy S., and Madeleine M. McGrady. "Shelby Foote, Memphis, and the Civil War in American Memory." *Southern Cultures* 21, no. 4 (2015): 13–27, www.jstor.org/stable/26220240.

Hughes, Alexander O. "Hidden History: The Ku Klux Klan in Troup County." *Georgia Historical Quarterly* 105, no. 4 (2021): 281–300.

Hurst, Jack. *Nathan Bedford Forrest: A Biography.* New York: Vintage Press, 1994.

———. "Tennessee Turning Point: Nathan B. Forrest Took Matters into His Own Hands at Ft. Donelson—and a Legend Was Born." *America's Civil War* 21, no. 6 (January 2009): 28–35, link-gale-com.scsl.idm.oclc.org.

Hutchison, Coleman. "In The Land Where We Were Dreaming." *South: A Scholarly Journal* 48, no. 1 (Fall 2015): 44–51.

Imes, William Lloyd. "The Legal Status of Free Negroes and Slaves in Tennessee." *Journal of Negro History* 4, no. 3 (1919): 254–72, doi:10.2307/2713777.

Jackson, Herb. "As Donald Trump Defends Confederate Statues, Cory Booker Wants Them Removed from Capitol." *Home News Tribune,* August 18, 2017.

Jacoway, Elizabeth, and David Colburn, eds. *Southern Businessmen and Desegregation.* Louisiana State University Press, 1982.

Janney, Caroline E. *Burying the Dead but Not the Past: Ladies' Memorial Associations and the Lost Cause.* University of North Carolina Press, 2008.

———. "War over a Shrine of Peace: The Appomattox Peace Monument and Retreat from Reconciliation." *Journal of Southern History* 77, no. 1 (2011): 91–120, www.jstor.org/stable/27919388.

J. C. M. "Just a Word About the Lost Cause." *Register of Kentucky State Historical Society* 1, no. 3 (September 1903): 91–92.

Jewell, K. Sue. *From Mammy to Miss America and Beyond: Cultural Images and the Shaping of US Social Policies.* New York: Rutledge, 1993. Accessed at ebscohost.com.

Johnson, Joan Marie. "'Drill into Us . . . the Rebel Tradition': The Contest over Southern Identity in Black and White Women's Clubs, South Carolina, 1898–1930." *Journal of Southern History* 66, no. 3 (2000): 525–62.

Jonas, Gilbert. *Freedom's Sword: The NAACP and the Struggle Against Racism in America, 1909–1969.* Routledge, 2005. Accessed at ebscohost.com.

Jones, Beverly W. "Mary Church Terrell and the National Association of Colored Women, 1896 to 1901." *Journal of Negro History* 67, no. 1 (Spring 1982): 20–33, doi.org/10.2307/2717758.

Jones, Jacqueline. *American Work: Four Centuries of Black and White Labor.* Norton, 1998.

Jones, Winfield. *Story of the Ku Klux Klan.* Washington, DC: American Newspaper Syndicate, 1921.

Jordan, Winthrop. *White over Black: American Attitudes Toward the Negro, 1550–1812.* University of North Carolina Press, 1968.

Joyner, Charles, and Evan A. Kutzler. "Furling That Banner: The Rise and Fall of the Confederate Flag in South Carolina, 1961–2000." In *Citizen-Scholar: Essays in Honor of Walter Edgar,* 21–33. Edited by Robert H. Brinkmeyer. University of South Carolina Press, 2016, doi.org/10.2307/j.ctv6wgcrh.10.

Kelley, Robin D. G. *Race Rebels: Culture, Politics, and the Black Working Class.* Free Press, 1996.

Kennedy, R. C., and H. Fuller. "The Cotton Kingdom: 1931." *New Republic,* December 16, 1931, 129–34.

Kinney, Martha E. "'If Vanquished I Am Still Victorious': Religious and Cultural Symbolism in Virginia's Confederate Memorial Day Celebrations, 1866–1930." *Virginia Magazine of History and Biography* 106, no. 3 (1998): 237–66.

Knowlton, Steven A. "'Since I Was a Citizen, I Had the Right to Attend the Library': The Key Role of the Public Library in the Civil Rights Movement in Memphis." In *An Unseen Light: Black Struggles for Freedom in Memphis, Tennessee,* 203–27. Edited by Aram Goudsouzian and Charles W. McKinney. University Press of Kentucky, 2018, doi.org/10.2307/j.ctt2111h1m.12.

Kramer, Steve. "Uplifting Our 'Downtrodden Sisterhood': Victoria Earle Matthews and New York City's White Rose Mission, 1897–1907." *Journal of African American History* 91, no. 3 (Summer, 2006): 243–66, www.jstor.org/stable/20064090.

Kwate, Naa Oyo A. *Burgers in Blackface: Anti-Black Restaurants Then and Now.* University of Minnesota Press, 2019.

Labode, Modupe, and Kevin M. Levin. "Reconsideration of Memorials and Monuments." *History News* 71, no. 2 (Autumn 2016): 7–11.

Lamon, Lester C. *Blacks in Tennessee, 1791–1970*. University of Tennessee Press, 1981.

———. "Black Public Education in the South, 1861–1920: By Whom, for Whom and Under Whose Control?" *Journal of Thought* 18, no. 3 (1983): 76–90, www.jstor.org/stable/23801725.

Larsen, Lawrence H. *The Urban South: A History*. University Press of Kentucky, 1990, doi:10.2307/j.ctt130hs49.

Lawson, R. A. *Jim Crow's Counterculture: The Blues and Black Southerners, 1890–1945*. Louisiana State University, 2010.

Lewis, Nghana tamu. "In a Different Chord: Interpreting the Relations Among Black Female Sexuality, Agency, and the Blues." *African American Review* 37, no. 4 (2003): 599–609.

Lewis, Selma S., and Marjean G. Kremer. *The Angel of Beale Street: The Biography of Julia Ann Hooks*. St. Luke's Press, 1986.

Lewis, Theodore. "Booker T. Washington's Audacious Vocationalist Philosophy." *Oxford Review of Education* 40, no. 2 (April 2014): 189–205, doi:10.1080/03054985.2014.889603.

Lindgren, James M. "'Virginia Needs Living Heroes': Historic Preservation in the Progressive Era." *Public Historian* 13, no. 1 (1991): 9–24, doi:10.1080/03054985.2014.889603.

Little, Kimberly K. *You Must Be from the North: Southern White Women in the Memphis Civil Rights Movement*. University Press of Mississippi, 2009.

Logan, Rayford. *The Negro in American Life and Thought*. Dial Press, 1954.

Lord, J. Dennis. "School Busing and White Abandonment of Public Schools." *Southeastern Geographer* 15, no. 2 (1975): 81–92, www.jstor.org/stable/44370631.

Lorenzini, Jack. "United by a Cause: Student Activists and the Memphis Sanitation Strike of 1968." *Tennessee Historical Quarterly* 78, no. 4 (2019): 266–91, www.jstor.org/stable/27148608.

Lovett, Bobby. *The Civil Rights Movement in Tennessee: A Narrative History*. University of Tennessee Press, 2005.

———. "Memphis Riots: White Reaction to Blacks in Memphis, May 1865–July 1866." *Tennessee Historical Quarterly* 38, no. 1 (1979): 9–33, www.jstor.org/stable/42625934.

———. "The Negro's Civil War in Tennessee, 1861–1865." *Journal of Negro History* 61, no. 1 (January 1976): 36–50.

Lowe, David. *Ku Klux Klan: The Invisible Empire*. Norton, 1967.

Marable, Manning, and Leith Mullings, eds., *Let Nobody Turn Us Around: Voices of Resistance, Reform, and Renewal*. Rowman & Littlefield, 2000.

Massey, Douglas. "Confederate Revisionist History." In *Antidemocracy in America: Truth, Power, and the Republic at Risk*, 191–97. Edited by Eric Klinenberg, Caitlin

Zaloom, and Sharon Marcus, Columbia University Press, 2019.

Maurantonio, Nicole. *Confederate Exceptionalism: Civil War Myth and Memory in the Twenty-First Century.* University Press of Kansas, 2019.

Mayes, Thompson. "Why Old Places Matter." *History News* 71, no. 3 (2016): 19–23, www.jstor.org/stable/44605943.

Mayfield, John. "'The Soul of a Man!': William Gilmore Simms and the Myths of Southern Manhood." *Journal of the Early Republic* 15, no. 3 (Autumn, 1995): 477–500, doi.org/10.2307/3124119.

Maxwell, Tonya. "Witness in Dylann Roof Trial: 'I Was Just Waiting My Turn.'" *Citizen Times* (Asheville), December 7, 2016.

McElya, Micki. *Clinging to Mammy: The Faithful Slave in Twentieth-Century America.* Harvard University Press, 2007.

McGehee, C. Stuart. "E. O. Tade, Freedmen's Education, and the Failure of Reconstruction in Tennessee." *Tennessee Historical Quarterly* 43, no. 4 (1984): 376–89, www.jstor.org/stable/42626481.

McGhee Heather. *The Sum of Us: What Racism Costs Everyone and How We Can Prosper Together.* Penguin Random House, 2021.

McLean, Robert Emmett. "Cotton Carnival and Cotton Makers Jubilee: Memphis Society in Black and White." MA thesis, George Mason University, 1994.

McMillen, Neil R. *Dark Journey: Black Mississippians in the Age of Jim Crow.* University of Illinois Press, 1989.

———. "Organized Resistance to School Desegregation in Tennessee." *Tennessee Historical Quarterly* 30, no. 3 (1971): 315–28, www.jstor.org/stable/42623247.

McMurry, Linda. *To Keep the Waters Troubled: The Life of Ida B. Wells.* Oxford University Press, 1998.

McPherson, James. *The Negro's Civil War: How American Blacks Felt and Acted During the War for the Union.* Ballentine Books, 1991.

McVeight, Rory, and Kevin Estep. "The Ku Klux Klan in American History." In *The Politics of Losing: Trump, the Klan, and the Mainstreaming of Resentment,* 19–54. Columbia University Press, 2019, www.jstor.org/stable/10.7312/mcve19006.4.

McWhiney, H. Grady, and Francis B. Simkins. "The Ghostly Legend of the Ku Klux Klan." *Negro History Bulletin* 14, no. 5 (1951): 109–12, www.jstor.org/stable/44212443.

M'Donnold, R. L., and R. L. McDonnold. "The Reconstruction Period in Tennessee." *American Historical Magazine* 1, no. 4 (1896): 307–28, www.jstor.org/stable/42657113.

Meier, August, and Elliott Rudwick. "The Boycott Movement Against Jim Crow Streetcars in the South, 1900–1906." *Journal of American History* 55, no. 4 (March 1969): 756–75.

Meier, August, and John H. Bracey. "The NAACP as a Reform Movement, 1909–1965: To Reach the Conscience of America." *Journal of Southern History* 59 (February 1993): 3–30.

"Memphis Makes War on CIO." *Christian Century,* October 13, 1937, 1273.

Mencken, H. L. "Uprising in the Confederacy." *American Mercury,* March 22, 1931, 379–81.

Meriwether, Elizabeth Avery. *Recollections of 92 Years.* McLean, VA: EPM Publications, 1994.

Michel, Gregg L. "Surveilling the Memphis Movement: Police Spying in Memphis, 1968–1976." *Journal of Southern History* 87, no. 4 (November 2021): 673–710.

Middleton, Stephen, ed. *Black Congressmen During Reconstruction: A Documentary Sourcebook.* Greenwood Press, 2002.

Minchin, Timothy J. "Making Best Use of the New Laws: The NAACP and the Fight for Civil Rights in the South, 1965–1975." *Journal of Southern History* 74, no. 3 (August 2008): 668–702, www.jstor.org/stable/27650232.

Mixon, Gregory. "Good Negro—Bad Negro: The Dynamics of Race and Class in Atlanta During the Era of the 1906 Riot." *Georgia Historical Quarterly* 81, no. 3 (1997).

Molyneaux, Peter. "The Second Civil War." *Forum,* August 1934, 100–102.

Moore, Kenneth Bancroft. "Fort Pillow, Forrest, and the United States Colored Troops in 1864." *Tennessee Historical Quarterly* 54, no. 2 (1995): 112–23, www.jstor.org/stable/42627193.

Moore, Winfred B., Jr., Kyle S. Sinisi, and David H. White Jr. *Warm Ashes: Issues in Southern History at the Dawn of the Twenty-First Century.* University of South Carolina Press, 2003.

Morrison, Minion K. C., ed. *African Americans and Political Participation Reference Handbook.* ABC-CLIO, 2003.

Morton, Patricia. *Disfigured Images: The Historical Assault on Afro-American Women.* Praeger, 1991.

Mullane, Deirdre, ed. *Crossing the Danger Water: Three Hundred Years of African American Writing.* Doubleday, 1993.

Murray, Charles. *Coming Apart: The State of White America, 1960–2010.* Crown Forum, 2012.

Myers, Peter C. "'A Good Work for Our Race To-Day': Interests, Virtues, and the Achievement of Justice in Frederick Douglass's Freedmen's Monument Speech." *American Political Science Review* 104, no. 2 (2010): 209–25, www.jstor.org/stable/40863717.

Napier, Cameron Freeman, and Charles Reagan Wilson. "United Daughters of the Confederacy." In *The New Encyclopedia of Southern Culture: Volume 13: Gender,* 351–53. Edited by Nancy Bercaw and Ted Ownby. University of North Carolina Press, 2009, www.jstor.org/stable/10.5149/9781469616728_bercaw.113.

"Negro Workers and the NRA." *Christian Century,* September 20, 1933, 1165.

Neiman, Donald. *Promises to Keep: African Americans and the Constitutional Order, 1776 to the Present.* Oxford University Press, 1991.

Newson, Ryan Andrew. "Epistemological Crises Made Stone: Confederate Monuments and the End of Memory." *Journal of the Society of Christian Ethics* 37, no. 2 (Fall/Winter 2017).

Newton, James. "Delaware's Reaction to the Nat Turner Rebellion." *Negro History Bulletin* 38, no. 1 (1974): 328–29, www.jstor.org/stable/44175624.

Ogbar, Jeffrey O. G. *Black Power: Radical Politics and African American Identity.* Johns Hopkins University Press, 2019.

Oldfield, J. R., ed. *Civilization and Black Progress: Selected Writings of Alexander Crummell on the South.* Charlottesville: University of Virginia Press. 1995.

Page, Brian D. "In the Hands of the Lord." In *An Unseen Light: Black Struggles for Freedom in Memphis, Tennessee,* ed. Aram Goudsouzian and Charles W. McKinney Jr. University Press of Kentucky, 2018.

———. "'Stand by the Flag': Nationalism and African-American Celebrations of the Fourth of July in Memphis, 1866–1887." *Tennessee Historical Quarterly* 58, no. 4 (1999): 284–301, www.jstor.org/stable/42627498.

Painter, Nell Irvin. *Southern History Across the Color Line.* University of North Carolina Press, 2002.

Parks, Joseph H. "A Confederate Trade Center Under Federal Occupation: Memphis, 1862–1865." *Journal of Southern History* 7 (August 1941): 289–314.

Parsons, Elaine Krantz. "Klan Skepticism and Denial in Reconstruction-Era Public Discourse." *Journal of Southern History* 77, no. 1 (2011): 53–90.

———. "Midnight Rangers: Costume and Performance in the Reconstruction-Era Ku Klux Klan." *Journal of American History* 92, no. 3 (2005): 811–36, doi:10.2307/3659969.

Pearcy, Mark. "Stepping Stones and Robert E. Lee—Using Memorials to Explore Contested History." *High School Journal* 103, no. 4 (2020): 201–20, www.jstor.org/stable/26986630.

Perlstein, Daniel. "Teaching Freedom: SNCC and the Creation of the Mississippi Freedom Schools." *History of Education Quarterly* 30, no. 3 (1990): 297–324, doi.org/10.2307/368691.

Perman, Michael. *Pursuit of Unity: A Political History of the American South.* University of North Carolina Press, 2009.

Phillips, Danielle T. *Putting Their Hands on Race: Irish Immigrant and Southern Black Domestic Workers.* Rutgers University Press, 2020.

Plank, David N., and Marcia E. Turner. "Contrasting Patterns in Black School Politics: Atlanta and Memphis, 1865–1985." *Journal of Negro Education* 60, no. 2 (1991): 203–18, doi.org/10.2307/2295611.

Proctor, Bradley D. "'The K. K. Alphabet': Secret Communication and Coordination of the Reconstruction–Era Ku Klux Klan in the Carolinas." *Journal of the Civil War Era* 8, no. 3 (2018): 455–87, www.jstor.org/stable/26483635.

Rabinowitz, Howard. *The First New South, 1865–1920*. Harlan Davidson, 1992.

Ramseth, Luke. "Mississippi State Flag with Confederate Battle Symbol Will Be Replaced with Magnolia Design." *Mississippi Clarion Ledger,* November 4, 2020.

Ramsey, Sonya. "'We Will Be Ready Whenever They Are': African American Teachers' Responses to the *Brown* Decision and Public School Integration in Nashville, Tennessee, 1954–1966." *Journal of African American History* 90, no. 1/2 (2005): 29–51, www.jstor.org/stable/20063974.

Reed, Toure F. *Not Alms but Opportunity: The Urban League and the Politics of Racial Uplift, 1910–1950*. University of North Carolina Press, 2008.

Restad, Hilde. 2016. "Donald Trump's Calls To 'Make America Great Again' Show That American Exceptionalism Is Still a Powerful Idea." LSE (blog). *American Politics and Policy,* 2016.

———. "Old Paradigms in History Die Hard in Political Science: US Foreign Policy and American Exceptionalism." *American Political Thought* 1, no. 1 (2012): 53–76, doi.org/10.1086/664586.

Ritterhouse, Jennifer. *Discovering the South: One Man's Travels Through a Changing America in the 1930's*. University of North Carolina Press, 2017.

Roback, Jennifer. "The Political Economy of Segregation: The Case of Segregated Streetcars." *Journal of Economic History* 46, no. 4 (December 1986): 912–29.

Roberts, Blain. "Uncovering the Confederacy of the Mind: Or, How I Became a Belle of the Ball in Denmark Vesey's Church." *Southern Cultures* 19, no. 3 (2013): 6–25, www.jstor.org/stable/26217030.

Roitman, Joel M. "Race Relations in Memphis, Tennessee, 1880–1905." Master's thesis, Memphis State University, 1964.

Rosen, Hannah. *Terror in the Heart of Freedom: Citizenship, Sexual Violence, and the Meaning of Race in the Postemancipation South*. University of North Carolina Press, 2009.

Rosenberger, John D. "Nathan Bedford Forrest: Lessons from a Master of the Science and Art of Warfighting." *Cavalry & Armor Journal* 7, no. 4 (October 2016): 30–39. Accessed at ebscohost.com.

Rushing, Wanda. *Memphis and the Paradox of Place: Globalization in the American South*. University of North Carolina Press, 2009.

Ryan, James G. "The Memphis Riot of 1866." *Journal of Negro History* 62 (July 1977): 243–57.

Saslow, Eli. *Rising Out of Hatred: The Awakening of a Former White Nationalist*. Doubleday, 2018.

Savage, Kirk. *Standing Soldiers, Kneeling Slaves: Race, War, and Monument in Nineteenth-Century America.* Princeton University Press, 1991.

Scales, John. *The Battles and Campaigns of Confederate General Nathan Bedford Forrest, 1861–1865.* Savas Beatie, LLC, 2017.

Schaefer, Richard T. "The Ku Klux Klan: Continuity and Change." *Phylon* 32, no. 2 (1971): 143–5, doi.org/10.2307/273999.

Seaton, Corey. "'W. E. B. Du Bois & Booker T. Washington: Approaches to Developing Citizenship Post-Reconstruction in America.'" *Kola* 26, no. 1 (Spring 2014): 51–59. Accessed at ebscohost.com.

Sehat, David. "The Civilizing Mission of Booker T. Washington." *Journal of Southern History* 73, no. 2 (May 2007): 323–62.

Sewell, George, and Margaret L. Dwight. *Mississippi Black History Makers.* University Press of Mississippi, 1984, doi:10.2307/j.ctt2tvh56.

Shackel, Paul. *Memory in Black and White: Race, Commemoration, and the Post-Bellum Landscape.* Alta Mira Press, 2003.

Shelton, Jason E., and Michael Emerson. "Extending the Debate Over Nationalism Versus Integration: How Cultural Commitments and Assimilation Trajectories Influence Beliefs About Black Power." *Journal of African American Studies* 13, no. 4 (December 2009): 312–36.

Sklaroff, Lauren Rebecca. *Black Culture and the New Deal: The Quest for Civil Rights in the Roosevelt Era.* University of North Carolina Press, 2010.

Smith, Douglas. *The New Deal in the Urban South.* Louisiana State University Press, 1988.

Smith, John David. "The Recruitment of Negro Soldiers in Kentucky, 1863–1865." *The Register of the Kentucky Historical Society* 72, no. 4 (1974): 364–90, www.jstor.org/stable/23378347.

Snowden-McCray, Lisa, et al. "110 Years: When We Fight We Win." *Crisis* 126, no. 3 (Summer 2019): 23–31. Accessed at ebscohost.com.

Steward, Rodney J. "Christian Manhood and Respectability: David Schenk and the Making of a Confederate Identity." *North Carolina Historical Review* 82, no. 1 (January 2005): 61–81, www.jstor.org/stable/23523245.

Stokes-Casey, Jody. "Richard Lou's *ReCovering Memphis:* Conceptual Iconoclasm of the Nathan Bedford Forrest Monument." *Tennessee Historical Quarterly* 75, no. 4 (2016): 322–47, www.jstor.org/stable/26540255.

Sullivan, Patricia. *Days of Hope: Race and Democracy in the New Deal Era.* University of North Carolina Press, 1996.

Sumpter, Amy. "Segregation of Free People of Color and the Construction of Race in Antebellum New Orleans." *Southeastern Geographer* 48, no. 1 (May 2008): 19–37.

Taylor, Alrutheus Ambush. *The Negro in Tennessee, 1865–1880.* Reprint Company, 1975.

Taylor, Alva W. "The Plight of the Southern Tenant." *Christian Century,* April 3, 1935, 427–28.

Terrell, Mary Church. "Lynching from a Negro's Point of View." *North American Review* 178, no. 571(June 1904): 853–68, www.jstor.org/stable/25150991.

Thomas, Jesse O. "The Negro Industrialist: The Effect of Changing Economic Conditions upon the Living Standards of Negroes." *Proceedings of the National Conference of Social Work* (1928), 445–78.

Thompson, Ashley B., and Melissa M. Sloan. "South Polls: Race as Region, Region as Race: How Black and White Southerners Understand Their Regional Identities." *Southern Cultures* 18, no. 4 (2012): 72–95, www.jstor.org/stable/26217396.

Thomsett, Michael C. *Slavery and Racism in American Politics, 1776–1876.* McFarland, 2020.

Thruston, G. P. "A Relic of the Reconstruction Period in Tennessee." *American Historical Magazine* 6, no. 3 (1901): 243–50, www.jstor.org/stable/42657535.

Toppin, Edgar. "Walter White and the Atlanta NAACP's Fight for Equal Schools, 1916." *History of Education Quarterly* 7, no. 1 (Spring 1967): 3–21.

Trelease, Allen W. *White Terror: The Ku Klux Klan Conspiracy and Southern Reconstruction.* Louisiana State University Press, 1999.

Tribbett, Marcus Charles. "'Everybody Wants to Buy My Kitty': Resistance and the Articulation of the Sexual Subject in the Blues of Memphis Minnie." *Arkansas Review: A Journal of Delta Studies* 29, no. 1 (April 1998): 42.

Tucker, David. *Black Pastors and Leaders.* Memphis State University Press, 1975.

Tucker, Richard. *The Dragon and the Cross: The Rise and Fall of the Ku Klux Klan in Middle America.* Archon Books, 1991.

Tusken, Roger. "'In the Bastille of the Rebels.'" *Journal of the Illinois State Historical Society* 56, no. 2 (1963): 316–39, www.jstor.org/stable/40190643.

Twelve Southerners. *I'll Take My Stand.* New York: Harper and Brothers, 1930.

Twitty, Michael. "The Persistence of Memory." *Journal of Negro History* 85, no. 3 (2000): 176–82, doi.org/10.2307/2649074.

Van West, Carroll, ed. *Trial and Triumph: Essays in Tennessee's African American History.* University of Tennessee Press, 2005.

Van Zelm, Antonette G. "'Too Much of the Yankees about Them, to Suit Me': Wartime Emancipation and Tennessee's Slaveholding Women." *Tennessee Historical Quarterly* 72, no. 4 (2013): 269–88, www.jstor.org/stable/43825503.

Vincent, Tom. "'Evidence of Womans Loyalty, Perseverance, and Fidelity': Confederate Soldiers' Monuments in North Carolina, 1865–1914." *North Carolina Historical Review* 83, no. 1 (2006): 61–90, http://www.jstor.org/stable/23522933.

Waller, Altina. "Community, Class, and Race in Memphis Riot." *Journal of Social History* 18 (Winter 1984): 233–46.

Ward, Andrew. *River Run Red: The Fort Pillow Massacre in the American Civil War.* Viking Press, 2005.

Washburne, E. B. *Memphis Riots and Massacres.* Arno Press and New York Times, 1969.

Watts, Micaela A. "Nathan Bedford Forrest Descendants Sue Memphis, Demand Return of Equestrian Statue." *CA,* December 18, 2018.

Webster, Gerald R., and Jonathan I. Leib. "What Would Robert E. Lee Do? Race, Religion, and the Debate over the Confederate Battle Flag in the American South," 103–24. In *Faith and Race in American Political Life,* edited by Robin Dale Jacobson and Nancy D. Wadsworth. University of Virginia Press, 2012, www.jstor.org/stable/j.ctt6wrkw4.7.

Weekes Schroer, Jeanine. "The Terrifying Tale of the Philosophical Mammy." *Black Scholar* 43, no. 4 (Winter 2013): 101–7, doi:10.5816/blackscholar.43.4.0101.

Weinberger, Stephen. "'The Birth of a Nation' and the Making of the NAACP." *Journal of American Studies* 45, no. 1 (February 2011): 77–93, www.jstor.org/stable/23016760.

Welter, Barbara. "The Cult of True Womanhood: 1820–1860." *American Quarterly* 18, no. 2 (1966): 151–74, doi.org/10.2307/2711179.

West, Cornel. "The Paradox of the Afro-American Rebellion." *Social Text* 9/10 (1984): 44–58.

West, Emily. *Family or Freedom: People of Color in the Antebellum South.* University Press of Kentucky, 2012.

White, Calvin. *The Rise to Respectability: Race, Religion, and the Church of God in Christ.* University of Arkansas Press, 2012. Accessed at ebscohost.com.

White, Deborah Gray. *Ar'n't I a Woman? Female Slaves in the Plantation South.* Norton, 1999.

———. *Too Heavy a Load: Black Women in Defense of Themselves, 1894–1994.* Norton, 1999.

Williams, Jim. Letters to the Editor. "Preserving Good, Bad, Ugly Past." *CA,* November 7, 2017.

Williamson, Joy Ann. "In Defense of Themselves: The Black Student Struggle for Success and Recognition at Predominantly White Colleges and Universities." *Journal of Negro Education* 68, no. 1 (1999): 92–105, doi.org/10.2307/2668212.

Wilson, Charles Reagan. *Baptized in Blood: The Religion of the Lost Cause, 1865–1920.* University of Georgia Press, 1980.

Winberry, John J. "'Lest We Forget': The Confederate Monument and the Southern Townscape." *Southeastern Geographer* 55, no. 1 (2015): 19–31, www.jstor.org/stable/26233718.

Winsboro, Irvin D. S. "Give Them Their Due: A Reassessment of African Americans and Union Military Service in Florida During the Civil War." *Journal of African American History* 92, no. 3 (2007): 327–46, www.jstor.org/stable/20064203.

Woodman, Harold D. "How New Was the New South?" *Agricultural History* 58, no. 4 (1984): 529–45, www.jstor.org/stable/3742805.

Woodward, C. Vann. *The Strange Career of Jim Crow.* Oxford University Press, 1966.

Wright, Sharon D. *Race, Power, and Political Emergence in Memphis.* Routledge, 2003. Accessed at ebscohost.com.

Zangrando, Joanna Schneider, and Robert L. Zangrando. "Black Protest: A Rejection of the American Dream." *Journal of Black Studies* 1 (December 1970): 141–59.

INDEX

INDEX

INDEX

INDEX

INDEX

www.ingramcontent.com/pod-product-compliance
Lightning Source LLC
LaVergne TN
LVHW091342110826
845155LV00044B/7
9780807186565